THE FREE PRESS

New York   London   Toronto   Sydney   Singapore

TAKING

JUDAISM

PERSONALLY

Creating a Meaningful Spiritual Life

JUDY PETSONK

THE FREE PRESS
A Division of Simon & Schuster Inc.
1230 Avenue of the Americas
New York, NY 10020

Designed by Carla Bolte

Manufactured in the United States of America

10 9 8 7 6 5 4 3 2 1

Library of Congress Cataloging-in-Publication Data

Petsonk, Judy.
    Taking Judaism personally: creating a meaningful spiritual life/Judy Petsonk.
        p.   cm.
    Includes bibliographical references.
    ISBN 0-684-82809-X
    1. Jewish way of life. 2. Spiritual life—Judaism. I. Title.
BM723.P47   1996
296.7'4—dc20   96-5267
                                                                    CIP

This Book Is Dedicated to

My husband, Steve Eisdorfer, who sustains me with his patience, wisdom, and love and enriches my work with his thoughtful comments;

My parents, Ed and Jud Petsonk, who taught me by example the love of family, of the Jewish people, of all human beings, and of the earth;

And Hope and Ben, who teach me about everyday miracles.

CONTENTS

ACKNOWLEDGMENTS

My deepest thanks to the friends who gave me invaluable feedback, even while completing their own writing projects: Rabbi Nancy Fuchs, who directed me toward sources, gently pointed out errors, and read many drafts of this book; and Roselyn Bell, Carole Kantor, and Jim Remsen.

To rabbis Zalman Schachter-Shalomi, Max Ticktin, Arthur Waskow, and to those friends old and new who taught me and opened their homes and their lives to me, especially Jay Rovner, Minette Weiss, Goldie Kopmar, Eric Friedland, Dottie Shapiro, Penina Adelman, Judith Plaskow, Martha Ackelsberg, and rabbis Rami Shapiro, Michael Paley, Julie Greenberg, Brian Walt, Sheila Weinberg, Mitch Chefitz, and Art Green. And to Marilyn Goldberg and Miriam and Matt Gehatia of blessed memory.

To Wendie Gabay and Eli Wise, librarians at the Reconstructionist Rabbinical College (RRC), Lisa Freitock, former curator of the RRC liturgy archive, and Emily Milner of the Jewish Women's Resource Center of the National Council of Jewish Women, New York section, for their help and patience.

To editors Adam Bellow, Alice Greenwood, and Abigail Strubel. To agent Diana Finch, who helped me grow from reporter to writer.

To the Middle Atlantic Federation of Temple Youth (now PAFTY), which gave me permission to add my thoughts to Jewish tradition. To the havurah movement, especially Fabrangen, the Germantown minyan, and the Highland Park minyan, my comrades and extended family, who helped me find my Jewish self.

ON NAMES,
PRONUNCIATION, AND TIME

This book is full of people who changed their names at various points in their journeys. With a few exceptions, I have identified them by the name they were using at the period of time under discussion.

Like many Jews of my generation, for the Sabbath I have used the Israeli (Sephardi or Middle Eastern) term *Shabbat* (accent on the last syllable) and the Ashkenazi or East European *Shabbos* (accent on the first syllable) interchangeably.

Hebrew and Yiddish have a sound like clearing your throat, as in the name "Bach." When this sound appears in the middle or end of the word, I have used *kh* (as in Shulkhan Arukh). When it appears at the beginning of a word, I have used *h* (as in Hanukkah, Hasidic, and hallah). In many Jewish publications, this sound is indicated by *ch* (as in Chanukah and Baruch).

I have followed the Jewish custom of indicating dates in the secular calendar by B.C.E. (Before the Common Era) and C.E. (Common Era) rather than using the conventional Christian terms B.C. (Before Christ) and A.D. (Anno Domini, or the Year of Our Lord).

PART I

BECOMING

CHAPTER 1

ENTERING THE GATE

In Which I Find God in a Pile of Laundry, Which Sounds Like a Comedown from Sinai, But Isn't

One sunny fall morning not long ago, while my baby dozed in his stroller and I folded sheets in the backyard, it suddenly occurred to me that I had some time for myself. I could pray with the prayerbook, something I hardly ever got to do anymore, or I could get some sorely needed exercise. But if I didn't finish the laundry, I would need to do that instead of play with the baby when he got up. What should I do? I felt paralyzed. I was in genuine danger of pacing the backyard for the whole of the baby's nap, trying to decide what I should do with the time while he was asleep. Oh, dear! I thought. I have a few free moments, and I'm going to end up doing nothing, because I'm so busy, so overloaded, that I can't handle even insignificant choices.

So I cast out a quick silent prayer and asked the Shekhina, the loving Presence of God, to help me do it all. I ran inside, grabbed a prayerbook, scurried back outside, wrapped myself in a sheet, said the blessing for putting on a prayer shawl, and felt the Presence gently embracing me with arms of sunlight. I danced around the yard, folding the laundry in great swooping dancerly motions, turning pages as I passed the prayerbook perched on a lawn chair, singing, laughing at myself. I could feel the Presence bathe me in Her loving laughter.

"I know you love me, I know you delight in me," I said to Her, "for you have given us this blessed sunlight, and you've given me my beloved husband and this beautiful baby and this moment to myself and you've placed me here, dancing in your presence, being a fool for you. And I know you are with me. You are my partner. Because when I asked your help, you showed me that when I laugh at myself, I can do it all."

Sitting here at my word processor, remembering that day, new thanks pour from my mouth and heart and my suddenly tearful eyes. I realize now that there was even more blessing in that luminous moment than I understood at the time. Often I have read the commandment to "Love God with all your heart" and wondered despairingly how it is possible for someone like me— someone to whom God is sometimes real and sometimes not real, someone whose faith glimmers and wanes—ever to love God. I think, "This very moment, dear Presence, you are showing me that I can."

How did I, raised in a stately Reform synagogue where God appeared a couple of times a year as an awesome Judge, come to such a moment: so viscerally sure of God's Presence with me, so free to serve God in my own way, with every part of me? How on earth did I, a woman who had ignored Judaism for so many years, get to the point where it actually mattered to me whether I opened a prayerbook or was able to keep the commandments?

My journey began nearly twenty years ago. One starry March night, I stood on a bank of frozen earth and threw out a challenge to Heaven: "If You are there, I am going to act as if I believe in You, and see what happens. If You are not there, then You can't laugh at me."

Early the next morning, as I jogged along the unfinished high-way, a monarch butterfly landed fifteen feet in front of me—and then another, and another. Stretching down the road in front of me, living orange lamps lined my morning path. "You've answered me," I said. The monarchs flew away. I added, "And You are also laughing at me."

I was just shy of twenty-eight years old. Raised on the East Coast, I had come to a farming community in the Pacific Northwest to build a new career. In the small town where I reported for a local newspaper, many people had never known a Jew before.

It was "Key '73," a year fundamentalist Christians had targeted for conversion of the Jews, and I was the only Jew around. My doorbell was constantly ringing with people wanting to be friendly, the only price being that I should listen to their message. Their message was offered in love, yet I felt they valued me not as an individual, but only as a potential convert, a "savable soul." How could anyone who really wanted to know me seek to ignore—or worse, to root out—the Jewishness that was an intrinsic part of my personality?

Yet why should I feel this way? I had done nothing Jewish on my own since early in college, which was many years ago. I was only marginally connected through holidays spent with my parents.

When I came to the Northwest, I discovered that a good friend, Jewish by birth, had converted to fundamentalist Christianity. She was happy for the first time in her life, so I was happy for her. But I didn't want her certainties. I loved the struggle and questioning that to me was part of being Jewish.

I had assumed I would have a Jewish home when I had children. But I was a career woman; I might never marry. If I were to be Jewish, then, I would have to do it for myself.

I began discussing this challenge with the hypothetical God to whom I was reaching out in my embarrassed way. Mornings as I jogged, and under the vast night skies of the plains, I yelled out my puzzles and my protests.

Looking back, I can see that my beginning was typical of the Jewish spiritual awakening occurring across America: I was accepting my own questions, opening to a spiritual search, rather than demanding of myself a faith I did not have. But it wasn't until I discovered the havurah movement that I learned how faith can grow from the process of asking questions.

In my heavenward yelling, I was praying. I had to find my own way of talking to God. And the God to whom I spoke had to make sense to a woman shaped by a liberal college education and by the antiauthoritarian youth culture of the 1960s. Not until I encountered Jewish feminism did I learn how renaming and reimagining the Source of Life could flower into revelation.

As I continued these jogging conversations with God over the months, frozen ruts melted, and trees burst into leaf and blossom. Being outdoors and moving while I talked to God opened the gates of my heart. Later I learned that traditional Jews sway and move constantly as they pray. Not until I encountered the new Jewish mysticism did I learn how melding movement, meditation, nature, and song could release fountains of transcendent joy.

Could the Jewish way of life enhance my new spiritual aliveness? This question came up in my daily dialogues with God. It wasn't until I began meeting traditional Jews (and those returning to tradition) that I saw how the investment of my mind—through study—and my body—through observance of Jewish law—could bring the Infinite into everyday life.

This is the story of my journey, and that of other American Jews of the late twentieth century who have found great riches by becoming open to our past and to the infinite dimensions of the Present. Once I began seeking the meaning of being a Jew, I pursued the journey wherever life took me: in Dayton, Ohio, where I reported for a large daily newspaper and took my first fledgling steps toward Judaism; in Washington, D.C., where I lived communally with other Jews; in Philadelphia, where I became part of a reviving Jewish community and met my husband; and in the little town of Highland Park, New Jersey, where I am raising my children. In each place I found new teachers, new questions, new dimensions of Jewish experience, and new companions who shared my search. Our journeys have taken some of us to feminism, others to neo-mysticism or Orthodoxy. But for many of us, the beginning—the permission to search deeply into the spiritual significance of our Jewish roots—came through the havurah movement. So that is where this story begins.

CHAPTER 2

HAVURAH

Community of Individualists

The havurah movement grew out of an experiment in Jewish democracy—an experiment that flowered into a mini-revolution. A havurah is a Jewish spiritual cooperative: Leadership is shared, and spiritual authority comes from the group. Havurot were born in the late 1960s when young people who wanted to organize something more enduring than massive protest marches began to form small, creative alternative institutions. There were food co-ops, and co-op bookstores—why not a spiritual co-op?

The youth culture of the 1960s faded within a decade, but havurot endured. The long hair of the founders is short and graying at the temples now. Some of the rebels in blue jeans now have their own kids in jeans. The egalitarian Judaism they gave birth to has also survived and grown.

How did Jewish tradition, that weighty and venerable matriarch, give birth to such a feisty offspring?

8

Some of the seeds were planted at the Conservative movement's Camp Ramah, where the schedule alternated sports with deep study of traditional texts and rousing, tune-filled daily prayer. At Ramah camps around the United States, boys wore the traditional skullcap (*yarmulke* or *kippah*) on playing fields, not just in Hebrew classes. Kids came out of Camp Ramah with a particular ideal of Judaism: It should be lived twenty-four hours a day. At Jewish services you should be able to sing your heart out, speak your mind, pray in sunshine under trees, and fall in love. These weren't things you could do in most synagogues of the 1950s and 1960s.

At Ramah, campers planned and led their own services. They were being trained for citizenship in a Jewish spiritual democracy. But there was a problem: The Jewish tradition of spiritual democracy had dropped overboard on the journey to America. Since the destruction of the Temple two thousand years ago, Judaism has had scholarly elites but no hierarchy. Jewish law has been created by a continuing conversation or debate among the generations; the younger generation talks back to its elders by citing the grandparents or earlier generations. Through this process of talking back to the classical sources—neither breaking from the tradition entirely nor being rigidly bound by it—the Jewish people evolved a spiritually centered lifestyle that has adapted to many countries and eras.

The migration to America, though, largely silenced that conversation. The spiritual and intellectual elite, the rabbis, stayed behind in Europe (and were eventually ground up by the Nazi exterminating machine), while the poorest and least educated Jews came to America.[1] Scrabbling for a living on a foreign shore, most were too busy, too tired, and too illiterate in terms of religion to pass on to their children anything but a nostalgic husk of the Jewish spiritual experience—even if they wanted to. The way of life in the European ghetto village (*shtetl*) was spiritually rich but confining. Excluded politically, economically, and socially from the rest of Europe, many Jews also felt shackled intellectually by a ghetto religion that refused to participate in European science or culture. Such feelings explain the story of the woman on the ship to America throwing her traditional head covering into the ocean.[2] And even when immigrants cared enough to pass on their heritage, their children—anxious to be accepted as full Americans—often shrugged off religious observance as just another set of Old World superstitions, as irrelevant and embarrassing as a foreign accent.

By the 1950s, when I was growing up, most American Jews didn't know or care enough to debate their heritage. Reform Judaism encouraged young people to create and debate, but it never taught them traditional texts. Orthodox Jews taught the texts but rarely encouraged young people to debate. Conservative Jews were both taught the texts and encouraged to debate, but when they emerged into young adulthood, they found that the leaders of American Jewry were not interested in debating with them or sharing the planning and execution of religious services. The only generally recognized leadership role for lay people in the established Jewish world was to raise money: for Jewish charities through the United Jewish Appeal and the local Federations of Jewish Philanthropies, or for synagogues by being on the board of directors.

Young Jews were in the forefront of all the movements of the 1960s and early 1970s, including civil rights, peace, and feminism. We got our vision of freedom and justice from the Passover seder. Even so, most of the young Jewish activists were more activist than Jewish.

Our families, by and large, had accepted the devil's bargain America offered: We will completely accept you Jews (especially the economically successful ones) as long as you don't look, sound, or act Jewish. Even the synagogues—especially those that moved out to the suburbs—were modified so as not to be "too Jewish."[3] The tradition of rabbi-scholars sitting around a table debating with their students was replaced by a Protestantized version of the rabbi as a robe-wearing minister, preaching from the pulpit to a silent and passive congregation. After a century and a half of social exclusion, Jews had finally begun to find social acceptance in America, but at the cost of becoming indistinguishable from everyone else.

Like Paul Cowan, who chronicled his return to Judaism in the book *An Orphan in History*, some of us had begun to ask, shouldn't Jewishness be a distinctive category, a meaningful identity?

We didn't realize at the time what a luxury it was to be able to ask such questions.[4] The Jewish immigrants who came to America from eastern Europe between 1880 and 1924 had been excluded from jobs in the Old Country, gone hungry, and watched their homes burn in pogroms. The German Jews who had come earlier, between 1840 and 1880, were anxious to acculturate their less assimilated brethren; they created a network of charitable and educational organizations to ensure that American Jews could always take care of their own.

Our parents' generation, appalled by the powerlessness of the American Jewish community to stop the Holocaust, tried to make sure this could never happen again. They created an effective political action and lobbying effort, financed the fledgling state of Israel as a haven for future Jewish refugees, developed organizations to fight quotas and combat anti-Semitism, worked doggedly to achieve economic status, and groomed their children to be socially acceptable ("Jews at home and Americans in the street") so they would not be lightning rods for anti-Semitism. In providing financial backing, professional help and early leadership to the civil rights movement, they worked to break down the barriers that kept Jews as well as other minorities out of certain schools, neighborhoods, or jobs. In creating religious education programs, they were concerned less about spirituality than about ensuring that their children were proud Jews who realized they were just as good as everybody else.

Paradoxically, as the generation who had benefited from these efforts, we could reject our education in blandness and afford to think about being visibly, affirmatively Jewish again. The Holocaust had made anti-Semitism socially unacceptable behavior among most non-Jews. In the 1960s, for the first time, young Jews could generally find equal opportunities in education and most occupations. Then came Israel's lightning victory in the 1967 Six-Day War, which bolstered Jews' status both in their own eyes and in the eyes of gentiles. It became possible for Jews to go public with their Judaism.

The revolution in contemporary Judaism was ignited by a cluster of outsiders, intensely individualistic loners who fell in love with Judaism but had to do it their way. Rabbi Arthur Green, founder of Havurat Shalom (one of the first havurot), felt like an outsider from the day he walked through the old brick and wrought-iron gates of Conservative Judaism's Jewish Theological Seminary.[5] Green's father and mother had both been atheists. From the time Art was eight years old, however, he was attracted to Judaism. He cherished his grandparents' little Orthodox storefront synagogue.

Green's mother died when he was eleven; drawing closer to his grandparents, he became passionately Jewish. When he was twelve, Art urged his father to throw away the Christmas stockings and observe Hanukkah. Despite his father's objections, he enrolled in Hebrew school and Camp Ramah. At fourteen Green fell in love with Rabbi Abraham Joshua Heschel's deeply humane contemporary philosophy. In high school his clique spoke only Hebrew among themselves. By age sixteen Art was an observant Orthodox Jew.

Then Green entered Brandeis University, and the fabric of identity he had woven so eagerly began to unravel. He read Herman Hesse and decided that there were many paths to enlightenment. Camus, Sartre, and Kafka were his idols; he talked with his friends ("beatnik" poets and actors) about the death of God. But even though he abandoned Jewish observance, he remained a Jewish Studies major. The writings of Jewish spiritual masters and philosophers like Martin Buber seemed more profound to him than anything he learned in the secular world. He felt pulled in two different directions—toward the intensity and intimacy of his grandparents' world, but also toward the freedom of the 1960s.

He enrolled in rabbinical school at Jewish Theological Seminary with the vague dream of creating "a synagogue for people who wouldn't walk into a synagogue. . . . I needed something for myself, for someone who didn't fit the categories." It was hard for such a maverick to stay in rabbinical school, where few of the traditional courses of study addressed his dreams or the social ferment outside the seminary walls. Every year Green threatened to quit, but he stayed on so that he could study with intellectual giants like Heschel and Mordecai Kaplan.

Meanwhile, within the fledgling Reconstructionist movement in which Arthur Green would someday be a leader, an idea was spreading that was both very new and very old—the idea of the havurah. Two rabbis, Jakob J. Petuchowski of Hebrew Union College and Jacob Neusner of Columbia University, had sounded a warning in successive articles in *The Reconstructionist:* The idea of a "holy community" voluntarily taking on religious obligations, which had been central to Jewish spirituality since the Jews accepted the Ten Commandments at Mt. Sinai, was falling victim to modern individualism.[6] The deep sense of belonging that had sustained Jews spiritually throughout their history had been lost in the welter of secular and religious organizations Jews had created in America.[7] The authors' solution was as follows: Imitating the practice of their Pharisee ancestors in the early days of the Second Temple in the first century B.C.E., small groups of Jews should form fellowships within and outside synagogues that would voluntarily take on a deeper, more intense commitment to Judaism. One rabbi, Shamai Kantor of Toronto, had already experimented with creating havurot for study and cultural activities in his congregation. Rabbi Ira Eisenstein, editor of *The Reconstructionist* and Mordecai Kaplan's son-in-law, praised the idea of havurot as an alternative to the "curse of bigness" that left many members of large congregations "without a spiritual home. They find it hard to relate to other members of such congregations, and often, too, to the rabbi who is very busy doing many things."[8]

Eisenstein and Neusner spoke about the idea at the national Reconstructionist convention, and in 1962 they published a pamphlet, "The Havurah Idea." Unaffiliated Jews—and some who were unhappy in their synagogues—began forming small fellowships that conducted their own services, without rabbis. Some havurot have continued for decades. The national Jewish Reconstructionist Federation, which includes these ad hoc groups, was initially called the Federation of Reconstructionist Congregations and Havurot.

In 1965, while exploring what he would do after ordination, Arthur Green got his first taste of the havurah idea in action. He visited a new, experimental congregation, the Upstairs Minyan at the University of Chicago Hillel Foundation. Rabbis Max Ticktin and Dan Leifer had uprooted the formal rows of seats and arranged the chairs in a circle; instead of giving sermons, they provoked discussions and encouraged people to read poetry at intervals in the service. Unlike anywhere else in the Jewish world of that day, women participated fully in all aspects of the service.

The idea of an alternative congregation crystallized in Green's mind in 1966 when radical priest Daniel Berrigan visited one of Heschel's classes. Green came home from that class to find a couple of surprise visitors: Barry Holtz, a camper to whom he had become close while serving as a counselor at United Synagogue Youth encampments, and Alan Mintz, who later founded *Response,* a magazine where havurah leaders worked out a lot of the movement's ideas. They joked that instead of starting an alternative synagogue Green should start a radical rabbinical school and give his younger friends draft deferments.

Green didn't think the idea was such a joke. He called Rabbi Albert Axelrad, the Hillel director at Brandeis, and they began setting up a board, recruiting faculty, and writing a brochure. A few months later, Holtz, who had forgotten about the conversation, got a call asking if he wanted to enroll in the new rabbinical school.

As part of the faculty Green recruited charismatic, eclectic Rabbi Zalman Schachter, who combined long Hasidic sidecurls and beard with a bright African dashiki or a long, flowing white robe. When he was on the faculty of Camp Ramah, Schachter had called himself "director of Jewish spiritual ecology." Zalman (who later added *Shalomi,* "my peace," to the name *Schachter,* which means "butcher"), had been a teenager in Europe during the rise of Nazism. His father had prepared him well to be a syncretist; he was sent to a classical Orthodox yeshiva in the morning and to a secular high school in the afternoons. After a brief internment in a Vichy labor camp, Schachter's family was able to get visas to the United States, where Zalman, drawn to its mystical, intense religiosity, entered the ultra-Orthodox Lubavitch yeshiva. After a stint as an energetic youth outreach worker for Lubavitch, he had become a Hillel college chaplain and brought his skills to Camp Ramah during the summer. When they weren't studying texts with the young Art Green, the Ramah kids were baking their own *hallah* (braided bread), making their own candles for Shabbat, tying the fringes for their own prayer shawls, and imbibing the ideology of do-it-yourself Judaism, all under Zalman's direction.

Havurat Shalom (the name means "fellowship of peace") was to be the year-round incarnation of this idea: like the first rabbinical academy founded at Yavneh after the Romans destroyed the Second Temple nearly two thousand years ago, it would confront ancient Judaism and ask what should be preserved. Their model was eighteenth-century Hasidism, a Jewish spiritual revival movement in eastern Europe that emphasized a joyful, spontaneous relationship to God. Schachter encouraged the men to express emotions, hug, and dance in ecstatic circles during prayer and holiday celebrations. Religious services were fairly traditional in content, but people sat on cushions on the floor, singing and clapping hands. The cover of the ark where the Torah was kept was not velvet (as in an "establishment" synagogue) but macramé, which was made by a member of the group. The Saturday morning service attracted eighty people by the end of the first year.

The goal of Havurat Shalom's founders, though, was not simply to experiment with the traditional service but to create a spiritual community. Anybody could come to the Saturday morning service. But to be a member of the community, a *haver* (comrade), eligible to come to the more intimate Friday night service, one had to make a substantial commitment. In addition to whatever college courses Havurat Shalom members were taking (many were students at Brandeis University), they had to take twelve hours of classes a week at the havurah. All the members ate together once a week; afterwards there was a community meeting with intense discussions about the relationship between their religious practice and their ideals.

Michael Paley was seventeen, a high school senior with pale blue eyes and wiry blond hair, when he came to Havurat Shalom for the first time in 1968. He had met Rabbi Everett Gendler, a member of the Havurat Shalom faculty, at a political demonstration where Gendler was blocking a busful of draftees by praying the Jewish liturgy in front of it. As Paley recalls his first Shabbat service at Havurat Shalom, "There were thirty people sitting on the floor, and this guy with flowers around his head and a little child on his lap [Reb Zalman] was leading them." Unlike in the regular synagogue, "he was singing so slowly I could actually read along with him. He passes the Torah around, and everybody gets to hug it; then he passes around a rose. Then he says, 'Now we're going to skip ahead thirty-five pages.'"

Art Green talked about the Torah portion. People asked questions, argued, and discussed. "It was incredible: the learning, the intensity, the beauty," says Paley. He was hooked. In his senior year of high school, he moved into the Havurat Shalom neighborhood with his girlfriend, who was going to nearby Tufts University.

"It was a tremendous luxury to have as the central activity of your life, community," recalls Merle Feld. She was a budding twenty-year-old poet/playwright with a swinging curtain of dark hair framing a ruddy face when she moved to Boston with her partner, newly ordained rabbi Eddie Feld, who was joining the faculty of Havurat Shalom. For Merle, who had grown up in a non-observant home and had only been in a synagogue two or three times before getting involved in the Hillel Foundation at Brooklyn College, immersing herself in Jewish ritual "was like saying to consumer corporate America, 'Fuck you, I reject your values. They don't sustain me. They don't create a world I feel joyful in.' But it was only a small part about rejecting all these norms. . . . It was [more about] creating another reality which was utterly positive, and exciting, and empowering."

Merle remembers when one Havurat Shalom member received a draft notice and, instead of taking an exemption as a rabbinical student, decided to stand up to the system by going to jail. The night before his heroic deed, havurah members stayed up all night with him, studying, singing, talking, and eating brownies. Then they marched to Cambridge City Hall, singing, so he could turn himself in. The only trouble was that he had eaten so many brownies and slept so little that his blood sugar was way off, and he flunked the physical. He was humiliated.

Havurat Shalom was founded on four pillars of Judaism: learning, prayer, celebration, and community. Always the haverim tried to forge a new synthesis for their generation. Freedom and tradition, the havurah's most ardently held values, tugged and jostled against one another in the classes and in the services. Gradually the goal of creating a spiritual community eclipsed the idea of a seminary. "Nobody wanted a rabbinical degree," said Green. "We talked about ordaining people as *haver*."

In spite of their passion for democracy, though, there was an unstated elitism. Sometimes it seemed as if what the community really worshipped was brilliant leadership in prayers and discussion. For Merle Feld, who was still looking surreptitiously at other people to figure out when to stand, sit, or bow, Havurat Shalom services were wonderfully exotic, but a struggle. "There was something very earnest and very serious about the enterprise," said Feld. "But it was also centered on self in a way that you don't get to be when you really undertake the business of serious adulthood."

More than twenty-five years have passed, and Havurat Shalom continues, though its membership has changed many times. Its graduates have exported the havurah model throughout the country. Michael and Sharon Strassfeld (who came to Havurat Shalom in its fourth year) and Richard Siegel captured the early havurah experience in the *Jewish Catalog.* Modeled after the *Whole Earth Catalog,* the *Jewish Catalog* was the youth culture's answer to the *Shulhan Arukh* (the authoritative guide to Jewish law). In its cartoon-and-photo-filled pages, you can learn how to bake your own hallah, sew your own prayer shawl, or make your kitchen kosher. There is even a lighthearted (but ultimately serious) chapter on how to bring the Messiah.

Along with its two sequels, the *Jewish Catalog* sold more than half a million copies. Havurot were started in New York, Philadelphia, Berkeley, Los Angeles, and Washington, D.C. In Madison, Wisconsin, and other university centers, young Jews began living together in kosher communal houses.

Three streams of young people came together to create the havurah movement: Reform or assimilated Jews (like me) whose Jewishness was a passionate mass of feeling, with no knowledge to shape it; Conservative Jews who were fluent and well-educated in the prayers but didn't have much sense of who or what they might be praying to; and Orthodox members of the 612 Club (committed to observing all 613 of the Jewish laws, except the prohibition on premarital sex) who needed an ideology that could reconcile a gut-level commitment to Jewish tradition with the equally burning need to modify it. Each of these groups needed the others to give it energy and direction.

TWO GIANTS of contemporary Jewish philosophy, Rabbi Abraham Joshua Heschel and Rabbi Mordecai Kaplan, were the spiritual grandfathers of the movement. Immigrants from Europe who were fascinated with the possibilities of American democracy, Heschel and Kaplan energetically and thoughtfully explored the directions Judaism should take in a free land.

Kaplan was the director of the Jewish Theological Seminary's Teachers' Institute from its beginning in 1909 to the mid-1940s, and continued to teach rabbinical students at the seminary until 1963. Raised in a traditional home (his family left eastern Europe when he was seven so that his father could serve on the rabbinical court of New York City), Kaplan had begun questioning the traditional view of God while he was a young student at the Jewish Theological Seminary and Columbia University. He became the founder of Judaism's newest and most experimental denomination, Reconstructionism. Kaplan believed that Jewish law was not the revealed will of God but the accumulated wisdom of the Jewish people, to which every generation must make its own new response. His daughter, Judith Kaplan Eisenstein, in 1922 became the first Jewish woman in the world to have a *bat mitzvah,* a coming-of-age ceremony equivalent to that of a boy.

Heschel had escaped the Nazis and come from Europe to America in 1940, where he taught first at Reform Judaism's Hebrew Union College and then at the Jewish Theological Seminary from 1945 to 1972. He taught that God cares deeply about human action and that people must act out the moral imperatives of the Bible in their own time. Influenced by Heschel and Kaplan, rabbinical students went out into the Conservative movement's synagogues, camps, and youth groups in the 1950s and 1960s carrying the message that it was time to forge a uniquely American Judaism. Young Jews must interpret for their own generation the covenant between God and Israel.

The *Jewish Catalog* transformed the scattered havurah experiments into a sort of movement, for which it became the informal guidebook. In its free-wheeling, eclectic way, the book began to answer one of the key questions members of the movement were asking: How can one find meaning in Judaism while carving out one's own twentieth-century identity?

For *Jewish Catalog* coauthor Michael Strassfeld, this was a personal quest. Michael was the son of an Orthodox rabbi, raised in an Orthodox home and neighborhood, educated in a yeshiva. While most of the Orthodox community is intentionally aloof from the rest of American society, Michael's father had marched for racial justice with Heschel and Martin Luther King in Selma, Alabama. When Michael was in high school, his father became rabbi of a Conservative congregation in the seaside suburb of Marblehead, Massachusetts, and got involved in the election campaign of a peace candidate. Rabbi Strassfeld had invited Reb Zalman Schachter to speak to his congregation and spend Shabbat with the Strassfeld family. When Green, Schachter, and others started Havurat Shalom, they asked Michael's father to be on the advisory board.

Michael's own struggle to reconcile Orthodox tradition with the excitement of the new, questioning approaches to Judaism intensified when he switched from Yeshiva University to Brandeis. He plunged into the youth culture. His wife, Sharon, recalls that, newly married during their senior year, they walked into an Orthodox "Young Israel" synagogue and felt people staring at their long hair and Michael's beard, thinking, "What are *they* doing here?"

Orthodox in practice but hippie in lifestyle, they, too, didn't fit the conventional categories. When he spent a Shabbat at Reb Zalman's house during the first year of Havurat Shalom, Michael realized, "This is the kind of Judaism I was looking for"—still involved with and cherishing the tradition, while participating fully in the larger American culture. In the *Jewish Catalog* he and his coauthors depicted "young, regular-looking Americans doing these Jewish things," recalls Michael. "They could be your neighbor or friend. You could make your own Jewish life and it was fine, and authentic. You don't have to ask a rabbi about every-thing, you don't have to feel guilty because you only want to do Shabbat [and not observe all of Jewish law]. You could explore Jewish identity in pieces, and feel good about the process, and not feel bound to do the whole thing or nothing. Ultimately, it was empowering."

Strassfeld became one of the informal architects of the havurah movement. In the mid-1970s the havurot began to organize pan-havurah weekend retreats three times a year at Weiss's Farm, an abandoned fresh-air camp in central New Jersey. The retreats brought together havurot from four East Coast cities to study, dance, sing, and argue about topics ranging from sex to charity to the future of Israel.

Havurah was an idea whose time had come. By whatever name they called it, Jews of all ages were seeking greater intimacy and freshness in their worship services, and more responsibility for their own religious lives. Havurot began springing up in small towns and among people who had never heard of the havurah movement. Even in the tiny Jewish community of Altoona, Pennsylvania, my parents—who never called what they did a havurah—met once a month with three other families for dinner and a creative Friday evening service they wrote themselves.

Merle and Eddie Feld moved to Princeton (where Eddie was the Hillel rabbi for nineteen years) and then to New York, where he took over the Society for the Advancement of Judaism, the first Reconstructionist synagogue, which had been founded by Mordecai Kaplan. Merle's poetry explored the connection be-tween the events of her life—childbirth, menstruation, or nursing her child through an attack of croup—and the Jewish stories, as well as the Jewish God. In October 1994 her play *Across the Jordan,* interweaving the Biblical story of Sarah and Hagar with the modern story of a Palestinian terrorist and her Israeli lawyer, was produced at Princeton University.

Art Green moved to Philadelphia to teach at the University of Pennsylvania. He became a well-known scholar of Jewish mysticism and author of books on contemporary Jewish theology. From 1987 to 1993 he was president of the Reconstructionist Rabbinical College. He was an influential member of a Philadelphia havurah, the Germantown minyan. He says wistfully that he never found a community equal in spiritual intensity, camaraderie, or learning to Havurat Shalom. In 1994 he quit the college and returned to Boston to teach at Brandeis.

Michael Strassfeld, while continuing to influence the havurah movement, became a writer and educator on Jewish topics. Recently ordained by the Reconstructionist Rabbinical College, he is now rabbi of Ansche Hesed, a havurah-style synagogue in New York that he helped to revitalize. With his oldest child now in college, he is working on an updated *New Jewish Catalog* that will include not only how-to-do-it but also "more of the whys," he said.

Michael Paley in some ways has traveled furthest from offbeat anti-establishment havurah Judaism: gray suits have replaced his T-shirts and jeans, and his frizzy sandy hair and mischievous blue eyes peek out from under a fedora instead of a baseball cap. While still a political radical and a mystic, he has become an Orthodox Jew and a rabbi. After a stint as chaplain of Columbia University, he is now a teacher at Bard College and at the Wexner Heritage Foundation, which seeks to reeducate Jews in their tradition.

But such changes should be no surprise. When one decides to take Judaism personally, it is always the beginning of a journey.

CHAPTER 3

LEARNING AS WORSHIP

The Question Is the Answer

There comes a point in the lives of some Jews when a question they had previously ignored begins to set the direction of their lives: What does it mean—or what should it mean—to be Jewish? The question hit Jeff Garden at age thirty-three almost as if someone had thrown an electrical switch, he says. Raised in Detroit, he had good health, boyish good looks, a good marriage, and a successful business supplying parts to the auto industry. As friends faced troubles he was spared, he asked, "Why am I so blessed? . . . How can I continue to take without giving back?"

To Jeff, who was raised in a traditional home, "giving back" meant charity, ritual observance, and study. Having gone to an Orthodox Hebrew school for twelve years as a boy, he said, "I could repeat back what it said in the book," but now Jeff had to decide Judaism's place in his adult life. His father, an immigrant from Europe, had felt pressed to work on the Sabbath while establishing himself in America and developing a business as a jeweler. When Jeff was a teenager, his father returned to Ortho-doxy, observing the Sabbath and the kosher laws with new fer-vor. Now Jeff, who admired his father greatly, felt the need to begin his own return. He began quietly dispensing financial sup-port for Jewish education. A rabbi he had known as a youngster helped him start a study group in his home, exploring *Pirkei Avot* (*The Ethics of the Fathers*), a book of wise sayings from the Mish-nah, the first great collection of Jewish law following the Torah.

A friend I'll call Susan grew up in a very different kind of Jew-ish home, but she felt the same thirst to understand what it means to be a Jew. Her family's sole Jewish observance was to roll down the blinds on Yom Kippur (the Day of Atonement) so no one in their Jewish neighborhood in Queens would see them eating lunch while others were fasting. The family religion was atheism: "My mother used to say if there's a God, he's an evil God," Susan recalls. But, she adds, "I was always jealous of religious people. At holiday times, Jewish people had their holidays, Christians had theirs, and we were out in the cold." And Susan knew she was Jewish.[1] After reading *The Diary of Anne Frank* at age ten, "I packed my bag and kept it in the closet in case the Nazis would come."

The political community of Communists and fellow travelers that had sustained Susan's parents at the start of their marriage had fallen apart. The family's isolation grew when, just after she graduated high school at age sixteen, Susan's father began dying of ALS, the progressive paralysis that killed Lou Gehrig.

When Susan started commuting to Queens College, she vol-unteered at the student newspaper, hoping she would find a community there. The first time she walked into the newspaper office, she met the quietly witty man I'll call Rick Bender, whom she would marry before graduation. They were intellectual spar-ring partners. When Susan said she was an atheist, Rick coun-tered: Did she *know* God didn't exist, or was she simply mouthing her parents' ideas? His question launched her on a search that would radically change the direction of both their lives.

Susan began asking whether anything had ultimate value. The idea of a person-God was as alien to her as it was to her parents, but she began to believe that "there must be some moral law for the universe, objectively true regardless of time and place. That was God to me—that moral absolute."

While doing graduate work at NYU, she began sitting in on a class at a large Orthodox synagogue. When she took a computer research job at Bell Laboratories in New Jersey, Susan plunged into the search in earnest. She signed up for as many synagogue classes as she could fit into her crowded schedule. She also stumbled across another, informal world of Jewish learning. In Highland Park (where she lived), as in many other Jewish communities, there were people studying together and sharing their knowledge of Judaism. And in a conference room of the sprawling glass-and-concrete research headquarters of Bell Laboratories in Holmdel, New Jersey, Chaim (Herman) Presby, a company physicist, led a Talmud study session during the lunch hour. As Presby went through many of the 613 commandments recognized by traditional Judaism, Bell employees as far away as Chicago dialed in on a conference-call line to participate.

Presby, who also taught Shabbat afternoon classes at his Orthodox synagogue, ran an evening course for women in his home. Susan started going. Presby's wife, Shelly, impishly humorous despite her sedate ultra-Orthodox wig, sat among the twenty or so hatted or wigged women around a basement table, chaperoning and providing a lively counterpoint to his remarks. When I attended several years later, Presby, who teaches in a question-and-answer style, asked, "Why did the *Kadosh Baruch Hu* ["the Holy One, Blessed Be He"] put us here?" There was dead silence—until Shelly ventured, "To shop?" No, smiled Presby. Citing the Ramhal, an eighteenth-century commentator, he asserted, "The purpose of human beings is to delight in God, to attach to God, to be the object of God's goodness." Susan eventually dropped out of Presby's classes because his Orthodoxy clashed too much with the approach to Judaism she developed. But, she adds, "When I was discovering the basics, everything seemed divine and holy."

Study was especially important to Susan because in some ways she remained very much the spiritual child of her parents. The idea of a personal God remained so remote to her that once when the leader of a havurah prayer group asked the members to imagine God as a loving father, all Susan could picture was "God as a toad hopping from rock to rock." When I interviewed her, she had been attending synagogue weekly for twelve years, but she said that at prayer, "I feel like a failure. . . . In the group, no matter how much I prepare ahead of time, I'm just going through the motions." She continued to go to synagogue because it helped her bond to the community ("I think of it as praying with the people"), but the world of study she could enter into fully and with growing excitement.

My background was midway between Jeff's and Susan's. As a Reform Jew, I grew up celebrating Hanukkah and Passover, knew many Bible stories, and was proud to be Jewish. But I knew almost nothing of Jewish law and observance, or the vast world of Jewish learning. My first tentative spiritual reaching out took place when I was completely uprooted—far from home, and embarking on a new career—and approaching my thirtieth birthday. Suddenly, when I was farthest from any Jewish community, I found myself wanting to understand this Jewishness which I had breathed growing up as unconsciously as the fragrance of chicken soup in the kitchen. As if to answer my prayer, the phone rang with a job offer from the *Daily News,* a newspaper in Dayton, Ohio, which had a medium-sized Jewish community. If I wanted to learn about Judaism, I would have my opportunity.

For years I had told my anxious parents (who wanted me to go to synagogue to meet Jewish men), that no man I would be interested in would be caught dead in a synagogue. (Well, maybe dead, but not under any other circumstances.) Overcoming my hesitations, I began attending Beth Abraham, the Conservative synagogue in Dayton. I was the only single woman I could see.

A friend,[2] sensing my confusion about where I fit in the Jewish world, introduced me to the just-published *Jewish Catalog*. The picture inside the cover showed long-haired people of my generation doing Jewish things together. I decided to organize a havurah for people like me who weren't comfortable in synagogues but hungered to connect with our Jewish roots.

At the first Shabbat morning service of the fledgling Dayton havurah we sat cross-legged on the floor of someone's apartment, wrestling sentence by sentence with the service. We started at ten o'clock in the morning and talked until nearly three in the afternoon. A line in Psalm 92 said, "The wicked may spring up as the grass, and the workers of iniquity may flourish/Only to be destroyed forever."

"I can't say this line," protested one man. "I don't think that's how the world works." So we talked about it. Should we skip the line? Or could we interpret it so we could say it honestly? Do wicked acts shrivel one's humanity? Do right actions strengthen the spirit?

I went home elated, thinking, "I've found a way to learn about Judaism *and* to think about its relevance to my life."

Because of the special circumstances of their history, Jews have been trying to figure out their relationship to their heritage for nearly twenty-five centuries. Study and worship circles like mine have been an important way of doing so.

When the Babylonians destroyed the Temple (the center of Jewish worship) and deported most Jews from their land in 586 B.C.E., it looked as if Judaism was finished. Cyrus of Persia defeated Babylonia fifty years later and invited the Jews to return to Palestine, but the wealthy, educated elite were too ensconced in Babylon. An impoverished band of returnees rebuilt the Temple, but they were unable to recreate the Jewish nation. In 445 B.C.E., Ezra the Scribe returned and launched the Judaism we know today—with Torah, not solely the Temple, as the unifying element. Sending messengers to all corners of the land, he assembled the people in Jerusalem on New Year's Day. The purpose? To hear their story, the Torah. For six hours Ezra read the book, and interpreters explained it, since the returned exiles spoke Aramaic rather than Hebrew. The people wept. Later that month, the people swore aloud to accept the Torah as their constitution; lay officials and priests sealed the agreement. Traditon says that Ezra had passages from the Torah read in town squares on market days (Monday and Thursday). The Torah is still read in daily services on those days, as well as on Shabbat and holidays.

Torah means "teaching." Since the time of Ezra, the Torah has been the central vehicle for teaching Jews to be Jews. The term has come to mean not only the original five books of the Bible but the twenty-five centuries of Jewish thought since, which are all seen as commentary on that original Torah.

The Second Temple was destroyed by the Romans in 70 C.E. By then Ezra's group of interpreters had grown into a whole class of rabbis (teachers). The rabbis decreed that prayer and study of sacred texts should replace the animal sacrifice of the Temple as the way to serve God. Rabban Yohanan ben Zakkai risked his life to organize a rabbinical academy at Yavneh; his students smuggled him out of Jerusalem in a coffin under the noses of besieging Roman soldiers. The majority of the people became part of the Pharisee movement, turning to the rabbis to interpret how the ancient law should apply to their time. Their discussions, stories, and rulings were compiled in the Talmud and later commentaries. For centuries, men have gathered in the synagogue (often called *shul*—"school" in Yiddish) morning and evening to study as well as to pray. Every Jewish community of any size had Talmud study circles. At one point, the Jewish community councils of Prague and Worms decreed that every man must study for a minimum of an hour a day.[3]

Rabbi Adin Steinsaltz, born into a secular Israeli family and now a leading Orthodox rabbi, says that fixed regular times of

study with a partner or a master teacher are also vital today, especially for anyone returning to Judaism: "No Jew is free of the
obligation to study [Torah] to the best of his ability. The Jewish
notion of 'a kingdom of priests and a holy nation' rests to no
small degree on the fact that Jewish knowledge is not restricted
to a separate learned caste but incumbent on all."[4]

This two-thousand-year tradition of Jewish study was different
from anything I had known. Traditional Jews learned sitting
around a table, arguing with each other. They argued with the
texts as well, bringing the insights of each generation into dialogue with teachers of previous years. Talmud says that the most
important things you need to deal with life are a spouse and a
study partner. And study was not just for the scholarly elite; one
of the books that survived the Nazi book-burning was inscribed
The Society of Woodchoppers for the Study of Mishna in Berditchev.[5]
The havurah extended this universality to Jewish illiterates like
me. From the first Shabbat in the Dayton havurah, my thoughts
were valued: I was valued.

Shabbat learning with the havurah only increased my desire to
learn more. In Dayton I found Torah *l'shma*—people sharing
their learning for the love of it. Matt Gehatia, an elderly Israeli
physicist, was an amateur Bible scholar and archaeologist. Sitting
on the flowered sofas of his suburban living room, we read parallel passages from the biblical books of Isaiah, Kings, and Chroni-
cles, noticing how the same events were described by different
players in the drama. We also read two inscriptions. One, from the
obelisk of the Assyrian king Sennacherib, described his siege of
Jerusalem in 700 B.C.E. A Hebrew inscription from the same time
described how the Hebrew king, Hezekiah, foiled the seige. Two
teams of excavators, working from opposite directions, dig a tun-
nel to bring water from a spring outside the walls into the city. I
could almost hear the clang of axes echoing through rock, and
see the flash of lights from answering torches as the water burst
through. Five years later in Jerusalem I waded through that tun-
nel, boots slipping on wet rock, my inner ear tuned to the clang

of long-ago pickaxes. The Bible world had come alive for me. This was my history.

After three years with the tiny Dayton havurah, which had to be reorganized every fall when two or three key people left, I took a sabbatical from my job to spend a year in one of the large East Coast havurot: Fabrangen, in Washington, D.C.

Learning was in the air at Fabrangen. I rented a room from Arthur Waskow, one of Fabrangen's leaders. The Talmud class met in Arthur's living room. Dressed in shorts and T-shirts on a warm fall day, we sat in a circle, with some members on the sofa, some on cushions on the floor. We read a sentence aloud in Aramaic and English, then threw out ideas. The talk flowed so freely that it took me awhile to perceive that we were being taught—or rather, that our discussion was subtly molded and directed by an elflike gray-bearded man with a gently teasing manner, Rabbi Max Ticktin. Though Max was national supervisor of all the college Hillel directors, he was not Fabrangen's rabbi but simply one of several members who shared their knowledge through informal classes.

For the first time in my life I found myself really wanting to know Hebrew. Now I understood why in eleven years of Reform Jewish Sunday school I had scarcely learned the alphabet; neither I nor my teachers thought I would ever use it. I had learned by rote the few Hebrew blessings in our Reform service. It didn't matter whether you said them, because the rabbi would say them for you. If I ever tried to reach out to God, these arcane formulae in a foreign language were not how I did it. In Fabrangen, though, I watched people struggling to enter into the meaning of the Shabbat service. I realized that I could never discover that meaning, or truly encounter the Bible and other classic texts, if I had to rely on translations. Max named a lively grammar text I could use to study on my own. I checked in with him monthly.

Max also suggested I study weekly with a young woman, Dottie, who was rediscovering Judaism, had a passion to teach, and could use the extra cash. Working with Dottie I found a reason to labor over this alien and difficult language. She helped me hear the music, to feel the holiness that breathed from the words of the Hebrew prayers. At my first lesson, as she requested, I began to read and translate the first words of the evening prayer— "Blessed art thou, Oh Lord, our God"—a formula I had been saying by rote since I was five years old. She stopped me. "'Blessed art thou'—what does that mean?" she asked. "Does God inherently call forth our blessings? Do our blessings make a difference to God? What does it mean to bless?"

I was stunned, stimulated, delighted. Later that session, I saw how the Hebrew verbs swept us through the cycle of day and night, as if we saw time through God's eternal eye. From Dottie I learned to inch up on the poetry of prayer, jumping from Hebrew to English and back, letting the few words I knew carry me to the transcendent levels glimpsed by the poet.

Beyond the skill I was gaining with the language, in the supportive environment of Fabrangen I was able to use the texts to begin a personal transformation. In Ta'anit, the Talmud tractate on fasts, was the story of Honi, who drew a circle and refused to step out of it until God gave the parched earth rain. With Max's encouragement, we free-associated about the story. That intellectual play made it safe for me to explore spiritually. The image of God as stern Father, Judge, and King had long been for me a barrier to prayer. Reading about Honi stamping his foot and God indulging his beloved child, I began to understand that in Judaism God was a unity containing infinite dimensions, and that the possibilities for relationship to God were also infinite.

I was a somewhat combative and defensive person. Growing up Jewish in a small town, I had felt different—and vulnerable—for as long as I could remember. At Fabrangen, I was listened to. I could begin to have the courage to ask how I needed to change. I began to apply the Shabbat Torah discussions to my own life. We talked about Joseph, favored son of the patriarch Jacob, who was arrogant and self-centered until personal setbacks forced him to see God and not himself as the center of the universe. I could examine my own family, where I had been the favored child for a period of time, and see some of the same dynamics at work.

Midway through the year, I joined a committee that was organizing an alternative Jewish study center where one could study Jewish feminism and Jewish folk songs along with more traditional subjects. I saw it as a Jewish extension of the Free Universities, the freewheeling 1960s version of adult education. Fabrangeners more knowledgeable than I were modeling our study center on the Free Jewish House of Learning (*Freies Juedisches Lehrhaus,* or Lehrhaus), founded in Frankfurt, Germany, in 1920 by Franz Rosenzweig and Martin Buber.

Rosenzweig had felt his parents' minimalist Judaism was empty. At the age of twenty-seven he was about to convert to Christianity when he attended an Orthodox Jewish service for the Day of Atonement and suddenly felt that what he was looking for had been in Judaism all along. Turning down a plum academic job in Berlin, he began intensively studying Jewish texts. He fashioned a new career as gadfly to established Judaism, urging both Reform and Orthodox establishments to confront the alienation of the modern Jew. Buber also had a spiritual crisis as a teenager and young adult. Rejecting the Judaism of law with which he had been raised, he turned to Zionism and Hasidism. Buber saw relationships as either one-way, exploitative "I–it" relationships or mutually transforming "I–Thou" relationships— dialogues. In an I–thou relationship, in that mutual transformation, one experiences God. Hasidic rabbis of the eighteenth and nineteenth centuries, he said, had discovered how to have a transforming I–Thou relationship with God.

By applying the idea of dialogue to Jewish learning, Buber and Rosenzweig hoped to create a cultural/spiritual renaissance of the Jewish people. At the Lehrhaus, said Rosenzweig in his opening speech, Jews could again experience their texts as central to their lives without sacrificing the intellectual freedom of modern society. Teachers were not Torah scholars but chemists, physicians, artists, historians, and politicians. Students and teachers would be partners, finding the meaning of the texts for a new generation.

Within a year of the founding of the Lehrhaus, Rosenzweig—only thirty-five years old, married for one year, and looking forward to the birth of his first child—was stricken with a progressive paralysis that rapidly robbed him of speech and immobilized him entirely except for one thumb. His friends enabled him to continue practicing Judaism by holding Shabbat and High Holiday services in his room. Using first a special typewriter, and then barely perceptible signals interpreted by his wife, Edith, he continued writing for the next seven years until his death.

The Lehrhaus was closed by the Nazis in the 1930s, choking off the hoped-for Jewish renaissance. Buber, who moved to Palestine, was active into his eighties. His writings about the possibility of encounters with God inspired a generation of not only young Jews but Christians as well.

Nearly fifty years after the founding of the Lehrhaus, Buber and Rosenzweig's educational vision was reborn in the havurah movement. In 1979 the havurot (working together through the National Havurah Committee) began holding a weeklong summer-study program. Subsequently called the Havurah Institute, it is open to members of synagogues and unaffiliated individuals as well as members of havurot. At Havurah Institutes, every teacher is required also to be a student in someone else's class. In addition to taking classes, all participants also study in pairs (*hevruta*). At various Havurah Institutes I have studied the poetry of the prayer book; written poetry from the point of view of a biblical character; helped develop an improvisational dance and oratorio based on a psalm; taken a mystical visionary journey meditating on the letters of the Hebrew alphabet; learned how to eat an apple like a Hasid; and torn (verbally, at least) into five of the Talmudic texts most demeaning to women. Teachers at the institute include mathematicians, doctors, poets, and dancers as well as rabbis.

Rosenzweig predicted it would take a special kind of teacher to help people find the connections between Torah and their lives. For part of one wonderful week, I stayed at the home of Rabbi Mitch Chefitz, former chair of the National Havurah Committee, and visited the network of groups he has woven into the Havurah of South Florida. In a class on "practical mysticism," a surgeon, a student, a wealthy widow, a young bride, and others pair up hevruta-style to discuss mystical texts and try out the meditation techniques of the Jewish mystics. Atop a chrome-and-glass office tower with a view of the ocean, business executives, lawyers, secretaries and an elderly retired woman study the medieval philosopher Maimonides. Regional havurot in the northern and southern suburbs study what they wish, with texts suggested by Mitch. (He has them dissolve every year, then regroup if there is something members really want to study together.)

Instead of a conventional Sunday school, parents and children study together in a family *Beit Midrash* (house of study). "Nowhere in the Jewish community do children see their parents as models for lifelong Jewish learning," says Chefitz (who is canny enough to suggest that adults study with other people's children, not their own). On a tree-shaded patio, a teenage girl, a nine-year-old boy, and I sat on a porch glider puzzling over Mitch's questions on the Torah portion: How did God write the commandments on the stones? How was Moses able to carry them? (The boy in our group suggested that maybe God's writing made the stones light.) Later we watched Cecil B. DeMille's Hollywood extravaganza *The Ten Commandments.*

I asked Mitch what makes hevruta different and more powerful than other forms of study. "There has to be total involvement in the text," he said. "You read it out loud. One person is the designated reader. Why is Rab So-and-so saying this? I take a position, give a theory. You attack the position; you don't attack the person. You can do *hevrusa* on any text. You have done hevrusa if you can never look at it the same way again."

By way of illustration, he grabbed a plastic seltzer bottle from the table. " 'Ritz Seltzer.' Hmmm. Why do they call it Ritz? What are they trying to convey? 'No salt.' Why do you think that's on there? 'One liter.' When I was a kid, there weren't any liters. The label is red, white, and blue. They want us to think drinking seltzer is all-American." I disagreed, saying that I thought they were eye-catching colors; we were off and running. Mitch was right—I would never see that label in quite the same way again.

A doctor's son under pressure to go to a good college, Mitch did badly in high school, got into the Massachusetts Institute of Technology anyway, flunked out, spent a year at Berkeley writing for the humor magazine, then dropped out and joined the navy. Developing a thirst to know his Jewish roots, he entered rabbinical school—an amazing commitment for a guy who had a serious study block. At graduation Mitch got a post as assistant rabbi at a large, wealthy temple in Miami. Although highly regarded by the congregation, he quit and spent a few years as a successful stock trader. Yet the navy uniform, the clerical robes, and the business suit all felt to him like disguises. Today his rabbi's "uniform" is a faded T-shirt and shorts, a scraggly graying beard, and a collection of idiosyncratic hats. He says he has decided to make his career "filling Jewish vacuums"—serving people who fall outside the margins of the established Jewish community.

Studying is still hard for Mitch, but he is glad that the havurah forces him to do so. Every week he studies Talmud with a black-coated study partner from Miami's ultra-Orthodox yeshiva. Mitch is convinced that study, especially hevruta, is the key both to community connection and to connection with God. "Learning Torah, you grab hold of God and go. Whatever or whoever is the author, it is written so it reveals level after level. . . . When two people learn and uncover a word of Torah, you know it: it's like lifting a rock off an angel," he said.

What happens when established denominations (often spurred by havurah "graduates" who have become rabbis and religious educators) adopt the very personal havurah learning style? At a regional Reform movement Kallah (retreat for study and prayer) in Montclair, New Jersey, discussing Jacob's dream of a ladder stretching to heaven, one man said, "Jacob was a mama's boy.

Now he's on the run, sleeping outside with a stone for a pillow. Maybe each of us has to get out, away from home, before we can claim our own spirituality." The discussion leader, Rabbi Steven Kushner, concluded that "discovery of God is intertwined with discovery of self. We have to discover the God within us."

The stories of the Jewish people are a soil in which this dual discovery of God and self can grow. At a discussion for young adults run by the National Jewish Center for Learning and Leadership (CLAL), Rabbi Steve Greenberg[6] pointed out that if you identify with the story of the exodus from Egypt—even if you think it is just a story—you see the world, justice, and history in a certain way, a way that links you to other Jews.

CLAL's mission is to reconnect Jews with our stories. At the invitation of local synagogues, Jewish Federations, other organizations, or simply groups of Jews, CLAL runs classes all over the country on subjects as diverse as "What does Jewish tradition tell us about how to spend our money?" and "How can we bring holiness into our daily lives?" Exile and the destruction of the Temple gave birth to Judaism's second evolutionary stage, the rabbinic era, says CLAL founder Rabbi Irving Greenberg. The Nazi Holocaust could potentially be the birth pangs of the third great era. Israel has been reborn as a modern state. In America, where Jews have achieved social equality and economic and political power, leadership has shifted from rabbis to laypeople—especially in the Federations. So it is to lay leaders that CLAL addresses itself. In the third era, says Greenberg, it is we who must choose whether to be Jewish, and what Jewish means. To find meaning for ourselves and a vision for our community, we must know our stories.

Like the woman who told me that "the Reform Kallah is a gift I give myself," Susan, Jeff, and I were seeking out the stories we needed to consolidate our identities. We needed to understand this Jewishness stirring inarticulately within us if we were to become whole persons. The Jewish stories were our stories, a lens through which we could understand the world and ourselves. To become more Jewish was to become more ourselves. By studying our heritage, Franz Rosenzweig said, Jews can "return home to your innermost self and to your innermost life."

As I was gathering material for this chapter, I convened several focus groups and asked people whether study was a spiritual experience for them. The men talked about flashes of insight, overcoming obstacles, things suddenly coming together—or a sense of encounter that bushy-browed Sol Moshowitz said he couldn't or wouldn't describe ("We Litvaks don't kiss and tell with the Almighty"). The women talked about a process of achieving wholeness, knitting together one's sense of self with the long span of the Jewish people.

In the havurah and Jewish feminist worlds, the goal of learning is not only to become rooted in Judaism's past but to shape its future. Bringing some traditional texts about women to a class at the 1993 P'nai Or Kallah, Rabbi Sue Levi Elwell (now rabbi of a feminist center, Ma'yan, at the Jewish Community Center of the Upper West Side in New York) commented that today's women must write their own stories, their own texts. Traditional texts, she said, "are the raw materials we need to build upon."

Study, of course, was a Jewish path to God long before the havurah. I wondered: How did traditional Jewish study, which wasn't intimate self-exploration like havurah study, bring people closer to God? To get answers, I would have to seek out people who were different from me—people who had been born into or chosen Orthodoxy.

Rabbi Eric Kroner was a twenty-three-year-old graduate student at the University of London, en route to a career in international law or public administration, when he took a side trip to Israel. The son of Jewishly active but atheist parents who were founding members of a "humanist" synagogue, he got into an argument with some yeshiva students at a concert. He ended up, on a dare, going back to their yeshiva. He was so touched by his conversations with the rabbi that he stayed on to study there. What were the arguments the rabbi used to draw Kroner to Orthodox study and practice? He was persuaded, he said, by Torah's view that history has a goal: "Man has responsibility, accountability. One's life is not wasted; it has purpose."

Kroner came back to his native Detroit for a master's degree in public administration. Instead of going into politics, though, he donned the traditional black coat and used his administrative skills to build a Detroit community education program for *Ohr Somayach* ("Joyful Light"), the Jerusalem yeshiva that had changed his life. Every day he makes "cold calls," phoning four to five hundred people a month from lists of lawyers, doctors, and contributors to the Jewish Federation, inviting them to attend "Lunch and Learn" programs (he now gets two hundred attendees at these monthly lectures), small study groups, and one-on-one tutorials. The young businessman Jeff Garden and his wife, Helen, were among his recruits.

Rabbis ancient and modern agree that Torah study should create a more moral person. In everyday Jewish speech, the word *mitzvah* (literally, commandment) has come to mean "good deed." The more I studied, the more I loved the ethical imagination of the Torah. With great richness of detail, the Torah helps one think about what might be hurtful to another: don't hold a laborer's pay overnight; shoo away the mother bird before you take her eggs. But if one were to read for ethics alone, we would chuck out a lot of Torah: poetry, colorful but ambiguous stories, arbitrary rules. Why is it holy to study the rest? Study of Torah, says Rabbi Steinsaltz, is a *mitzvah* commanded by God, and as such creates a link between the doer and the One who commanded it.[7]

The rabbi of my Conservative synagogue, Yaakov Hilsenrath, had a similar view: "God reveals himself through knowledge. This is how God talks to us." I was touched by what he said, but it raised a conundrum for me. If I don't believe the Torah is the word of God, why study? Could study be holy activity even for someone like me? As I thought over my experiences, I realized it was—that the texts gave me new intuitions about holiness.

When my sabbatical was over (and I was unable to find work in Washington) I took a job in a suburb of Philadelphia, where I could be part of another large and vital havurah: the German-town minyan. Germantown was a somewhat more traditional community than Fabrangen. In Fabrangen we passed the English translation of the Torah around, and each person read a paragraph. Germantown members wanted the Torah read in Hebrew, and a service with most of the traditional prayers in Hebrew. To do that and still rotate leadership, they needed a good supply of skilled volunteers. Those who knew taught the rest to chant Torah and lead services. In the minyan women took every role I thought had been reserved for male rabbis: chanting from the sacred texts, leading the service, giving the brief sermonette (*d'var Torah*, "word of Torah") that opened the Torah discussion. I did not feel confident enough to play a part. But I decided for my thirty-sixth birthday I would have an adult bat mitzvah and learn to chant the Torah and Haftarah ("Prophets"). My bat mitzvah speech would be my first *d'var Torah*, my first leadership role in a minyan service.

Rabbi Art Green, founder of Havurat Shalom, was then teaching at the University of Pennsylvania and was a member of the Germantown minyan. I asked him to review my bat mitzvah speech. Instead, he did what the best teachers do: He posed me a question. In my Torah portion was a line I hadn't thought much about, a troubling line: "God will fulfill to the fourth generation of those that hate him and to the thousandth generation of those that love him." What did I make of this verse? Art asked. I went home and puzzled over it, and came back the next day with an answer. The word translated as "fulfill" was *m'shalem,* which is related to the word *shalom* ("wholeness"). Perhaps those who hated God were in some way incomplete. Though each person struggled to become whole, he or she couldn't help passing at least part of the hurt on to the next generation. It might take four generations to heal that hurt and create once again a whole person.

Art smiled his approval—I had received the bat mitzvah gift he was trying to give me. With one well-placed question, he had taught me two ways in which Jewish learning creates a spiritual moment. First, the rabbis assumed that just as God contains all possibilities, every word of the sacred texts contains infinite possibilities. Stories, phrases, even letters can be interpreted and reinterpreted. There were not only the literal meanings of stories and laws but moral teachings, allegorical meanings, and hidden meanings that only one skilled in mystical codes could uncover. By teasing me into looking more closely at the ambiguities and multiple meanings of a single Hebrew word, Green taught me that each word has the potential to teach one how to live in the image of God. Since then, I've seen this unfolding of meanings many times. Jewish tradition says God is in the details; each fragment of the universe is holy and reflects the Whole.

The second thing Green's question taught me has been even more useful: Don't skip the hard parts, because what is most troubling is potentially the most fruitful. Judaism's great sages could see the Torah as the word of God and still look at it critically. They noticed the contradictions—two passages that seem to say opposite things, an apparently needless repetition, even places where a noun and verb don't agree in number or gender. But unlike modern scholars who ascribe scripture's unevenness to multiple authors or mistakes by the editors, the rabbis believed that every contradiction has a higher purpose that people, through reason, can discover. Time and again, struggling with an obscure bit of text, I've come to an insight that has helped guide me in life. Once, while reading one of the boring lists of sacrifices (Prince X brought a bullock and Prince Y brought a bullock), I wondered, why do they have to name every prince? Suddenly I thought of those equally boring United Jewish Appeal dinners where they name every contributor. I realized, "People need credit for the good they do. They needed it three thousand years ago and they still do. So don't judge someone harshly when she needs to beat her own drum. Try to understand."

In preparing for my bat mitzvah, I had acquired the skills to contribute more actively to the service. When I began to do so, I found the texts entering my heart in a new way. For the week or two weeks before the service, I would live with the text of the service and the Torah selection, meditating and asking God to show me what meaning was there for the community and for me. I would make several false starts, and then a meaning would begin to unfold while I was jogging, showering, driving to work one day. Multiple levels of meaning would become apparent—levels that often slide past during the momentum of a service. When I heard and said the words during the service, they would radiate meanings within meanings.

Sometimes, in the midst of leading the Torah discussion, I would sit bolt upright, realizing that I was saying something I needed to hear. This message coming out of my mouth was from God to me. Yet it nearly always turned out to be relevant to others as well. It was as if, when I reached out to try to help the community find meaning, the Source of Meaning reached out to me.

The same Torah portions and the same themes came up year after year, but they always seemed to yield new meanings. Rabbi Larry Kushner says the text of the Torah is like a dream; every character, every aspect is analogous to some part of yourself and can reflect back something that you need to learn at this moment in your life. I was changing, and so were the questions I was asking. Because I was in an environment where I could keep asking questions—indeed, where the community needed me to keep asking questions—my religion could grow with me. "It's a process," says Rabbi Kroner. "It requires an open heart and an open mind."

I got married, wrote a book, adopted a child, and found that I had less and less time to contribute to the minyan. In practice, this also meant that I was not studying. I continued to enjoy minyan discussions, but I was not pushing myself to grow in relationship to the text. I had never studied texts for their own sake—as a form of *avodah,* service to God. When my husband's job necessitated our moving to New Jersey, though, I had an opportunity to step across that threshold. My husband, Steve, got involved in a Talmud study group that met at our house. I had no interest in participating. Despite the taste I'd had with Max in Washington, I still thought of Talmud as dry and abstruse, and I knew I was no scholar. But I used to eavesdrop while doing the dishes.

The group was studying Brachot, the Talmud tractate on blessings. One evening I heard a shout of laughter and came to the doorway, my wet hands still clutching a towel. They were reading a passage about the law of food fights. One of the long-ago rabbis (I picture him as a sixteen-year-old student with a bare wisp of beard) had thrown some food at another, and now the students were throwing biblical quotes at each other to prove what foods you were or were not allowed to throw. I felt transported to the rabbinical academy of two thousand years ago, dodging imaginary flying chunks of bread. I was touched that the lives of these students were so full of the Torah that even their wisecracks explored the limits of holy and profane.

In the next passage the rabbis were talking about what to do if you've started eating and have forgotten to say the blessing over the food. Should you spit out the food to say the blessing? That would be both wasteful and disgusting. Should you shove the mouthful into one cheek and say the blessing? One of the scholars objected. Scripture says your whole mouth should be filled with God's blessing. Chuckling, I hung up my dishcloth, sat down at the table, and began the first of four years' study with the class. Later I learned that the Talmud was edited from discussions that took place over centuries and that the scenes I imagined might never have taken place, but I still think it's a wonderful way to study Talmud: to imagine that you're there and might throw your two bits into the conversation.

As my husband has pointed out to me, that mental time travel we do every time we gather around the table is part of what makes Talmud study sacred. The thread connecting that long-ago time to our own weaves us into a family that transcends time, distance, oppressions, and ideological differences. In addition, we eavesdrop on a place where God is real. Steve, though very committed to Jewish practice, is a nonbeliever. But in Talmud class, he says, we suspend disbelief. We enter a world where people believe they can use their minds for the sacred task of understanding God's will.

One night the passage we studied concerned mental preparation for prayer. Members of our group asked, how could *we* prepare ourselves to really pray? Another night the Talmudic rabbis discussed which biblical figures were proper models for prayer, including Moses, King David, and Hannah (who prayed for a son and eventually gave birth to the prophet Samuel). Members of our group asked, what linked these diverse figures? We realized that all of them had prayed with no holds barred. They argued, bargained, and manipulated, not weighing words, presenting themselves to God just as they were. Profoundly moved, we began to talk of our own struggles with prayer.

Week after week we sat around the table in our drafty dining room, drinking tea, translating word by word from the often elliptical and puzzling text, and arguing our way onto tangents that covered our work and our families. When we talked about the duties of children toward parents, Susan talked about her mother's struggle to decide whether to put her grandmother in a nursing home. We gradually developed a wonderful camaraderie, with inside jokes based on phrases that came up in our study, and our own traditions (such as beginning and ending with a brief discussion of the problems people were having with their computers). We often covered only a few lines of text, spending the rest of the two-hour session on a tangent. But the tangents were fruitful.

Now that I had broken the barrier of Talmud study, I wanted to explore hevruta—studying text with a partner—more deeply. I began studying with a good friend from Philadelphia, Rabbi Nancy Fuchs, who teaches at the Reconstructionist Rabbinical College. Since I now lived in New Jersey, every two weeks

Nancy and I would load a pile of books, Hebrew-English dictionaries, and notebooks into our respective cars and meet in the parking lot of a motel on the Pennsylvania Turnpike, halfway between our two houses. That first summer day we found a dilapidated picnic area near the river, spread out our texts on a weathered wooden table, and got to work. We were using *Sefer HaAggadah* ("The Book of Legends"), a collection of Talmudic stories and quotations grouped by topic. We started with the section on study. The tradition said we should study Torah *l'shma*, for its own sake, without any goal except fulfilling God's commandment to study. Could we really do that? I thought of Nancy as the perfect scholar, but that idea turned out to be as hard for her as for me. The study that meant most to her, she said, was study in order to change, to become a better person.

We left our questions standing and went on to another topic— anger, something we both agreed we needed to work on. As we puzzled over the texts, all of which seemed without qualification to condemn anger, we talked about our own anger: when it was good to express it, when it was important to control it. Our conversation spun back and forth, from the texts to us: her daughter going through an angry phase, and my struggles to handle my son's tantrums without throwing a tantrum myself.

Just before Yom Kippur, the Day of Atonement or Judgment, while studying over the telephone, we found ourselves discussing (without having planned it) a section on judging others charitably. I suddenly realized that many of my bursts of temper come from snap judgments I make about others and about myself. We talked about reconciling the images of God's unconditional love and judgment. We talked about our children: We love them unconditionally, but still we often push them and judge them. In fact, we judge them more harshly sometimes because we see them as reflections of ourselves (and judge ourselves for their actions).

Nancy recalled a Hasidic story in which the master tells the disciples that Judgment Day will be no more and no less than a long chat between each individual and God, reviewing that individual's whole life. That conversation, the master concluded, will be both heaven and hell. Such a homey, loving image—God there with you, the two of you working it out, fully facing the imperfections and celebrating the growth and triumphs of spirit. I went into Yom Kippur with something to pray for: If I could see myself as God's child, beloved and forgiven, perhaps I could forgive myself, and in turn be the loving parent I wanted to be for my own children.

From Nancy, my Talmud class, and Fabrangen, I realized that Jewish study is communal. As sociologist Samuel Heilman points out, for all their vehemence, the arguments of Jewish study are always a game.[8] Rabbi Mitch Chefitz had explained the rules to me: Ideas are attacked, but never people. In fact, in challenging the ideas of the study partner, one is actually communicating respect and delight in sharing this exercise of mind and spirit. The communal, intimate nature of Jewish study is an important part of its spiritual power. Hevruta is a partnership; it makes study into an experience of I and Thou.

In wrestling with ideas, laughing, and trying to connect our lives to the text, we connect with each other differently than in the side-by-side beauty of communal prayer. For me, God is in all the ways that people learn to respect, delight in, and care for one another. Studying together is very special, because it forces us to go beyond the routines that usually dominate everyday conversation and deal with the ultimate questions of life. Said Rabbi Michael Paley, "The relationships with people I learn with are my most intense, precious, transformative relationships. They have a medium in which to grow."

Our sages said:

When two sit together and words of Torah pass between them, the Divine Presence dwells between them.

—R. Hanania ben Teradyon, *Ethics of the Fathers* 3:3

and

> Three who have eaten at one table and have said over it words of
> Torah are as if they had eaten from the table of God.
>
> —R. Simeon, *Ethics of the Fathers* 3:4

For me these sayings turned out to be true. Study was a way of intensely experiencing community, and in community I could encounter the presence of God.

CHAPTER 4

COMMUNITY AS SANCTUARY, CALENDAR AS CATECHISM

Jewish Time and Jewish Space in an American Life

When Sarah Schandelson was a little girl going to a Reconstructionist synagogue in Buffalo, New York, she tried to listen very carefully during High Holiday services when the congregation spoke in unison. As she explains, "I thought somehow in that rumble I would hear the voice of God." Sarah eventually began to hear that voice in the tight embrace of an Orthodox community.

Havurahniks, too, felt that a community was the place to hear the voice of God. But the synagogues where they had grown up had become so large and bureaucratic that "the very institution of the synagogue itself threatens to destroy the religious life it purports to sustain," wrote havurah movement mentors rabbis Lawrence Kushner, Arnold Jacob Wolf, and Everett Gendler in the *Third Jewish Catalog*.[1]

The problem was not only what had happened to synagogues,

but what had happened to Jews. We were the first generation of truly American Jews. As second- and third-generation Americans, we were fully integrated into and shaped by a Protestant culture that sees the encounter with God as an individual one. But community is as central for Jews as Jesus is to Christianity; it is our primary way of feeling God's presence. Community is to our spiritual life as the sea is to fish. Was it possible to reconstitute the sea so that each fish had a vote? Unlike synagogues, Ramah and other summer camps gave young Jews a taste of a community where they felt affirmed as individuals while they were embraced as Jews. Through the havurah movement, they tried to make that embrace last the year round.

Barbara Laster was one of these seekers. From the time she was a youngster, Barbara searched for a Jewish connection. She eventually found her way to Fabrangen in Washington, D.C., but it took a long time. The family she was raised in gave mixed messages about Judaism: for example, her father would make sarcastic comments while her mother said the Sabbath blessings. In elementary school Barbara made a quiet personal decision to keep the Sabbath by not doing any homework that day. At age eleven she took the bus by herself every Saturday morning from her non-Jewish neighborhood in Miami to a synagogue where she could participate in Junior Congregation.[2] She was so entranced with the taste of Jewish community she got as a counselor-in-training at a United Synagogue summer camp that she persuaded Miami's Central Agency for Jewish Education to hire one of the teachers, havurah poet Danny Siegel, to teach at the local Hebrew high school for a year. Once she had her driver's license Barbara began visiting the home of a traditional rabbi in Miami Beach, where she loved the singing, storytelling, peace and companionship that were part of Shabbat afternoon. "That's what I wanted," she said.

The Orthodox Hillel at University of Florida, though, didn't prove to be the community Bellows was looking for. When a National Teacher Corps job after college took her to a remote section of Appalachia where there were no Jews, she used to drive more than an hour to attend High Holiday services at a college campus to the north. "I was trying to find something. I wasn't going to give up until I found it," she recalled.

The man Barbara married had no interest in Judaism. When his job took them to Boston, she participated in Havurat Shalom and got her first taste of the kind of unorthodox but intensely spiritual community she was seeking. To really be part of Havurat Shalom, however, required a commitment that Barbara's family responsibilities didn't allow. Because she had to rush back to her family every Saturday morning after the musical and beautiful service, she could never be part of the real in-group, the haverim. When Bellows and her husband moved again in 1977 to Washington, D.C., she tried getting involved with Fabrangen. Not only were the services moving, but the community seemed more welcoming. Community members who lived in her neighborhood invited her for Shabbat dinners. She got involved in a women's Rosh Hodesh (New Moon) group. She was learning to chant the Torah from one woman, reading commentaries on the Torah under the guidance of another havurah member, and had gone on a couple of community retreats when her husband's job uprooted her once again and took her to California.

After eleven years of marriage, Barbara and her husband separated, and she came back to the District of Columbia as a single mother with two small daughters, aged one and three. "It was very sad. But sure enough, Fabrangen was there. My community rallied around." She went almost immediately to a Fabrangen retreat. Everyone was so loving and comforting to her that "I realized I was going to get through it." Community members took on the role of aunts and uncles to her children.

Life got complicated for Barbara when she began to date John Laster, a member of Fabrangen. Because the community was so small and interconnected, and she didn't want her daughters to be hurt, she and John kept their relationship hidden until they actually decided to get married. During a Fabrangen Shabbat retreat Barbara called her daughters, by this time six and eight years old, into her room and told them that she and John planned to marry; the girls burst out into the hall, flinging open doors and yelling into classrooms, "Mom and John are getting married." The community was gathering for Havdalah, the lovely ceremony of candles, wine, spices, and song that ends the Sabbath. Everybody started spontaneously singing and dancing in a circle around them.

The community was in a similarly ecstatic state during the couple's *aufruf* (the Torah ceremony the Shabbat before the wedding) and their wedding. The minute the ceremony was over, joyous line and circle dancing began and continued for five hours. The community lifted her, John, and the girls up on chairs and danced them around. When Barbara and John had a baby, the naming ceremony overflowed with the same communal joy. Feeling their community so genuinely rejoicing with them, Bellows said, "I've been so blessed. It's remarkable to me. . . . I always knew that within Judaism I could find what I wanted. I just had to keep looking." The community was there in a different way, to support and help, when she had a car accident. This support at both low and high points in one's life makes it easier to take on the petty not-so-spiritual tasks that are necessary to the functioning of any community, Barbara said.

When Fabrangen member Paul Lichterman disappeared on the coldest day of the year in 1985, police insisted on waiting twenty-four hours to search for him, assuming it was probably just another case of a man abandoning his family. The Fabrangen community, though, didn't wait. They formed a search team of nearly one hundred people that combed the District of Columbia metropolitan area, eventually finding Lichterman's car in a nature reserve (where he had apparently fallen through the ice while hiking). Fabrangeners then created a memorial service and provided emotional support for his family through the year of mourning. Ten years later Fabrangen members were still helping out, coaching the man's young son for bar mitzvah.

Just before Passover in 1993, Donna (not her real name), a thirty-five-year-old Fabrangen member, learned she had a lymphoma. Shabbat morning she asked to be called up to the Torah for an *aliyah,* the honor of standing beside the Torah while it is read. There, beside the Torah, she told everyone the news. "It seemed the obvious thing to do, to tell your community if you're having a crisis," said Donna. "Part of the havurah is that people are open and familial with everybody." After services, Donna said, people lined up "like a wedding reception" to find out more and ask how they could help. To her embarrassment and gratitude, within twenty-four hours four committees had formed to provide rides home from chemotherapy, baby-sitting for her four young children, help with cooking, and fundraising (to hire a nanny to assist with the children).

People stocked a freezer at one member's house with frozen home-cooked meals. Donna went when she needed and chose what she wanted; she didn't have to ask for help every day. Friends sat with her during chemotherapy. As she got to know other cancer patients, Donna realized how isolated many of them were. She felt lucky that people in her community didn't shy away, worrying about what to say. After her second chemotherapy treatment, one friend called up and joked, "Well, are you bald yet?"

One person did a computer search for the latest information on treatment of Donna's particular cancer. Others brought her articles about alternative treatments. One group sewed a lap-size "friendship quilt," which all community members signed in indelible ink—"a great moral support," commented Donna. When it was announced that Donna was in remission and would help lead High Holiday services, the community rejoiced.

Not only the havurah, but more established Jewish communities can rally around to provide support for members who need it. Donna and her husband also belonged to a large Conservative synagogue near their home. On days Donna had chemotherapy, a member of the synagogue would arrive that evening with a hot meal for her family. "Looking at my own experience, it's impossible for me to imagine how difficult it would have been without community," said Donna.

WHAT IS THE CORNERSTONE, the defining element of Jewish community? "We have to create a caring community," said Rabbi Burt Jacobson, a former faculty member of Havurat Shalom and founder of Kehilla ("Community"), a politically radical synagogue in Oakland, California. "A community is a group of people who are together, not necessarily because they are friends, but because they are there for one another during times of tragedy and joy. . . .You can't have community unless you have responsibility for each other in an ongoing way."

A member of Mishkan Shalom ("Sanctuary of Peace"), a politically radical congregation near Philadelphia, said that the first time someone asked her to join a *shiva* minyan for someone who was in mourning, she wondered how her presence could possibly be comforting to someone who did not know her. But in time she came to feel a spiritual connection when she brought food to someone who was ill or drove a carpool for a woman who had just given birth; she was creating the web of community that would sustain her in turn.

It wasn't easy for havurahniks to build that kind of community. Havurat Shalom in 1968 and the New York Havurah, founded a couple of years later, tried to make it happen by creating a small, self-contained Jewish spiritual community—a pond for a select group of very committed fish. They interviewed and admitted to membership only gifted, Jewishly well-educated, iconoclastic students and teachers.

Martha Ackelsberg, like most New York Havurah members, was a graduate student when she joined the group. Members ate dinner together every Thursday, *davened* (prayed) together every Shabbat, had a retreat once a month, and took at least one havurah class. "It was a wonderful, very intense community," she said. "The idea was to overcome the fragmentation of life, so the people you *davened* with were also the people you studied with and did politics with [mostly opposing the Vietnam War]. It didn't overcome the fragmentation; we all had other lives. [But] it was one of the central, orienting lodestones of our lives."

As one person said of the havurot, "Relationships [are] our spirituality. We can't seem to find God so easily; we find it in the relationships."

The spiritual glue of the havurot was the same as in traditional Jewish communities: the year-round cycle of holidays. The German-Jewish scholar Rabbi Samson Raphael Hirsch said, "The catechism of the Jew is his calendar."[3]

Jewish holidays build community. From the weekly Sabbath to the nature-based and history-based holidays that occur nearly every month, the holidays must be celebrated with other people. As Kushner, Wolf, and Gendler wrote, "Jews must gather, not because they are friends or even because they agree, but simply because they need each other to go on being Jews."[4]

At synagogue services, a *minyan* (a quorum of at least ten adults) is required for certain prayers to be recited.[5] Shabbat and holidays also have home celebrations, each with its festive meal. At least three must be present to say the special introduction to the blessing after the meal.

I had grown up in a classical Reform synagogue where holidays were celebrated only by short tepid services, with prayers and observances so indistinguishable that I could never keep straight the difference between Tu B'Shvat, the birthday of the trees, and Tisha B'Av, the mournful memorial of the destruction of the ancient Temple in Jerusalem. There wasn't much there to make me feel compelled to come to synagogue and be with other people. When I joined the Germantown minyan in Philadelphia I understood for the first time how it felt to be swept along on the tides of the Jewish year.

For most of the previous six years I had been a newspaper reporter, living from deadline to deadline. Now my life took on a new rhythm. Every Shabbat we had lunch or dinner in each other's apartments, singing Sabbath songs until late afternoon. With the larger community, we built leafy booths outdoors and ate in them during the fall harvest holiday of Sukkot. We danced in circles with the Torah on Simkhat Torah ("Rejoicing in the Law"). We slogged through winter slush to spin dreidels and cook *latkes* (potato pancakes) at the minyan Hanukkah party. The late winter holiday of Purim found us gathered in crazy costumes to read the book of Esther, spoofing each other in skits, and sending each other baskets of sweet treats (*shalah manot*). I felt bathed in love as unsolicited goodies piled up outside my apartment door.

At Passover in early spring, we stretched out the seder until the wee hours of the morning, sharing readings from different *haggadot* (books retelling the story of the exodus from Egypt) and debating how this story should guide our actions in the political struggles of our own day. At Shavuot (the late spring holiday celebrating the giving of the Torah at Mt. Sinai), we stayed up all night studying the meaning of revelation, then put on prayer shawls and stood on a grassy embankment to accept the Torah anew by the light of a dawning sun. I finally learned, indelibly, about the summer fast of Tisha B'Av when we sat on the floor barefoot, like mourners, and by the flickering light of memorial candles wailed the agonized verses of the biblical book of Lamentations, which describe the horrors of a city under siege. Toward the end of summer, nearly every regular member of the community would contribute in some way toward putting on the High Holiday Service. The service was open and free, and people from the surrounding community who had no other Jewish connection would show up and feel they belonged. After the final, piercing call of the ram's horn (*shofar*) at Yom Kippur, our little group of friends came back to someone's apartment and broke the fast together. The rhythm of my life became a Jewish rhythm.

Returnees to Judaism often say that the most dramatic life change they experienced was a sense of living in Jewish rather than American time. As Lisa Newell of Fabrangen said, "Until now, the only markers of time in my life were weekends and exams." Like other returnees to Judaism, I was absorbing a key element of Jewish spirituality—a sense of God's presence in the order, cycle, and flow of the calendar. Though I lived in the city and got my connection to nature in two-week chunks during summer vacation, the Jewish calendar brought the physical cycle of the seasons into my home, into my heart, and into my identity. The holidays linked the physical seasons to Jewish history, which was becoming my history.

And these holidays were all tied to emotional and spiritual meanings that were becoming the ways in which I found meaning.

At Sukkot, squeezing with my guests around the table in my breezy outdoor booth, I connected with the tradition of hospitality my ancestors carried from desert tents to harvest shelters on terraced hillsides of ancient Israel and later to urban ghettos in Europe and Arab lands. During the Passover seder, the parsley I dipped in salt water connected me to the tender spring leaves uncurling outside my window, the tears of oppressed people everywhere, the long saga of my people, and the affection of my friends who sat elbow to elbow around the table singing about freedom. At Purim, waving my *gragger* (noisemaker) to drown out the name of the wicked Haman, I was claiming victory over all the manipulative tyrants throughout the ages who for their own political purposes had roused mobs to anti-Semitic rampages.

The holidays covered the full range of human emotions—from Passover's joy to Tisha B'Av's abject despair and horror, and from the regal solemnity of the High Holidays to the giddy silliness of Purim. In celebrating the holiday cycle, I felt myself acquiring permission to be the full, many-sided human being I am. I grew more confident that I could live with the heights and depths, the angers and envies and ebbs of confidence that were all part of me, and still be a fine and decent human being, contributing to making the world a better place. I felt valued and whole as I celebrated each holiday surrounded by friends. I felt blessed as each holiday delighted my senses with its special foods, fragrances, candles, and songs. I found myself constantly anticipating the next holiday or the next Shabbat, taking sustenance from one sweet island of joy and holiness and moving forward toward the next.

Celebrating the holidays over the years, I've come to sense a larger heartbeat of time in which we live. Coming back over and over to the same holiday makes me feel as if I have a home in time, not only in space. And there's a wonder in finding that it is never the same, because every year I have grown and changed. This sense of connection, not only to this community but to the community of all Jews who have ever lived, is itself a very beautiful manifestation of the Divine Presence.

In traditional communities, the way of life prescribed by religious law was another part of the glue that bound Jews together. Since Jews were not permitted to ride on the Sabbath, homes clustered around the synagogue. Since people could buy only kosher meat and eat only in kosher homes, they had to support their peers economically and socialize within the community. Even clothing set them apart: while their neighbors favored a mixture of linen and wool, Jews were not allowed to wear fabrics of mixed threads, so it made sense for them to buy cloth from a Jewish merchant.

When Sarah Schandelson entered the Orthodox world, she was struck by the intensity of community. One reason for the bonding: "You are with people who share the same assumptions. There are certain things you don't have to talk about."

In the havurah movement, the assumptions were being worked out as we went. We did have to talk about things; in fact, talking was part of what held our communities together. Though havurah members did not demand the Orthodox world's uniformity of observance, we voluntarily adopted many of its customs and restrictions, such as walking on the Sabbath. A helicopter flying on Saturday over our section of Philadelphia would have seen bright skullcaps (*yarmulkes*) creeping like so many multicolored ladybugs toward the synagogue where we met, and a forest of strollers parked at the front door.[6] Various havurot added their own community-building traditions, such as potluck dinners after Sabbath services.

We learned to handle differences in observance. Before Neil Reisner and Ruth Honigfeld, who don't have a kosher kitchen, held a housewarming, Neil questioned the Orthodox members of our Talmud class: What would make it possible for them to attend and eat? Paper plates? A new metal grill for their barbecue?

Many university neighborhoods had *batim,* kosher communal houses with both Orthodox and non-Orthodox egalitarian students. At Shabbat services in the *bayit* where attorney Jonathan Zimet lived, if ten egalitarian men and women arrived first, the service would be egalitarian. If the Orthodox were first to gather a minyan of ten men, the service that day would have separate prayer areas for men and women and follow Orthodox traditions.

Allowing each member to determine his or her own level of observance fit nicely with the havurah attempt to balance individualism and community. But to compensate for the fragmenting pull of individual choice, the havurot needed to generate additional forces to pull the community together. They did this by turning the potential liability of their individualism into a community-building asset.

The community became a forum for affirming the worth of each individual in it. Running the community was the responsibility of each member. Havurah was Judaism on a shoestring. The Highland Park minyan where I am a member now has met for twenty years in people's living rooms. The minyan's combined assets consist of a homemade wooden ark that holds our borrowed Torah, a cheap set of stainless steel flatware for potluck lunches, eight folding chairs, and several boxes of hand-me-down prayerbooks and Bibles turned over to us by local synagogues. If havurah Judaism is Orthodoxy without rules, it is also Reform without dues. There is no rabbi's salary, no building fund, and no monied leadership.

Though havurot were sometimes dominated by people who knew Hebrew and had a good Jewish education, the best way to achieve influence was to have a strong dialing finger and enough *sitzfleish* (flesh on your buttocks) to make it through lots of meetings. People who didn't know Hebrew could contribute to Sabbath services by leading some sections in English while another leader led sections in Hebrew. (Some havurot experimented with stereophonic prayers: English coming in one ear, Hebrew in the other.) Those who knew taught those who didn't have skills such as chanting the Torah or leading the service. Three or four of us would sit in someone's living room, tape recorders rolling, while the volunteer teacher walked us through the service.

We tried to make sure everyone had a chance to speak in meetings and Torah discussions. When people at the Germantown minyan realized that men were dominating most discussions, they made a simple rule. Each man who spoke had to call on a woman to speak next, and each woman had to call on a man.

The most important forum where everyone could contribute was the Torah discussion. Services and study sessions were personal explorations; instead of affirming ideas they didn't believe in, havurahniks built an intimate community by sharing their doubts. Folklorist Chava Weissler described the process in *Making Judaism Meaningful,* her doctoral dissertation on the Germantown minyan.[7] A typical *d'var Torah* would begin with the phrase "I had trouble with this portion because. . . ." After explaining the doubts, the havurahnik would describe some metaphorical way in which the text was relevant to dilemmas with which she was struggling. The discussion leader set a tone that encouraged others to share. In one Torah discussion described by Weissler, the story of Joseph and his brothers stimulated an intense discussion on handling sibling rivalries left over from childhood. Martha Ackelsberg's gay and lesbian havurah focused on a different aspect of the Joseph story: his decision to reveal to his brothers that the man they thought was an Egyptian prince was really their brother. The havurah talked about being in hiding and "coming out," telling their families that they were gay.

IN A *d'var Torah* at the Germantown minyan, Chava compared our simple circle of folding chairs to the portable sanctuary carried by the biblical Jews as they wandered through the desert.[8] Our small circle and the thoughts and feelings shared here, she said, do for us what the sanctuary did for the ancient Jews: allow us to feel God's Presence in our midst. Underlying the sanctuary of shared selves was Martin Buber's notion that all real sacred experience is a kind of meeting—not the type with an agenda but a meeting of minds, in which people are able truly to understand and accept one another without surrendering their differentness. Jewish spirituality is about finding God in this world, and relationships are the most important way we do it. The Jewish emphasis on ethics flows naturally from the notion that we are to find sacredness by treating each other as holy.

The havurah was such an accepting community that many people who had to leave one because of job or marriage hungered to find another. Since the havurah had given them on-the-job training in creating community, "graduates" who couldn't find a havurah in their new town often organized one.

It is not easy, though, to keep alive a community that refuses to be an institution. The Westwood minyan in Los Angeles had been going strong for ten years when Riv-Ellen Prell made it the subject of her doctoral dissertation, *Prayer and Community*.[9] By the time her book appeared in print, the minyan, plagued by burnout and loss of leadership, had disbanded.

The fluidity of havurah communities has been both their strength and their weakness. As Rivkah Walton, former coordinator of the Havurah Institute, pointed out, the communities were "permeable both ways." It was easy to get in, but if you were on the margins—or even if you were very active and gradually got less active—you might disappear without anyone pursuing you to see what happened.

Many havurah communities have divided at least once. The democracy of the havurot encourages the development of many leaders, and these leaders cannot always coexist. The Highland Park minyan split after one member took offense when another got angry and yelled at the first member's son, who was misbehaving. Although many factors contributed to the split (differences in philosophy about how much to include young children, how traditional a service was desired, differences in age between newcomers and veteran members), the underlying problem was that these two members were both leaders: one a founder of the minyan, the other a woman with a strong Jewish education and her own style of leadership.

A crisis in the Germantown minyan was triggered by a dispute between one of the founding couples and some newcomers. The founding couple was upset at having to share the stage on the weekend of their son's bar mitzvah with some relative newcomers who were getting married that weekend and wanted to be called to the Torah for a blessing (*aufruf*). Shortly afterward, a small group of havurah veterans split off to form the Home Minyan, a group that was by invitation only. Home Minyan members explained that its growth had stripped the Germantown minyan of the intimacy they had cherished. The bitter feelings, though, have lasted to this day.

The year before there had been another split. Some of the minyan members wanted a more traditional service (what a member of our group referred to as "peas-and-carrots" or "mumble" prayer). Despite the splits, we tried to maintain that we were still one community; for example, our phone list ("the United Germantown Minyanim") included members of all three groups. Four times a year—for the High Holidays and for the festivals of Passover, Shavuot, and Sukkot—we planned and prayed together. But it was a fragile union. One year, when I, representing the less traditional minyan, had spent about three weeks negotiating with members of the more traditional minyan about the format for festival services, a group from my minyan got up and announced unilaterally that, following the Reform and Re-constructionist custom, they would hold end-of-festival services a day before the traditional minyan. Our attempts to agree on joint services were shattered.

Women, gays and lesbians also began to organize their own prayer communities. Martha Ackelsberg, a former New York Havurah member who helped to found both a gay/lesbian havu-rah and a feminist spirituality collective, B'not Esh ("Daughters of Fire"), says spirituality is a search for wholeness. Some women and gays felt they could experience wholeness only in a commu-nity that explicitly embraced the parts of themselves that tradi-tional Judaism rejected.

Such divisions are painful, but I choose to see them as resulting in an array of choices, a variety of ways to express one's spiritual-ity. I pray mostly with my havurah, but sometimes with a women's group and sometimes with a mystical group.

Because they were equally committed to individual self-ex-pression and community, the ability of some havurot to struggle through differences could be one of their great strengths. When members of B'not Esh held their first retreat, they were stunned to see how deep the divisions could be among women who were all very involved with both Judaism and feminism. After the first rather traditional Shabbat evening service, wrote Ackelsberg (who had led it), "Some members were 'high' with the power of an all-women's davening, [while] others felt alienated and an-gered by the fact that we had followed so closely the hierarchical, male-dominated aspects of the liturgy."[10]

The tensions came out the next morning: "What began as a five-minute discussion turned into a two-hour session, during which almost everyone expressed strong feelings of alienation and exclusion, and many people were in tears."[11] That day, and over the years, the members resolved their differences by exper-imenting with a mix of the elements each woman felt she needed: some traditional, some eclectic. They held discussions about what each wanted from prayer, acknowledged their differences, tried to come to each retreat and prayer session with an attitude of openness, and listened afterward to each other's reactions. "At our best, we transform the sources of our confrontations into the topic of our conversations . . . [and] turn painful confrontations into sources of growth."[12] Though they did not succeed consistently in creating services that satisfied everyone, they came to realize that the experience of learning to understand each other was as powerful and spiritually significant as any prayer experience.

Though communal houses, potluck dinners, and self-revelatory discussions are very contemporary ways of creating community, the struggle to find a balance between individualism and community is as old as Judaism. In fact, it is fundamental to Jewish belief.

Jewish moral vision is rooted in the experience of being outsiders, what Simone de Beauvoir calls "the Other." The very name Hebrews, according to some scholars, means "the ones who crossed over" from the other side of a river. From our first ancestor, Abraham, who was commanded by God to leave his home, to go to a new land, we Jews have been strangers in a strange land. As outsiders we were forced into slavery in Egypt. Liberated, we entered a promised land where we struggled to maintain our cultural and religious separateness from the indigenous peoples. We lived as an independent nation in our own land for only about six of our thirty-two centuries as a people. For the last nineteen centuries we have been scattered among other nations all over the world. The commandment to treat the stranger kindly is repeated thirty-six times in the Bible, more than any other commandment.[13] As the Bible says, "You know the feelings of the stranger, having been strangers in the land of Egypt" (Exodus 23:9).

From our experiences as outsiders rose the two poles of Jewish theology. One pole is a vision of wholeness: Beyond all divisions is a unity in which no one is a stranger. Though God seems to speak with so many voices—from the stars, the sea, the earth and its fruits and creatures—beyond all these manifestations of power and goodness God is one, uniting them all. All humans are children of God, one family, descended from one set of parents. God creates the first humans as partners because "it is not good for man to be alone" (Genesis 2:18).

Our communal life mirrors this image of wholeness underlying all diversity. The great medieval scholar Moses Maimonides pointed out that Jews are the only people whose theology is built on an encounter between the entire nation and God. At Mount Sinai, tradition says, the Jewish nation accepted the Torah with one voice. We entered a covenant, a mutually binding commitment between the Jewish people and God.[14] But most details of the covenant concern our relationship to other members of our Jewish and human communities. As Rabbi Irving (Yitz) Greenberg has pointed out, we come to know God by seeing and dealing with another human as an image of God. We are to know God through our relationships with each other, as family and community. Jews traditionally consider themselves members of one family descended from the patriarch Abraham, who made the first Jewish covenant with God. Our scriptures are about brothers and sisters, constantly in conflict yet inextricably connected. The Jewish community has the intensity, the sense of obligation, the complex bonds of a family.

After the encounter at Sinai, we wandered through the desert carrying our sanctuary with us, a concrete symbol that God was to be found not "out there" but in our midst. In Jewish tradition, the worst punishment other than death was to be cut off from the community.

Yet the second pole of Jewish ideology is that individuality is sacred. In our creation story, each person is created in the image of God (Genesis 1:27). Each person is whole, complete in himself or herself. Tradition says that to save one person is equivalent to saving the whole world, and to cause one man to perish is like causing a whole world to perish (Mishnah *Sanhedrin* 4,5). The covenant embodies that paradox. Each Jew is individually responsible for fulfilling the covenant, but each is also responsible for seeing that other community members do their parts. In both the positive sense of helping each other and the negative sense of being blamed for each other's misdeeds, "all Jews are responsible for one another" (Babylonian Talmud, *Shevuot* 39a).

Other nations and religious traditions, operating from a fixed center in their own lands, developed concentric hierarchies. Jews in exile elaborated the theme of community as unity embracing plurality.[15] We lived in a web of villages and ghettos connected by threads of kinship, commerce, language, religious law, and custom that crossed the formal boundaries of other nations. At times, pressured by the larger gentile society, each community acted like an island. When the surrounding gentile nation strictly regulated the number of Jews allowed, Jewish community councils would not allow anyone to settle in the town except by a vote of the council. But at other times, within the web of communities, hospitality was the law—there were to be no strangers. Students might travel to another country to study with a particular rabbi. Matchmakers arranged weddings linking families in different towns or countries. When Jews from one country were persecuted or expelled, doors opened and other Jewish communities took them in.

This pattern probably began to develop after the destruction of the First Temple. With worship no longer in the hands of the priests, a lay leadership bloomed. In exile in Babylonia, the merchants and nobility apparently organized the community to maintain a Jewish way of life. By the time they returned to build the Second Temple seventy years later, there seems to have been a profound shift in the nature of the Jewish community. Piecing together the record from biblical and other sources, many scholars believe the reestablished kingdom of the Jews for at least part of the time was a constitutional monarchy. Nationally the council of sages known as the Sanhedrin (or Men of the Great Assembly) elaborated the civil and religious law, confirmed the king and high priest, and decided when the country would go to war.

The Sanhedrin continued as the high court of the Jewish people even after the destruction of the Second Temple, until 425 C.E. In villages and towns, community life centered around the congregation or synagogue, often led by a council of elders and a teacher-judge, or rabbi. Spurred by exile and opportunities for trade, Jews began traveling all over the world, organizing themselves wherever they went to take vital aspects of the Jewish way with them.[16] In order to follow Jewish law, the community needed to develop a source of kosher meat, to acquire land for a Jewish cemetery, and to collect and distribute charity. These were organizing tasks that laypeople could do.

After the destruction of the Second Temple, we replicated this form of self-government in the communities we established all over the world. The Hellenic and Roman empires, the Moslem and Christian empires, and the other nations in which Jews lived frequently allowed Jewish communities a considerable measure of self-government in matters of everyday life. In Babylonia for twelve centuries the lay head of the Jewish community was the exilarch, or *Resh Galuta,* who was supposed to be a descendant of King David, while the spiritual heads were the *Geonim,* the heads of the academies of scholars. Sometimes competing and sometimes cooperating, they balanced each other's power in setting up the courts and other organizations of Jewish life. The further away Jewish communities were from Babylonia, the more lay control and decentralization there tended to be.

Outside of Israel, Jews were often restricted to living in certain areas and were considered aliens, neither serfs nor citizens. From the Middle Ages on, as the *Encyclopedia Judaica* points out, Jews in effect lived in self-governing "Jewish cities" within the Muslim and Christian ones.[17] Since it was easier for monarchs to simply demand a lump tax payment from each Jewish community and let the Jewish community figure out internally how it would raise the funds, Jewish communal governments often had the power of taxation. While tyranny reigned throughout the world, many Jewish communities were laboratories for democracy. In Europe, "Each community was conceived as the Jewish people in miniature, having sovereign rights," according to the *Encyclopedia Judaica*.[18] Every community, or *kehilla,* had its own constitution. Major decisions were made not just by the representatives, but by an annual assembly of all heads of households—a Jewish town meeting. In some communities even the decision to excommunicate someone could only be made by a majority vote of the town assembly. And if someone (such as a tenant being evicted by a landlord) failed to get justice, he or she could come to the synagogue on the Sabbath and stop services until the grievance was dealt with.

In eastern Europe, for about two centuries, we had three levels of elected representatives: the council of elders or community board (*kahal*), which ran the day-to-day communal administration in each town; the regional councils, held annually during spring or fall fairs; and national councils which dealt with the monarchs and regulated commerce. Communities in Spain, the Middle East, and northern Africa had similar elected councils, though more power was held by the hereditary aristocratic leadership. Jewish communities traced the tradition of elected leadership back to Moses, who had been told by God to have each tribe elect elders to help him do the work of judging disputes.[19]

Within our communities, we developed voluntary associations for particular purposes such as prayer, study, and charity, including artisans' guilds and the *hevra kadisha* (holy fellowship) to care for and watch over the dead awaiting burial. At a time when few gentiles outside the nobility and clergy could read, we ran our own systems of elementary and secondary schools and schools for advanced learning. We frequently had our own civil and criminal justice systems, with our own courts, and in some communities our own police and prisons. The elected council coordinated all community activities, taxing everyone to take care of the poor, and distributing the funds.

It was, by today's standards, an imperfect set of experiments. Many communal governments were dominated by an entrenched oligarchy. Voting was often indirect, similar to the U.S. electoral college.[20]

There was no separation between secular and religious life. The law by which civic leaders and everyday citizens conducted their lives was interpreted by rabbi/scholars, for whom every detail of life was a religious matter. Rabbis were judges in the communal courts. In the traditional Jewish community you might have had a choice about what to believe, but you didn't have a choice about whether to be involved. Weddings took place in the town square. In some communities, every head of household was required to attend the annual assembly—and no one was allowed to leave until it was over.

Though the power of communal governments was undermined in the nineteenth century by the lure of secular learning and enfranchisement (Jews gaining the right to citizenship in the countries where they lived), communal governments continued to have a powerful role in many Jews' lives until World War II. In parts of Latin America and the Middle East, Jewish communal councils still exist.

When Jews came to America, we brought our talent for organization with us. We founded educational associations, charitable organizations, synagogues, and burial societies. From the middle of the nineteenth century to the 1930s, and again for a short period after World War II, the *landsmanshaft* (association of people from the same village) helped eastern European immigrants get started, providing loans and money for education and funerals. In the twentieth century we organized national groups to combat anti-Semitism (such as the B'nai B'rith Anti-Defamation league), for the different synagogue denominations, and for the fundraising organizations (such as the Council of Jewish Federations). As of 1970 about 95 percent of American Jews lived in communities where there were community-wide federations to collect and distribute Jewish charity.[21] Zionism—fundraising and political support for Israel—particularly after the Holocaust, became a

major focus. Hadassah, a women's Zionist and social organization, is the largest Jewish mass organization in America.

The Holocaust spurred us to think about how we could mo-
bilize a rapid nationwide response to issues affecting us. The
Conference of Presidents of Major Jewish Organizations, representing twenty-two different groups, was organized in 1954. This
form of national organization—an association of associations—
reveals a lot about the American Jewish community. There has
never been in the Jewish communities of America, either at the
local or the national level, anything like the cohesion and organization that existed in eastern Europe and the Mediterranean
world in prior eras. There are several key differences in America.
We are free and we are mobile. Our communal organizations
have also lost their essential power—the power of involuntary
taxation. Now we have a choice both of what to believe and of
whether to belong.

Perhaps the ghetto world excessively emphasized community
at the expense of the individual, says Rabbi Burt Jacobson, one of
the original faculty members of Havurat Shalom. Yet the America
we grew up in had "overemphasized the individual to the point
where it destroyed the possibility of community."

As second-generation families became economically self-sufficient, "they thought they could be psychologically self-sufficient,
too," said Nancy Fuchs. The third generation, striking off to far
corners of the country without the support of either an extended
family or a strong Jewish community, felt something was missing.
In the havurah, we sought to create a blend of both.

It wasn't until we had separated from our parents and established our own communities that we were able to look back and
appreciate the strength of the bonds that held together the established Jewish community of our parents' and our grandparents'
generations. Even in my parents' small-town Reform congregation—where there was very little Jewish observance, and a service that was more social than spiritual—there was an amazing
amount of bonding and community loyalty. When during her

seventies my mother had a series of illnesses, members of the community showered her with calls and cards and as many visits as she could handle. They invited my father to dinner when my mother was in the hospital. When it became difficult for my parents to drive, friends would call and offer to pick them up for community events. The intensity of love and concern was overwhelming.

As they acquired jobs and young families, more havurahniks began to join synagogues, where they wouldn't have to take all responsibility for choreographing their communal religious life. They began to ask how they could combine the spiritual strengths they had learned in their havurot with the community-building strengths of more conventional synagogues. When they sought synagogue membership, they tried to find intimate settings with opportunities for active participation. Some created havurah-like structures (personalized adult study groups, family holiday groups, or women's support groups) in the synagogues they joined. When Gerry Gorelick and Susan Leviton moved from the Germantown minyan to Harrisburg, they joined a small congregation known for its *haimish* (homey) quality. They became members of the burial society. There was a special bond among the members because they felt themselves to be engaged in a holy task: instead of turning the dead over to the impersonality of a funeral parlor, they lovingly bathed, dressed, prepared, and watched over the body until the time of burial.

For people who don't feel able to organize their own havurah inside or outside the synagogue, there are now other ways to experience havurah-like intimacy and creativity. The National Havurah Committee runs a weeklong program of study and prayer each summer. The Havurah Institute is an immersion experience. Participants spend all day in classes and have the opportunity to *daven* morning and evening in a wide variety of styles: there are traditional egalitarian, creative, feminist, and beginners' services. In workshops and classes, the discussion is personal, asking "How does this text apply to me"? Institute-wide events each evening help build a sense of community. During communal discussions a panel stakes out various positions on a topic, and other people voice opinions at an open microphone. A discussion on community responsibility for addictions, for example, forced us to consider how we—the generation that had inhaled[22]—should handle our children's explorations with drugs.

Some creative rabbis tried to restore the sense of spiritual community to synagogues by using havurah techniques. Harold Schulweis, charismatic rabbi of a large Conservative congregation in Los Angeles, pioneered a new pattern: havurot within synagogues. Some rabbis, like Burt Jacobson of Kehilla in Oakland, California, and Mitch Chefitz of the Havurah of Southwest Florida, created their own alternative communities. Both Jacobson and Chefitz gathered their first groups by advertising in the newspaper that they were holding High Holiday services for unaffiliated Jews.

Other maverick rabbis took jobs at conventional suburban synagogues and nudged the members toward a sense of spiritual partnership. Havurat Shalom faculty member Everett Gendler, who wanted to be a part-time farmer so he could keep a living connection to nature, became part-time rabbi of a small Reform temple, Emmanuel, in Lowell, Massachusetts. In the forty-five years since the congregation was founded it had never had a full-time rabbi, so congregation members were used to experimenting and taking a fair amount of responsibility.

Several years ago Gendler began asking families to bring an object sacred to them to share with the community during the opening candle-lighting ceremony. One person brought a leather-covered hammer that his father had used in the little jewelry shop where he eked out a living. "The whole immigrant generation was suddenly present," recalled Gendler, "the immigrant parents working so their kids could go to college."

One person brought a diving regulator and spoke of the extraordinary experience of descending into the deep, with the regulator as lifeline. One person brought nothing, explaining she was the daughter of Holocaust survivors who had nothing material from their former home.

In a short-lived havurah journal, *New Traditions,* Kushner spelled out a key idea: Synagogues should exist to help Jews perform the three kinds of "primary religious acts" that they "should not, and probably cannot, do alone . . . communal prayer, holy study, and good deeds."[23] The structure of many American synagogues pulls people away from these three key purposes; some groups (like the board) have power, and other groups (like the men's and women's clubs) are for social gatherings and auxiliary fundraising. The subgroups in havurot and alternative synagogues tend to focus on the three intrinsic spiritual purposes. Women of Congregation Solel, a synagogue formerly led by Rabbi Wolf, organized and led a summer day camp that brought Jewish children together with black children from the inner city. They then helped other congregations and churches to organize similar programs. At Kushner's Congregation Beth El in Sudbury, Massachusetts, congregants have written their own prayerbooks for Sabbath, sitting *shiva* (mourning), and High Holidays. Bar and bat mitzvah parents study along with their children. Groups of families with children of similar ages have grown into family havurot that meet independently for various activities. Kushner says he is trying to help the congregation evolve into "a confederation of semi-independent religious family groups."

Even without the centralizing force of a charismatic leader, some of the havurot have lasted for more than twenty years and have achieved their goal of creating a community that is emotionally supportive, spiritually alive, and open to experiment and growth.

Dealing with illness, divorce, and death helped the havurot mature as communities. Debra Cash, a longtime member of Havurat Shalom, has not been active there in recent years. ("I'm not into praying at the moment.") But a few years ago when she had major surgery, a havurah friend came over and did her laundry. After years in the community, "I can look at people on *Kol Nidre* night

[Yom Kippur] and remember when they lost their parents. I've been there at baby namings, *aufrufs,* funerals, celebrations of Ph.Ds. I've been there crying, I've been there laughing."

I began to understand this after about five years in the Germantown minyan. Within the space of a month, my husband's mother died, and—after a month in bed trying to stave off the birth, followed by an emergency Caesarian section—I gave birth to a premature baby who lived only half a day. While I was confined to bed, minyan members, some of whom I did not know well, came in to cook, clean, and visit. At the *shiva* for Steve's mother, there were people I loved and people I had barely met; the house was full. Helping hands took over everything. Someone even went around covering the mirrors, as is traditional in a Jewish house of mourning, and leaving the traditional pitcher of water at the door for people to wash their hands after returning from the cemetery. Our baby died right before Thanksgiving; one of our minyan friends, Rabbi Nancy Fuchs, brought a complete Thanksgiving dinner to our house.

One day, about a week after the baby's death, I saw through my tears how the circle of community came together. Sitting across the breakfast table was Dr. Deborah White, holding my hand and crying with me. About a year after I came to the minyan, Debbie, her husband (Dan Piser), and I had shared a very special day: the *aufruf* for their wedding was also my adult bat mitzvah. A few years later I came to the baby-naming ceremony for Deb and Dan's first child and heard her talk about the miracle of seeing the infant's profile on ultrasound while it was still in her belly. Now she was mourning the death of my child with me. (I did not know it yet, but within a year, we would adopt a baby girl, Hope. Deb and Dan and all our community would crowd into our house, set food on the table, and rejoice with us.)

I hated to leave the Germantown minyan. Because I had learned the habit of community, though, the next move was easier. Within a month of moving to New Jersey, it seemed we had been members of the Highland Park minyan for years. Within a year I was co-chair of programming for children's High Holiday services. When I walked into Yom Kippur services with our newly adopted second child, Ben, the whole community stood and the leader called us up for a Torah blessing to welcome Ben into the community.

Nearly four years later, a family crisis again made me realize how deep is the blessing of community. Playing pirates with Ben, jumping off the bleachers at the high school, I tore the ligament of my knee and was confined to the couch in my living room. A stream of friends arrived from the many communities I now belonged to: the minyan, my women's Rosh Hodesh group, the neighborhood. Friends ferried my kids home from school, did our grocery shopping, and stuffed our refrigerator and freezer with homemade casseroles. I felt bathed in God's love, which was made almost palpably present through the caring of my communities. I had a little taste of the paradise that is possible when all Israel—and indeed all human beings—are responsible for one another. I had never felt more in the presence of God.

CHAPTER 5

ACTION AS PRAYER

The Judaism of Justice

Behold, on the day of your fast you pursue business as usual, and oppress your workers. . . . Is this the fast that I have chosen . . .? This is My chosen fast: to loosen all the bonds that bind men unfairly, to let the oppressed go free. To break every yoke. Share your bread with the hungry, take the homeless into your home.

—Isaiah 58:3–7

Judaism is inherently a political religion. . . . Sharing one's bread with the hungry is every bit as powerful a way of connecting to the tradition as lighting the Sabbath candles.

—Leonard Fein, "What Is Required of Us," *Reform Judaism,* Spring 1991

Justice is a central moral value of Judaism. The Torah commands it; the prophets demand it. Our key story is the Exodus from Egypt, the freeing of an oppressed people. "Justice, justice, shalt thou pursue," orders the Torah (Deuteronomy 16:20). Young Jews of my generation thought their parents had given up the pursuit, and they were determined to take it up again.

Arthur Waskow, a barrel-chested lion with a roaring laugh and scraggly mane of beard and hair topped by a cocky beret, was a full-time activist/writer/political analyst, marching against the war in Vietnam, against the bomb, and for civil rights. Except for the annual Passover seder, Waskow had long abandoned the tepid Judaism of his childhood. But in April 1968, as Washington, D.C., smoldered from the rioting that followed Martin Luther King's assassination, Waskow felt the Passover story was happening again. Martin Luther King had been the Moses of his people. The soldiers with machine guns guarding every corner were Pharaoh's soldiers. The seder, Waskow told himself, had to celebrate the hope of freedom—not just for Jews, but for blacks, Vietnamese, and all oppressed people. Jotting a few additions to the Haggadah he would read from that night, he began making the transition "from Jewish radical to radical Jew."[1]

Jews for Urban Justice (JUJ), a group of activist government workers, lawyers, and professionals, helped Waskow organize an interreligious Freedom Seder the following year; eight hundred black, white, Jewish, and Christian activists came. Published in 1970, the Freedom Seder swept the activist community.[2]

JUJ members began to realize that every Jewish holiday has an ethical and thus a political dimension. That fall, at the invitation of a Washington synagogue, JUJ introduced into the Yom Kippur liturgy a new confession of sins (*Al Chet*):

> Hear the sins that we have sinned together. . . . By paying soldiers to burn Vietnamese babies alive
> > —*without forcing our rulers to stop the war machine;* . . .
> By using chemical products that poison the air and give people cancer—ourselves and our families included
> > —*without forcing our rulers to change these products;* . . .

By keeping Black people out of our neighborhoods, and not keeping rats out of the Black neighborhoods, so Black children are bitten to death by rats
> —*without forcing our rulers to end the existence of slums.*

So in all these ways
We have murdered, O Lord;
We have killed real children;
We ourselves have done it,
And we have allowed others to do it while we turn our eyes away;
> For . . . some of us own real estate, and murder;
> And some of us drive automobiles, and murder;
> And some of us use pesticides, and murder;
> And some of us serve on draft boards, and murder;
> And all of us pay taxes, for murder.[3]

These were strong words. Members of JUJ were speaking in the tradition of the prophets.

Some conservative members of the congregation, infuriated by the service, charged forward to attack. With locked arms, JUJ nonviolently resisted. A well-known slumlord shouted, according to Waskow, "I paid for this synagogue, and this is never going to happen in this synagogue again!" Waskow and other JUJ members realized that "the fusion of religious and political feeling into a single whole—in short, a revivification of the old meaning of the Jewish tradition—carried an enormous emotional charge, was far more explosive and far more productive of spiritual and social change than either religion-in-a-box or politics-in-a-box."[4]

Exploring the connection between political action and religion was as explosive and life-changing for Waskow as for the politicians and citizens he was trying to touch. He began going to Fabrangen and living an increasingly Jewish life.

Politics was part of the religious language at Fabrangen. In Torah discussions, people would note how the Torah story was relevant to current political actions. Marches and rallies were announced at the end of services. Many of the havurot had organized *tsedakah* collectives, giving their pooled funds to Jewish and secular environmental, peace, or social-justice groups. The Fabrangen collective gave money to a group of steelworkers trying to buy their failing mill and run it as a workers' co-op.

The issue that really split the radical Jewish groups from their elders was Israel's relationship to the Palestinians. Waskow got involved in starting Breira ("Alternative"), a name referring to Israel's slogan, "*Ayn Breira*" ("There is no alternative"). Breira proposed alternative policies such as separate Israeli and Palestinian states. Breira's leaders, especially Waskow, were vilified in the Jewish press.

It was a tense time; the lion roared often, in anger and anguish. But the seeds of Waskow's personal and spiritual transformation were already sprouting. He delighted in imagining how his two worlds—Judaism and radical politics—might fit together. Could you take the idea of kosher and fuse it with the modern concern for ecology, looking at whether products were "eco-kosher"? (The term was coined by one of Waskow's mentors, Rabbi Zalman Schachter-Shalomi). Could Torah insights and modern socialism be brought alive on an American kibbutz? (Kibbutz Micah, in south-central Pennsylvania, provided some wonderful weekends of gardening and some great political discussions but soon fizzled.)

Most important to Waskow was celebrating Shabbat every week. Its powerful lesson of rest, play, companionship, and renewal shaped the way he saw the world, political action, and himself. The alienation of modern life, he came to feel, grew from insistence on goals and achievement. Shabbat, a time of *not* doing and peaceful acceptance, had given Jews a vision of the heaven that could be created on earth, the wholeness that people could create in their own lives.

Shabbat was a lesson radicals needed to learn if they were to continue in the unrewarding work of playing prophet to an unheeding world. "I worked on [opposing] the bomb before from 1959 to 1963," Waskow said. "Then I burned out. Couldn't stand it. But I've now worked on the bomb since 1980, and I haven't burned out. I think the reason is . . . I do make Shabbos. I do celebrate. I do Rosh Hashana and Purim and all the rest of the craziness. Someone asked me once, 'Do you really believe we can keep from blowing ourselves up?' And I said, 'On weekdays I hope, and on Shabbos I know.' On Shabbos there's no question."

When he moved to Philadelphia in 1982, Waskow founded the Shalom Center to enlist Jews from mainstream synagogues in peace action. Now part of ALEPH: The Alliance for Jewish Renewal, the center is one of a cluster of Jewish activist organizations in Philadelphia, including Shomrei Adamah ("Guardians of the Earth") and the Shefa Fund, which, among other things, helps Jewish funders channel foundation grants to social-change organizations.

Working closely with Reb Zalman, Waskow began to describe his work with a traditional Jewish term: *tikkun olam,* which means repair, healing, transformation of the world. In October 1995, twenty-seven years after he began to link social action to his Jewish roots, Waskow received rabbinic ordination from a religious court (*bet din*) composed of Rabbis Zalman Schachter-Shalomi, Max Ticktin and Laura Geller, and feminist theologian Judith Plaskow.

For some of the Jewish activists, religion and social justice went hand in hand from the beginning. Growing up in a family of Democratic party activists, political involvement came naturally to Michael Lerner, a short, intense man with dark curly hair and a square jaw that juts forward pugnaciously when he talks. He remembers arguing politics with an underwear-clad Adlai Stevenson when the Democratic candidate for president was resting up in Michael's bedroom before a fundraising speech.

Lerner's commitment to Judaism blossomed at Camp Ramah. After the first summer, he came home keeping kosher and observing an Orthodox Shabbat, though his family did not. By the end of the second summer he had decided to be a rabbi, an idea to which his mother was bitterly opposed; she wanted him to go into politics. Ultimately Lerner managed to do a bit of both. In 1986 he cofounded the magazine *Tikkun* as a forum for discussions among progressive Jews. *Tikkun's* national conferences brought together secular and religious progressive Jews from around the United States. As Lerner explained to the sometimes skeptical secularists at the 1993 conference, for centuries organized religion was allied with the feudal hierarchy, an integral part of an oppressive system that deprived people of political, intellectual, and economic freedom. Today, however, it is important for political activists to reconnect with the religious roots of their values. Our society teaches us that the way to survive is to be selfish—to stand alone, and to compete with each other for food, shelter, status, even love. Torah, in contrast, teaches us to take care of one another.

The ethic of selfishness, said Lerner, has created a profound moral and spiritual crisis in America. The right wing is the chief proponent of the ideology of selfishness; ironically, though, right-wingers are the only ones talking about the moral crisis, using phrases like "family values." In his magazine Lerner exhorted Democratic leaders to develop a "politics of meaning" that would address these as well as purely economic issues. He urged *Tikkun* readers to form havurah discussion groups and to create a new progressive movement based on "the politics of meaning." First Lady Hillary Rodham Clinton, a regular reader of *Tikkun,* invited Lerner to the White House to discuss his ideas. In November 1995 he was privately ordained as a rabbi.

The pursuit of justice could take Jews the length of the political and religious spectrum, from left to right. Glenn Richter was turned on to an active Judaism by an Orthodox Yeshiva University series of retreats for high school students. While a freshman at Queens College in 1962–63, he began carrying out the mandate to let the oppressed go free by working in the office of the Student Non-Violent Coordinating Committee (SNCC). A tiny demonstration by a group of Yeshiva University students in front of the Soviet embassy convinced him that among his own Jewish brethren there were also oppressed who needed to be freed. Anti-Semitism, a centuries-old Russian tradition, had found its way into Soviet policy. In the 1960s the Soviet government backed a vicious anti-Jewish and anti-Israel propaganda campaign, complete with mass rallies and stereotyping cartoons. Jews who tried to emigrate to Israel were refused permission (earning the nickname "refuseniks"), fired from their jobs, and then arrested for "parasitism," with the added charge of "hooliganism" if they resisted arrest. Jewish students were expelled from or denied admission to universities. Study of Judaism, training of rabbis, manufacture or import of religious objects, and even the baking of Passover matzoh was prohibited.

Feeling that SNCC had begun advocating violence, Richter, disillusioned, decided to focus all his energies on the cause of Soviet Jewry. In 1967 he married the chairwoman of the Stern College chapter of the Student Struggle for Soviet Jewry. They agreed that Lenore, a teacher, would support the family so he could work full-time as national coordinator of SSSJ. For many years he worked for no salary, and after that for a pittance.

The work was full of danger and drama. In November 1974, Richter made the first of five trips to the Soviet Union. Walking toward a Moscow apartment building to meet with a leading refusenik, Vladimir Slepak, he saw two KGB cars slowly trailing him. He and his companion ducked into a subway and changed trains several times to evade their pursuers, finally coming back at midnight for the meeting. Slepak then showed him that the room was "bugged," transmitting their meetings to the KGB. He looked Richter in the eye and said, "We're not afraid. Why should you be?"

Slepak was exiled to a labor camp in Siberia for several years, but he is now in Israel. Richter thought, if this man can risk his life to be allowed to live as a Jew, "we can do our bit."

In order to confront the Soviet Union, SSSJ leaders felt that they would have to confront the U.S. government, the Israeli government, and the "Jewish establishment" in the United States.

The Israeli Labor party government, trying to develop friendly relationships with the Soviet Union, seemed reluctant to push hard to get rights for Soviet Jews. Some Jewish organizations, like B'nai B'rith and the World Jewish Congress, had protested the treatment of refuseniks without success; many other organizations remained silent. SSSJ members turned up the volume of protest dramatically, using tactics learned in the civil rights and antiwar movements. Wearing sackcloth, they chained themselves outside the Soviet and Polish missions to the United Nations. They sat in at the offices of Hadassah and other Jewish organizations, demanding that they devote staff time and money to freeing Soviet Jews.

The SSSJ took its slogan from the Passover story: "Let my people go!" When Soviet athletes were to compete in a California swim meet, SSSJ members poured red dye in the water, recalling how God turned Egypt's waters to blood to teach the Pharaoh that he must let the Jews go. Reenacting another of the plagues, they sent frogs hopping all over the offices of Aeroflot, the Soviet airline. In spite of the opposition of a number of mainstream Jewish organizations, the SSSJ lobbied Congress to link trade with the Soviets to improvements in human rights. The 1974 Jackson-Vanik amendment, which tied Soviet trade benefits to the freedom to emigrate (and was also supported by the mainstream National Conference on Soviet Jewry), provided the key leverage for changing Soviet policy.

A growing proportion of the American Jewish community had become concerned about Soviet Jews. Elie Wiesel won the Nobel Peace Prize for his book, *The Jews of Silence* (1966), a scathing indictment of the American Jewish community's failure to aid their Soviet brethren. In 1970 twenty Soviet Jews were arrested, and two sentenced to death, for attempting to steal a small plane in order to escape. American Jewish organizations lobbied strongly for President Richard Nixon to intercede, and the executions were stayed.

From then on, the movement grew rapidly. Synagogues all

across the United States "adopted" Soviet Jewish families, writing them letters of encouragement, pressing for their release, and helping them to find jobs and housing when they came to the United States. Bar and bat mitzvah kids "twinned" with Soviet Jewish kids, remembering during their celebrations youngsters of the same age who were unable to practice their religion. Federations of Jewish philanthropies allocated money and staff to resettle Soviet emigres. On December 6, 1987, when Soviet Premier Mikhail Gorbachev was about to meet with President Ronald Reagan, two hundred thousand people from all over the United States and Canada came to a demonstration in Washington, D.C., to demand freedom for Soviet Jews. Vice President George Bush spoke, and President Reagan sent a letter of support. The rally made the front page of the *New York Times.*

The remarkable thing, says Richter, is that "we won." Since 1971 nearly a million of the 2 to 3 million Jews in the Soviet Union have emigrated to either Israel or the United States. Many of those remaining in the former Soviet Union are again learning and celebrating their religion and culture. Recently, as fascist and anti-Semitic tendencies have emerged in the former Soviet republics, the Soviet Jewry movement has again intensified efforts to get people out.

Richter continued as coordinator of SSSJ for more than twenty years, despite tragedy in his personal life. In 1979 and 1983 his wife gave birth to two daughters, both of whom were afflicted with an undiagnosed neurological ailment. One died at age two, the other at age three. In hopes of stimulating brain function in their first daughter, Glenn and Lenore turned to patterning, a program of around-the-clock rhythmic exercises. The program required teams of five people to move the baby's arms, legs, and head in a motion that imitates crawling. The Richters' friends from SSSJ provided the troops for this struggle too.

As the Soviet Jewry movement became mainstream, Richter and his companions began to look for other arenas where it seemed necessary to confront anti-Semitism. Former SSSJ president Rabbi Avi Weiss formed Amcha ("Your People"). When the Vatican established a convent in Auschwitz in 1989, Richter and other Amcha members went over the fence to disrupt it. In August 1994, when Pope John Paul II knighted Kurt Waldheim, a former Nazi who had been elected premier of Austria, Richter was there as part of an Amcha protest demonstration.

Richter believes the success of the refuseniks helped inspire the rebellions in the Eastern European satellite countries, leading to the fall of the Soviet government. Fighting for Soviet Jewry taught him, says Richter, that "you're not just a spectator in Jewish history. You can't just watch. . . . By participating, you can change the course of history."

As they pursued their various interpretations of justice, Jewish activists sometimes found themselves confronting each other. In the summer of 1991 the Crown Heights neighborhood of Brooklyn exploded in racial tension after a car in a Hasidic entourage killed a black child, and a black rioter killed a yeshiva student in retaliation. While other, more liberal activists were working overtime trying to heal the rift in black–Jewish relations, Amcha members were heckling New York's black mayor David Dinkins, accusing him of going easy on the black rioters instead of protecting the Jewish population. Waskow and other members of the Jewish religious left had been working for decades toward a negotiated peace between Israel and the Palestinians, trying to build bridges between Palestinian moderates and the Israeli peace movement; as the September 1993 preliminary plan for peace negotiations became a reality, Amcha members were demonstrating against an agreement that they saw as suicidal.

Over more than twenty-five years of political action, many Jewish activists of both the right and the left moved from criticizing the "Jewish establishment" to becoming part of it—and leading it in new directions. Their goal was not only to influence American politics but to transform American Judaism. What some of its veterans call "the revolution" began in November 1969. A couple of hundred Jewish students crashed the national meeting of the Council of Jewish Federations and Welfare Funds, picketing and threatening to disrupt unless they were given a chance to speak.

My parents were attending that meeting in Boston. I happened to be riding the escalator with them through the large glass atrium while the students picketed below. Having never met politically committed people who were also religious, I couldn't figure out what was going on. What were kids with scruffy beards, long hair, and picket signs doing wearing yarmulkes? And their signs demanded more money for Jewish education—why on earth was that something to picket about? Had I cared to sit in on the speech by their representative, a young Yale University rabbi named Hillel Levine, I would have found out.

> The black awakening reminded us that the melting pot dream was a
> fool's fantasy and that differences were legitimate. We woke up from
> the American dream and tried to discover who we really were. . . .
> Yet where can we find inspiration in the multi–million-dollar Jewish
> presence of suburbia?[5]

Federation, Levine said, had built a mammoth and effective philanthropic organization but allowed American Judaism to become spiritually bankrupt. Individual Jews had no connection to the poor except through their checkbooks. Jewish education was "insipid and irrelevant." Federation spent more on camps and sports than on educating young Jews to understand the texts in which the Jewish vision is rooted.[6]

In the decade following the 1969 "revolution," concerned students and their mentors scored some notable successes. A 1976 Conference on Alternatives in Jewish Education (CAJE) launched a new organization bent on radically changing Jewish education. Cherie Koller-Fox, one of the organizers of CAJE, recalls the shock of her first day as a teacher in the very same Akron, Ohio, classroom where she had gone to afternoon Hebrew school. Experiences in Israel during high school and college had opened her to a vibrant world of Jewish life and culture.

"I could not imagine why it was that Judaism was so wonderful and the classroom I was teaching in was so terrible. Even the smell of it." It became her lifelong quest to make the classroom reflect the living Jewish world she had come to love.

Within eleven years CAJE became so widely accepted that its name was changed to Coalition for the Advancement of Jewish Education. CAJE brought the ideal of grass-roots democracy to Jewish education. Instead of being "handed a curriculum and told what to teach,"[7] as Koller-Fox put it, teachers came to CAJE to learn from each other. For one week a year, CAJE encourages Jews to cross the boundaries that normally divide them: Orthodox, Conservative, Reform, and secularists, teenage Sunday school instructors and Ph.D.s teaching in colleges share ideas. CAJE pioneered creative teaching strategies, got teachers of Hebrew school involved in their own quests for Jewish understanding, and grew into the largest organization in the United States dealing with Jewish education. Many federations now pay the cost for teachers in local Jewish institutions to attend the CAJE conference. Among many other activities, CAJE has generated curricula on special topics: "Feed the World"; "Life and Choice: Jewish Views on Abortion"; "AIDS: Our Responsibility as Jews"; "Power, War, and Peace in the Jewish Tradition" (produced during the Persian Gulf crisis of 1990) and "The Pursuit of Peace" (following the signing of the preliminary agreement between Israel and the Palestine Liberation Organization). Koller-Fox and other members of CAJE pioneered family education, where parents and children learn about Judaism together. Some CAJE members have even developed a Jewish philosophy discussion course for teens by pairing film clips from "Star Trek" with readings from the Talmud. In 1995, Koller-Fox, who had been serving as unofficial rabbi of a congregation that grew up around a school she headed, completed rabbinical studies and was ordained.

Rabbi Irving Greenberg, who had been an adviser and spokesman for the students during the 1969 "revolution," eventually formed his own organization to change the perspective of the leaders of the Jewish establishment. The National Center for Jewish Learning and Leadership (known as CLAL) gives lively classes for leaders in Federations, synagogues, and other organizations relating Jewish tradition to issues the leaders are concerned about, such as how to set priorities for distributing funds. By the 1950s the state of Israel had become the focus of the Jewish Federation's fundraising efforts, as well as of Jewish identity in America. Many federation leaders, and staff members of Jewish social agencies, were secular. Their main point of identification with the Jewish people was through Israel; they knew little of Jewish texts, tradition, or way of life. But Greenberg saw in their passionate defense of Israel a deeply spiritual need for connection and meaning. Now ideas like covenant are part of the discussion at Federation meetings. In 1993 hundreds of people participated in Torah and Talmud study at the Jewish Federation's General Assembly, where students once had to threaten a sit-in to discuss the need for Jewish education.

When I began my return to Judaism, I straddled two communities: the New Left, representing my ideals, and the Jewish community, representing my roots. In college, as I was busy organizing grass-roots civil rights organizations and antiwar rallies, I didn't feel estranged from Judaism, but it clearly wasn't where the action was. From my very first Shabbat with the Dayton havurah, though, I began to see how naturally my ideals and my roots fit together. The Torah portion for that week concerned the Sabbatical year (every seventh year, when the land was to lie fallow), and the Jubilee (every fiftieth year, when slaves were to be freed and land taken away from large landholders and returned to its original small family holdings). I couldn't believe that in the Bible, the sacred text of the Jewish people, was a plan for preserving ecology and redistributing wealth.

The Bible text answered a question that was crucial for me as a pacifist and social-justice activist: How could one achieve a social revolution without bloodshed? The biblical answer was to consider the needs and fears of all parties involved. The Jubilee passage gave a brilliant example of this approach; land in the years immediately preceding the Jubilee was to be sold for less, because it would soon have to be returned to the family to which it had originally belonged. If one believed Jefferson's idea about the need for a revolution in every generation this might be the most humane and realistic model for bringing it to pass.

In my other world, the world of political action, times were tough. The New Left was splintering, and provocative hard-line factions were emerging. When I compared Jewish tradition with some of the New Left rhetoric, Judaism made a lot more sense. Parts of biblical politics were anathema to me, including the sexism, xenophobia, and exclusion of homosexuals. But overall the Bible seemed to contain a wise, nuanced path to social change, in contrast to the rigid, simplistic politics of some of my peers.

The Bible says "Love your neighbor as yourself" (Leviticus 19:18), a dictate that is surely the basis for the kind of society I would like to see. But what would that mean in practice? In one of his CLAL study papers, Greenberg wrote:

> The heart of Judaism is a vision of perfection. . . . The freeing of the Hebrew slaves . . . teaches us that every human being is entitled to peace and freedom and dignity. . . . The process of achieving the dream is . . . the covenant . . . the binding commitment made by the Jewish people and by God to carry on until the perfection is achieved. . . . Each generation will have to do its share of redemption and pass it on to the next generation until the redemption is complete.[8]

The Bible and subsequent rabbinical commentaries, says Greenberg, don't assume that the just society can come about instantaneously. In a world economy based on slavery, they start by liberating the slaves every fifty years. In a world where wars occur, there are still rules: When you besiege a city, you may surround it only on three sides, so people can flee if they wish. You may not cut down the fruit trees, because after the war people will still have to eat. In the just society every family will have its own vine and fig tree. Until we get there, however, farmers must leave the corners of their field unharvested so the poor can gather food. Providing for the poor was not a matter of individual conscience; it was the law.[9]

> When there is a poor person from your brethren among your gates. . . . you must open your hand and provide for him what he lacks. (Deuteronomy 15:7)

From the time of the Talmud and probably before, most Jewish communities had a community tax, collected and distributed by the elders, to provide for the poor. From medieval times until they were destroyed by Hitler, most European Jewish communities had an interest-free loan fund, a shelter for homeless wanderers, and a soup kitchen where gentiles as well as Jews could get help. As long as the *kehillot* (Jewish community organizations) existed, these charitable institutions were supported by compulsory tithes of up to 10 percent of income—a contribution called *tsedakah* (justice).[10] Similar charitable institutions existed in Jewish communities throughout the world. Pogroms, exile, and laws excluding them from farming and many trades ensured that there would always be a good supply of wandering Jewish strangers needing the help of their community. My neighbor Milton Frant, who fled Poland just before the Holocaust, remembers the beggars lining the wall of his village synagogue on Shabbos, knowing that even the poorest families would feel obligated to invite one of them home for dinner. Poor as they were, his family managed before every Shabbos to put at least a penny into the *pushke* (charity box) for needy Jewish communities in Israel and elsewhere. In the Passover Haggadah it says, "Let all who are hungry come and eat"; in our great-grandparents' world, this was not an empty phrase.

But the extraordinary network Jews wove to care for one another could be ripped as easily as a spider's web by the hostile societies in which they lived. For centuries Jews yearned for a Messiah to usher in a world where poverty and hate would disappear, and they would no longer be vulnerable just because they were Jews. In the nineteenth century, Russian Jews began to think about bringing in the Messianic age in a new way: by joining the revolution. Many young Jews joined the populist party in the 1880s. In 1897 they formed their own organization, the Jewish Labor Bund. When radicals assassinated the tsars in 1881 and 1905, though, reactionaries blamed the Jews and incited brutal pogroms; tens of thousands of Jews were murdered or left homeless. The Russian radical organizations in which Jews had been active deserted them. In fact, during the 1882 pogroms, populist party leaflets praised the "revolutionary energy" shown by peasants attacking Jews.[11]

My grandmother left Poland after the 1905 pogrom, walking with a group of teenagers across Europe to Denmark. She was fifteen. At eighteen, with two infant sons, she stowed away in a ship to America.

As in Europe, Jews in America had created a unique social welfare network, including the *landsmanshaft,* the Hebrew Immigrant Aid Society, and settlement houses. But with a million refugees flooding in from Russia in the last two decades of the nineteenth century[12] and even more to follow, American Jewish social service agencies were overwhelmed. Jews working for pitiful wages in squalid sweatshops sought their own redemption in labor unions and the right to strike.

Though only a small number of Jews actually joined socialist organizations, their ideas for a time captivated the Jews of the Lower East Side. Clara Lemlich, the "working girl" whose fiery speech ignited the shirtwaist-makers' strike of 1909, was every Jewish family's daughter. From 1914 to 1920 Jews elected the only Socialist congressman, Meyer London. Jews in New York City elected ten state assemblymen, seven city aldermen, and a municipal court justice who were socialists, and they gave a large portion of their votes to a socialist candidate for mayor. In working-class Jewish New York until World War II, to be a right-thinking person was at least to have socialist leanings.[13]

The grandchildren of the struggling Jewish workers were reared on the same egalitarian visions as their parents. Some social researchers estimate that one-third of the participants in the New Left were Jews, including one-third to one-half of the students taking part in the Mississippi Freedom Summer project of 1964, one-third of the demonstrators in the Berkeley Free Speech movement, and nearly half of those taking part in a University of Chicago sit-in against the military draft.[14]

Many of the young Jewish activists of the 1960s and 1970s followed in the Jewish social welfare tradition. They did it their way, though: low on budget and bureaucracy, high on face-to-face involvement. The Ark, a free clinic in Chicago started by a group of Maoist Jews, stocks its pharmacy with free samples collected from doctors. Dorot, started by Columbia social-work students on the Upper West Side of Manhattan, holds a conference-call seder for elderly shut-ins and helps them find long-term relationships with "Friendly Visitors" from the suburbs. Ezra, which gets working-class Jewish elders together in a crafts co-op, classes and kosher lunch programs, is still a 1960s-style "participatory democracy," with secretaries, social workers, and the executive director receiving the same salary and having the same vote on policy. Poet Danny Siegel became a one-man mitzvah-generating machine. At synagogues and youth programs all over the United States, he talks about the work of "mitzvah heroes": individuals who, in creative, low-budget, person-to-person ways, are making the world a better place. He has written a whole series of books about how young people and adults can find their own ways to make the world better.

For Siegel, all mitzvot are clearly rooted in the Jewish concept of *kavod,* the dignity and worth of every human being. But not all the social activists had such clear ideas about the connections between their political work and their Jewish roots. Having benefited from the economic and political miracle wrought by their first-generation American parents, most 1960s activists grew up in the middle class. Unlike all generations of Jews before, they weren't forced by a hostile surrounding society to see the struggle for justice as their own struggle. They would have to figure out for themselves what it had to do with being Jewish. Many had dropped Judaism entirely and focused on radical politics—until the New Left itself forced them to rethink their relationship to their heritage.

The first United Nations International Women's Decade Conference in 1975 passed a resolution equating Zionism—support for the state of Israel—with racism. Many left-wing organizations followed a similar line. They passed resolutions condemning Israeli mistreatment of Palestinian prisoners, but did not criticize Palestinian terrorism directed against the civilian population of Israel. Jewish radicals who tried to support Israel were isolated. Like their Russian and Polish grandparents, Jewish radicals were discovering an ugly streak of anti-Semitism among the people they had thought of as comrades and allies.

One of those awakened to her heritage was feminist writer and activist Letty Cottin Pogrebin. Pogrebin reentered the Jewish world for the same reason she'd opted out—to assert her dignity as a full human being from those who tried to exclude or diminish her.[15] As a youngster, her family attended a synagogue (the Jamaica Jewish Center) that was her "second home." When, as a fifteen-year-old struggling to cope with her mother's death from cancer, Pogrebin was told she could not be counted in the minyan to say the memorial kaddish, she walked away from Judaism. She continued to attend High Holiday services and to celebrate Hanukkah and Passover, but this minimalist Judaism was an amputation of the deeply Jewish identity with which she'd grown up. As an adult she immersed herself in feminist political action and became one of the founding editors of *Ms.* magazine. At a workshop on identity issues, when asked to stand under the sign that most represented her self-concept, Pogrebin unhesitatingly walked past the "Jewish" and "American" signs and stood under the sign that said "Woman."

Two things brought her back to Judaism. In 1970 a small group of Fire Island vacationers was getting together to hold informal High Holiday services in one family's living room. It turned out that Pogrebin was the only person—male or female—with enough Jewish education to lead the prayers in Hebrew. Over the years, as the group mushroomed to two hundred members holding services in a borrowed church sanctuary, she continued to lead the prayers, five years before even the liberal Reform movement ordained its first woman cantor. If an imaginary sign had read "Keep Out" when Pogrebin's mother died, now it said, "Please Enter—and Come to the Front of the Room."

Even so, her Judaism remained a once-a-year, private matter until the first United Nations International Women's Decade Conference in Mexico in 1975 equated Zionism with racism. Things were even worse at the second UN women's conference in Copenhagen in 1980. Vietnamese, Chilean, and Afghanistani refugee women told horrifying stories of rape and starvation. But when an Iraqi Jewish woman tried to tell how her husband was executed without a trial, women shouted, "Israel kills babies and women! Israel must die." When a representative of the International Council of Jewish Women tried to speak, another woman shoved a fist into her face. Mormon activist Sonia Johnson, who roomed with an Israeli, told Pogrebin that she heard people saying, "The only way to rid the world of Zionism is to kill all the Jews."

Pogrebin realized that "the world will not allow a woman to say, 'Being female doesn't matter,' nor a Jew to say, 'I used to be a Jew.' The Jewish woman who does not take possession of her total identity, and make it count for something, may find that others will impose upon her a label she does not like at all."[16]

From 1975 on, Pogrebin began to take possession of her total identity as a woman and a Jew. Her political activity expressed that new integration. After signing a petition with feminist leaders protesting the "Zionism is racism" resolution, she was invited to Israel in 1976 and had her first contact with the fledgling Israeli feminist movement. In 1978 she led a *Ms.* magazine trip to Israel. In 1982 *Ms.* published her eleven-page article on "Anti-Semitism in the Women's Movement."[17] In her speeches she urged Jewish feminists to confront Jewish organizations that don't promote women to executive positions, and to give money to projects that advance the status of women in the Jewish community, from battered women's shelters and the Israel Women's Network to *Lilith,* the American Jewish feminist magazine.

She also got involved in supporting the Israeli peace movement. In writing, Pogrebin began calling for the creation of separate Israeli and Palestinian states. Using skills learned in the women's movement, she organized dialogue groups involving Jewish, black, and Arab women. Her first attempt was a disaster; Pogrebin and a Palestinian journalist ended up screaming at each other. Eventually she realized that "if I had been born a Palestinian, I too would be demanding liberation, self-determination, and freedom in just those words—for I have used the same words to argue on behalf of women and Jews."[18] Gradually Israeli and Palestinian women have begun cooperating in the Women and Peace Coalition. There have been marches and vigils, lectures and conferences, demonstrations and parlor meetings.

Awakened by the anti-Semitism of the left, other radical Jews who had never had any use for organized religion now sought a way to reconnect with the Jewish community. But it wasn't so easy for them to identify the twentieth-century Jewish community with their ideals. All through the first half of the century, Jews had been leaders of liberalism. B'nai B'rith's Anti-Defamation League fought not only against anti-Semitism but against all forms of prejudice. Kivie Kaplan, a Jew, was the founding president of the National Association for the Advancement of Colored People. The American Jewish Congress, the American Jewish Committee, the National Council of Jewish Women, and

the National Jewish Community Relations Council all were active in pursuit of social justice for all Americans.[19] But after the
revelations about the Nazi Holocaust, much of the Jewish community turned inward, focusing on self-preservation and support of Israel. "We are a people suffering from post-traumatic
stress disorder," explained Leonard Fein recently. "We are a battered people, a people that has taken as its slogan, really as its
oath, two words: Never again. . . . [But] 'Never again' is . . . an
insufficient slogan; it tells us what to avoid, but does not tell us
what to embrace."[20]

What could Jews embrace? The Judaism of the prophets, said
Rabbi Gerald Serotta, founder of the Committee for a New Jewish Agenda (known informally as Agenda). Serotta had grown up
in an activist Reform synagogue and a home where the connection between Judaism and social justice was fundamental.
Though Reform Judaism had always had a strong commitment
to social justice, he saw the commitment lapsing in many parts of
the organized Jewish community, while Jewish social activists
didn't recognize their work as stemming from Jewish values. So
he created an organization where people could work together
publicly as Jews for social justice. Agenda organized political actions not only on Israel and Soviet Jewry but on such issues as
energy and the environment. I got involved in another aspect of
Agenda's work: consciousness-raising groups to help Jewish men
and women overcome the internalized prejudice that keeps us
from loving ourselves and each other.

As the idealism and passion for justice of the 1960s and 1970s
gave way to the me-firstism of the 1980s and the paralysis and
cynicism of the 1990s, it got harder to keep alive the connection
between Judaism and justice. One Yom Kippur at our Highland
Park minyan, I listened to Isaiah's words, "This is My chosen fast:
to loosen all the bonds that bind men unfairly, to let the oppressed go free." I asked myself, "How long has it been since I really worked for justice?" We had young kids, demanding jobs.
Just maintaining a havurah community took so much time and

energy. But action for justice hadn't disappeared; it had shifted location.

By the 1980s and 1990s many former student leaders had become the professional staff of major Jewish organizations. Instead of confronting the Jewish community, they were changing its policies and providing it with new projects. Social action was more and more deeply a part of mainstream Judaism. The Reform movement, as Leonard Fein has pointed out, has always focused on ethics and has a long tradition of social action. Inspired by the student activists, many synagogues deepened their commitment to social justice. The Reform movement supported the rights of homosexuals and welcomed gay synagogues, individuals, and rabbis. Some six hundred Reform synagogues have social action committees, with projects to help the elderly, the homeless, AIDS sufferers and endangered Jewish communities. Through the annual High Holiday Hunger program, Reform synagogues collected nearly a million pounds of food in 1993. At the fall holiday of Sukkot, many congregations go to farms to "glean" fresh fruits and vegetables to donate to food pantries. Synagogues in Washington, D.C., alone collected ten thousand pounds in 1993.[21]

When members of my havurah looked for a place to get involved, we discovered that Anshe Emet, a large Reform congregation nearby, housed the homeless during January and March at a makeshift overflow shelter in its multipurpose room. I will never forget the night I volunteered there, talking to a black man who woke at 4:00 A.M. to walk ten miles (he didn't have bus fare) to a job that didn't pay him enough for the first month's rent on an apartment, and a Jewish man with an accounting degree who couldn't hold a steady job because of manic-depressive illness.

I found social action organizations I wanted to support with my cash, too. The Jewish Fund for Justice (JFJ) gives grants directly to coalitions of poor people working for better conditions in their own communities: from East Harlem teenagers rehabilitating abandoned buildings to farmers' cooperatives in Kentucky.

JFJ builds partnerships between synagogues and such groups. The Spring Hill Avenue Reform Temple in Mobile, Alabama, worked with the Mobile Community Organization to pressure the local government to deal with abandoned housing in the inner city. Members of Conservative Congregation Rodeph Shalom in Bridgeport, Connecticut, marched with the Greater Bridgeport Interfaith Action to protest the lack of inner-city trash pickup and the existence of "Mount Trashmore," a toxic forty-five-foot-high block of garbage.

Another organization, Mazon ("Food") was born when *Moment* magazine founder Leonard Fein saw a caterer's big black BMW parked outside a Los Angeles synagogue and started speculating about how much money Jews spend annually on catered celebrations. Funded through donations of 3 percent of the cost of weddings, bar mitzvahs, and other celebrations, Mazon gives $1.65 million annually to soup kitchens, food banks, agricultural assistance, and job training in the United States and abroad.

Instead of simply criticizing the Israeli government or the policy of American Jewish organizations, other activists created the New Israel Fund to aid organizations working on Israeli problems not being dealt with by established charities, including rape crisis centers, shelters for battered women, and civil rights, education, and housing for Arab Israelis.

Homelessness and protection of the environment have been two chief concerns of American Jewish social activists of the 1990s. When the Soviet Union collapsed and antinuclear work no longer seemed so urgent, Arthur Waskow expanded the work of the Shalom Center to include environmental problems such as global warming and the destruction of the ozone layer by chlorofluorocarbons. Calling together a coalition of environmental activists and clergy from all four of the major Jewish denominations, the Shalom Center and B'nai Jeshurun (a Conservative congregation in New York) organized a movement urging Jewish organizations of all types to adopt environmentally conscious purchasing and investment policies. The Eco-Kosher Project rooted its work in Jewish ideas such as *bal tashchit* (do not destroy), the principle of not wasting anything that comes from the earth.

The Religious Action Center of the Union of American Hebrew Congregations (Reform) has issued a guidebook on the environment for synagogues. A number of congregations have started environmental committees and have taken such steps as not using styrofoam cups, which release chlorofluorocarbons. The National Jewish Community Relations Council has convened a Coalition on the Environment and Jewish Life.

When Rabbi Michael Paley, one of the first Havurat Shalom students in the 1960s, became chaplain of Columbia University, he started "Community Impact," through which more than six hundred students are involved in work on homelessness and other issues. The University of Pennsylvania has a similar program. Dorot in New York and the Ark in Chicago established programs to house and rehabilitate the homeless. (Dorot's transitional housing program, with 30 percent Jewish residents, was started after a homeless Jewish woman was found collapsed on the steps of a New York synagogue.) New York Conservative congregations Ansche Chesed and B'nai Jeshurun are also involved in work with the homeless.

As Fein points out, however, many people still saw their synagogues as places to escape from the world rather than as platforms for changing it. Even in the activist Reform movement, much of the political work was being done by national organizations rather than by local synagogues. Unlike the 1960s, when people were fired by a vision of the world transformed, most social action of the 1990s was charity rather than change-making. "The pursuit of justice," wrote Fein, "is quite different from devotion to acts of charity or of loving-kindness. . . . Kindness leads us to contribute to the relief of hunger; justice points us towards the elimination of hunger. A thousand times a thousand points of light do not add up to justice."[22] Fein argued for the idea of a political synagogue where politics and spirituality would be fully integrated—where lighting Shabbat candles would not be seen as a substitute for political action, nor political action as a substitute for lighting Shabbat candles. In such a synagogue Shabbat would be seen "as a resting place, not a stopping place, a place to gather energy for the holy work of the week to come."[23]

As they worked with mainstream Jewish organizations on social action projects, some havurahniks also clung to the ideal of creating communities where prayer and social action would be inextricably mixed—where social action would be a central part of what makes the community a holy place. After lengthy discussions on what they as a small congregation could do, Fabrangen made a commitment to help some homeless families keep from having to return to the city shelter. For several years they have had a relationship with two families: helping with food, clothing bills and school supplies, sending the children to camp, taking them to cultural activities. But beyond that, they have attempted to provide a support network. They sent one boy to private school, and when he failed there, raised money to move the family to a better section of town where he could go to a good public school. The children of these two families come to Fabrangen services, play with children of the Fabrangen community and stay on to be tutored in reading or other school subjects. "We have brought them into our Shabbos," said Fabrangen member Barbara Laster.

One of the most ambitious activist synagogues is the Reconstructionist congregation Mishkan Shalom in Havertown, a suburb of Philadelphia. Mishkan was founded by Rabbi Brian Walt, a big, ruddy frizzy-haired man whose eyebrows dance when he talks excitedly (which he frequently does). "I wanted," he said, "to create a community that believes in something." For him, that "something" was "the connection between God and justice." Since its founding in 1988, Walt's congregation has sponsored dialogues between Israelis and Palestinians, held forums on Judaism and homosexuality, and participated in an interfaith coalition trying to rebuild urban Philadelphia.

Walt grew up in South Africa. The son of the lay leader of the Jewish community organization in Capetown, he loved Bible, prayers, and Jewish celebrations. When he got involved in the struggle against apartheid, however, he became disillusioned. One day, on the way to his Jewish day school, he saw blacks standing in line at a newsstand being searched and carted off to jail if they did not have the proper working papers or "passes." It struck him that Jews in Nazi Germany had gone through the same experience. Around that same time, at age fifteen he was studying the prophet Amos and read the words: "I hate, I despise your feasts, and I will take no delight in your solemn assemblies. . . . Take away from Me the noise of your songs, and let me not hear the melody of your psalteries. But let justice well up as waters/ And righteousness as a mighty stream" (Amos 5:21, 23–24). Remembering the beautiful choirs in his family's congregation, Walt thought, "This is about me."

The yellow stars of the Holocaust, the prophets, and Judaism's teachings about the sanctity of life came together for Walt in a clear message: A Jew is born with the obligation to fight injustice. He founded *Strike,* a Jewish student newspaper examining issues of apartheid, and organized a strike of white students in support of black students' struggles against apartheid. When sixty "white privileged kids" were arrested for refusing to leave the steps of Parliament, it made the front pages of the papers. The strike quickly spread, and the government banned all meetings of more than eleven people. Walt asked his rabbi to join the protests, but the rabbi was afraid. Maybe Christians can afford to fight the system, he told Walt, but it's too dangerous for Jews.

Angry South African police charged the student demonstrators, banging heads and drawing blood. In the midst of one of these clashes, Walt got word to rush home: his family was in crisis over his actions, and his father had suffered a heart attack.

Walt felt that there was no place for him in South Africa. Other Jews who were involved in resisting apartheid had abandoned Judaism, and within the anti-apartheid movement there was a considerable amount of anti-Semitism. He went first to Israel and then to America, where he realized that he would have to fight the dragons of racism and injustice wherever he lived.

After completing rabbinical studies at the Reconstructionist Rabbinical College, Walt had taken his first congregational pulpit when the same crisis of conscience reappeared in a different form. Divisions started to appear in his suburban Philadelphia congregation when he encouraged them to become a sanctuary for an illegal refugee family from El Salvador. Some members were very enthusiastic; others felt he was improperly injecting politics into what should be a purely spiritual enterprise. Then, at Yom Kippur in 1987, he gave a sermon called "A Generation of Occupation" about the rights of the Palestinians in the West Bank and Gaza. Occupying these territories was "eroding Jewish morality, the Jewish soul," Walt told his congregation. American Jews should "dissociate ourselves from any support" of it. The sermon created a furor. All that fall there was a series of congregational meetings about what Walt did or didn't have a right to say. On December 9th the *intifada,* the Palestinian uprising against the occupation, started. On December 24th New Jewish Agenda held a service outside the Israeli consulate, lighting a *yahrzeit* (memorial) candle for each of the twenty-four Palestinians who had been killed thus far in the uprising. Walt led the service.

"Rabbi," one of his congregants said to him, "You're such a good rabbi. You really helped me at the time of my son's bar mitzvah. Why can't you just stay out of politics?"

Walt replied ("perhaps somewhat self-righteously, but also accurately," he says) that as much as he cared about the bar mitzvah boy, he also cared about the twelve-year-old Palestinians being killed by soldiers from Israel, the nation to which he felt most deeply connected. As he explained, "I believe in a God who takes sides. God takes the side of the slaves in Egypt. . . . The moments in which I've seen God most manifest are when I've seen human beings courageously stand up for justice."

Walt and his congregation agreed not to renew his contract.

With a core of congregants who supported him, though, he began to develop a plan for a new congregation that would be explicitly committed to action for social justice. All summer they held meetings to develop a statement of principles that would embody their shared commitments. They decided to call themselves Mishkan Shalom ("Sanctuary of Peace"), firmly committing themselves to the kind of political activism embodied in the sanctuary movement for Salvadoran refugees.

Their statement of principles, said Walt at the congregation's first Rosh Hashana service that fall, was their covenant with one another. Many of the congregants were secular political activists not much interested in services and prayer. Walt persuaded them, though, that any successful Jewish community must integrate all three foundations of Jewish spirituality: Torah (study), *avodah* (prayer, ritual celebration), and *gmilut hasadim/tikkun olam* (acts of loving kindness/repair of the world). Many congregants who had never before been involved in religion found themselves discovering spiritual sides of themselves. On repair of the world, the statement said:

> Our experience as slaves teaches us that we have a special responsibility to the stranger and the powerless. . . . After the Holocaust, the Biblical commandment "Do not stand idly by the blood of your neighbor" assumes a new and urgent meaning. . . . To be neutral on issues of justice is to side with the oppressor. Our passion for justice must be applied not only to Jews but to all peoples. If we are not for ourselves who will be for us; if we are only for ourselves, what are we?

Each event at Mishkan Shalom, from services to classes to public forums, contains echoes of its statement of principles. The weekend I visit, the fourth-graders are leading the Friday night service. Before services, the kids and their families get together for a potluck meal, where (in a quiet challenge to traditional Jewish sex roles) a boy lights the candles and a girl says the blessing over the wine, the *kiddush*. Both boys and girls wear the yarmulke traditionally worn only by males. After the meal, in the spirit of synagogue as co-op, some parents clean and vacuum the room where they have eaten. (The vacuum, an electrical appliance, is forbidden by traditional Jewish law, but this congregation does not choose a traditional relationship to tradition.) Other parents go upstairs to set up a semi-circle of folding chairs for services. With the glow of a few candles, they convert a rented classroom into a sanctuary.

This is a special Shabbat, the weekend before the holiday of Purim. Walt invites all the children at services that evening to come to the front of the room and sit with him on the floor.

"Let's talk a little bit about the Purim story," he says. "It sounds like this Purim story is just a story, right? There's this king, and he wants his wife to dance naked in front of him, [giggles from the kids] and she won't do it, so he gets another wife and they're having a party, and he gets this evil minister Haman who wants to kill all the Jews, and it sounds like it's just a story. That a king would let someone kill a whole race of people, that's just a story, right?"

One boy answers, "Well, there have been people who wanted to kill all the Jews. Like Hitler and the Nazis."

Walt: "So the story of Purim is really a story about a big word that means hating Jews. Does anybody know that word?"

A girl: "Anti-Semitism?"

Walt: "Does anti-Semitism still happen? Has anybody ever been in a situation where you heard someone do or say something anti-Semitic? We've all been in that situation together. Remember?"

A boy: "Someone wrote something bad on the back wall here."

Walt: "Last year, when someone saw our sukkah in the back yard here, they wrote, 'Kill the Jews.' Probably it wasn't someone who really could kill Jews, but it's someone who thought it."

A woman then talks about a speech by a leader of the Nation of Islam calling Jews bloodsuckers.

Walt: "Have you ever heard someone say something bad about other groups of people?"

Kids talk about slurs against gays and African-Americans. Adults talk about prejudices toward Moslems or Germans.

Walt: "So Purim is about prejudice. One of the hard things, living in this world, is to be proud as a Jew. Because people may have hurt Jews and said bad things about us. Purim is about being proud to be a Jew. And Purim teaches that to be a Jew we must not only be against anti-Semitism but against all forms of prejudice. One thing to think about this Purim is the ways we may be prejudiced. Because we all have prejudices, whether we want to or not—I even more than you. When I grew up in South Africa I learned, whether I wanted to or not, that black people aren't as good as white people. No one ever took me to a class and said, 'Black people aren't as good as white people.' But I grew up with that prejudice. Purim is a day on which we try to get rid of all the prejudices within ourselves. We turn everything upside down. We turn the painful things into silly things."

Woman: "Did you unlearn that idea that black people aren't as good as white people?"

Walt: "I'm still working on unlearning it. I still react differently to black people than white people. And that's common amongst many people. If I see black teenagers I react differently than to white teenagers, whether I want to or not. When I notice it, then I can work with it."

Woman: "How do you work on that within yourself? How do you fight against it?"

Walt: "I have close connections with people who are black. Having people that I work with makes me operate very differently."

The congregation's commitment to fighting prejudice is reflected in their membership. Lesbian parents sit with their partners. Christians married to Jews play an active role. Among the group of thirty or so youngsters who troop in from the religious school to the main service the next morning are a sprinkling of Korean, Chinese, and mixed-race African-American kids and one severely disabled girl in a wheelchair. People along the aisle push back chairs as she joins her class at the front and listen patiently as she explains in labored speech the picture she has drawn for her class's crayoned version of the Purim story.

Vicki, a Mishkan Shalom member who grew up in the South, has started a club at the suburban high school where she teaches to help the small group of minority students confront prejudices in their white peers and in themselves. When Walt "stood up as rabbi in front of the congregation" and admitted that he had to struggle constantly to overcome his own prejudices, Vicki felt he validated her and the work she was doing.

Of Walt's congregation, she said, "I have really lived my Judaism since the day I walked in."

CHAPTER 6

JUSTICE IN JUDAISM

The Feminist Revolution

One group of revolutionaries dramatically changed the face of Judaism: the young women. In 1971, when some women from the New York Havurah studied how women were viewed in Talmudic texts, what they read made them angry. "A man could divorce his wife if he found a fly in his soup," said Martha Ackelsberg, while a woman couldn't divorce her husband even if he abused or abandoned her.

For two thousand years, women's status in traditional Judaism had remained largely unchanged. But change was in the air. In June 1972 the Reform movement ordained its first woman rabbi, Sally Priesand. Among Conservative Jewish youth, Ackelsberg and other women from the New York Havurah were the cream of the crop. They had been the stars of classes at Camp Ramah and Prozdor, the Jewish Theological Seminary's program for high school students. They were used to voicing their opinions. They had gained organizing skills from their activity in the civil rights and peace movements. They had the boldness of a generation that felt it was making an impact on its elders. But as soon as they completed the bat mitzvah ceremony, they had been demoted to mere women.

A male member of Havurat Shalom had invited a number of havurahniks from other cities to gather in Boston to talk about the future of the havurah movement. The group he selected consisted entirely of men. Outraged, a group of women from New York Havurah drove to Boston to hold their own meeting with women there. The talk quickly moved from the future of the havurah movement to their anger and frustration about the status of women in Judaism. When the New York women got home, someone pointed out a golden opportunity: The Rabbinical Assembly of the Conservative movement would hold its 1972 meeting soon at the Concord Hotel in the Catskills. The women decided to write the chairman of the program committee to ask if they could make a presentation at the meeting. He said no, the program was all set, but they could try again next year. "But this was the 1970s," recalls Ackelsberg, "so we said 'To hell with you' and decided to go anyway."

They mimeographed a one-page statement to distibute: "Jewish Women Call for Change." It outlined an "equal access agenda": Women should be rabbis, presidents of synagogues and major Jewish organizations. They should be counted in the quorum of ten required for Jewish prayer (the *minyan*) and receive the honor of being called up to the Torah (*aliyah*). The women called themselves Ezrat Nashim—a phrase meaning "help for women," and also the name of the women's section in the ancient Temple in Jerusalem. Their group had ten members. They called the media, and on the day they left for the Concord, the story—with their pictures—appeared in the *New York Post*.

They drove to the Concord with gray clouds hovering overhead, wondering if they would be forced to turn around and drive home in a snowstorm. When they got there, they were given a room to speak in. A hundred rabbis showed up for one meeting, a hundred rabbis' wives for another. (The only slated activity for the wives was a fashion show.) Discussions were lively. Some rabbis said calling women to the Torah would be the end of Judaism: Men's lust would be aroused, and they would not be able to concentrate on prayer. But several rabbis said women in their congregation would be interested, and they asked to be put on Ezrat Nashim's mailing list. One older woman stood and said, "Where have you been all these years? We've been waiting for this!"

Ezrat Nashim began receiving letters from all over the United States, with many people asking if they could join the organization. But there was no organization, just ten women with chutzpah. They quickly put together a packet of information and suggested that people start study groups in their local synagogues. Members of the group began writing articles in journals and speaking at conferences of Jewish organizations. Within two years, the Rabbinical Assembly's Committee on Jewish Law and Standards issued opinions permitting women's equal participation in all Jewish rituals. In 1983 the Jewish Theological Seminary ordained its first female rabbi.

For many Jewish women, the claims of feminism made sense precisely because their Jewish education had taught them to demand justice not only for others but for themselves. As the great teacher Hillel had said some two thousand years before, "If I am not for myself, who will be for me? If I am for myself alone, what am I? And if not now, when?" (*Ethics of the Fathers,* Chap. 1, Par. 14).

The American feminism that emerged in the late 1960s was largely a movement of educated women who felt that they deserved the dignity of an individual life, a life not valued solely by their status as wife, daughter, or mother. Poet Merle Feld remembers the moment when the new feminist feeling made its first tentative appearance at Havurat Shalom. One Shabbat at a retreat, everyone pitched in to help make the lunch. As soon as it was over, the men rushed off to engage in an ethereal discussion, leaving the women to do the dishes. The havurah ideology was fiercely egalitarian: Students and teachers were all comrades, *haverim*. But all the *haverim* were men. The women associated with them (like Merle, whose partner, Rabbi Eddie Feld, was one of the faculty members) could participate in the discussions, but they didn't lead services. When Merle confronted the men at the retreat about the dishes, there was a little instant consciousness-raising, and the egalitarianism of the havurah stretched a bit. It stretched further when one of the *haverim* broke up with his girl-friend, who applied and was accepted for membership in her own right.

But it was a death in the family that forced the havurah to break formally with the patriarchal rules of traditional Judaism. A mother of one member had died, and he needed to say the mourning prayer, *kaddish*. Mona Fishbane, the wife of a faculty member, noted that there were ten people present—nine men and herself. She suggested that this did indeed constitute a minyan. The group left it up to the member saying *kaddish,* and he decided that his mother would have approved. Without fan-fare, all the traditional ritual roles that had been reserved for men in the havurah became open to women.

The year that Havurat Shalom started, 1968, was the same year in which feminism became a fundamental force in my life. I had gone to college to become a writer, but at my parents' insistence I had ended up becoming a teacher because they felt I needed "something to fall back on" in case I didn't get married. In 1968, a few years out of college and working not very successfully as a teacher, I read Betty Friedan's *The Feminine Mystique,* which al-tered the course of my life. I realized she was talking about me: I was one of those bright college graduates who would be slated for misery and neuroses unless I carved out a career where I could use my energy and talent. The next year I visited my fresh-man-year college roommate, who asked me, "Why aren't you writing?" I started freelance writing, and at the end of the semes-ter I had landed a newspaper job.

In the early 1970s feminism spread through consciousness-raising groups. There were a lot of Jewish women involved in feminism in that era, and not so many Jewish feminists involved in Judaism. But gradually the two paths began to converge, both in America and in my life.

My first assignment as a brand-new reporter at the Dayton *Daily News* was to write about the Conservative movement's decision to count women as part of a minyan. It was an assignment that brought me back to Judaism—and, inevitably, to the question of how Judaism could be reconciled with feminism. In Dayton, I spent one part of my private time with the havurah, discovering myself as a Jew, and another part in a consciousness-raising group, discovering myself as a feminist. I and the other women in the group, in growing anger, discussed the many times in which men had regarded us (and we had regarded ourselves) as services, there to nourish and support the lives of men.

Egalitarianism quickly became a moral imperative of the havurah movement. While I was at Fabrangen in Washington, D.C., one of our members, Esther Ticktin, proposed that men refuse the honor of being called to the Torah (*aliyah*) in any synagogue where women did not have this right.

But while the gates of participation were opening in the havurah, some women were beginning to look more critically at the structure behind the gates. Some Jewish feminists believed that the bias against women in Judaism wasn't simply a matter of a few privileges to be equalized; it was fundamental to the religion. In 1973, the same year that the Conservative movement agreed to allow women to be counted in the minyan, Rachel Adler wrote a scathing article in *Response* magazine, "The Jew Who Wasn't There."[1] She pointed out that in Jewish law, women were nonpersons, equivalent in status to slaves and children—except that women could never expect either to be freed or to grow up.

Adler sometimes calls herself a "round-trip *baalat teshuvah*": someone who became Orthodox, then changed her mind. A fifth-generation Reform Jew, she grew up in Chicago. Her family was only marginally Jewish; her mother had never seen a Passover seder until Rachel invited her to one. Rachel went to Sunday school for only one year, when she was about nine. It hadn't worked out. She was bored. Being fond of Greek myths, "I kept asking why this God was better than Athena. The Sunday school teacher was not up to answering that question."

Despite her impatience with the way Sunday school teachers dealt with the question, ever since she was a small child, Rachel had wanted to know about God. She read everything she could find about God, from the lives of the Roman Catholic saints to Jewish texts. She taught herself to read and write Hebrew. She picked up whatever classes about Judaism she could, adopting new Jewish practices as she learned about them. By the end of her teens she was participating in the Orthodox community. She eventually married an Orthodox rabbi, moved to Minneapolis, and gave birth to a son. In her thinking and writing, she tried to integrate Judaism and feminism. She wrote about *mikveh,* the monthly immersion after the menstrual period, as a ritual with positive spiritual meaning for women: Mikveh should not be seen as purging some taint associated with menstruation, but as a purification, an affirmation of life, after the encounter with a small death—the egg that might have become a baby but didn't. "Menstruation is an autumn within, the dying which makes room for new birth."[2] The article convinced many Jewish feminists, including me, to adopt the practice of mikveh and to think of it as an important part of women's spirituality, rather than as something men imposed on us.

In some ways Rachel found Orthodoxy tremendously satisfying. It gave her "an orderly universe in which everything fit and everything made sense." But as a college-educated woman, she knew that when technology and ways of living changed, beliefs and social roles changed. She had more and more difficulty accepting the Orthodox view of the world, of laws and social roles that were set at Sinai and could not be changed.

Although her deep faith in God never wavered, Rachel could

no longer accept the Orthodox view of God or women. She could no longer pray in a community where she was regarded as a nonperson. In some ways, she said, her break with Orthodoxy was even more painful than the breakup of her marriage.

Rachel was divorced in 1984. She moved to Los Angeles, where she remarried. She now teaches Talmud at the American Jewish Congress's Jewish Feminist Center, prays in a havurah that includes both Reform and Conservative Jews, and has just received a doctorate from the University of Southern California. Her thesis was on Jewish feminist theology. In an article in *Tikkun* magazine she critiqued her previous writing on mikveh,[3] but the ideas she had generated had already taken on a life of their own. Mikveh was a key part of my spiritual practice, and that of other Jewish feminists. We were not about to give it up.

Being excluded from the recitation of the mourner's kaddish was the most fundamental experience of nonpersonhood for many Jewish women. Grieving the loss of a parent, they turned to Judaism for strength and comfort but were told that a man—sometimes a man they did not know, hired for the occasion—would have to say the prayer in their stead. That exclusion had been enough to drive Letty Cottin Pogrebin out of Judaism, and challenging that exclusion was part of what launched former Congresswoman Bella Abzug into feminism. Insisting on saying kaddish in her Orthodox synagogue taught her, she said, "that one had a right, indeed an obligation, to try unconventional paths and that no one would or could stop me. I can say that it was there behind the *mehitza,* standing to say Kaddish, that a Jewish feminist was born."[4]

So it's no accident that Arlene Agus thinks one of her most important tasks as a feminist is to teach Orthodox women that they have a right to say the kaddish, and to teach them how to conduct themselves with dignity when others do not think they have that right.[5] Agus was raised in an Orthodox home, educated in yeshiva, and is by faith and practice an Orthodox Jew. She came to feel that the exclusion of women from full participation was against God's will, however, and that it was part of the work God had given her to change it.

Agus was seven years old when a "croaky" cousin was asked to lead the closing hymn at services, and she realized that even though she had a much nicer voice, she would never be asked because she was a girl. In her Orthodox high school, she led a revolt of teenage girls demanding to be taught Talmud, a subject that is still reserved for boys in many Orthodox schools. When she went to Brooklyn College and then to Columbia, she found that there was no place where women could study Talmud at an advanced level, though there were many programs for men. So she persuaded David Eliav, a beloved teacher from her high school, to set one up, and she studied there in the evenings after her college classes. That program, Midrasha, eventually developed into Drisha Institute, an Orthodox program of advanced classical Jewish studies for women.

In 1971, Agus began meeting in a consciousness-raising group with some Upper West Side women (mostly raised in the Conservative movement) to see how they could bring feminism to traditional Judaism. The following year this group, Ezrat Nashim, would demand the Conservative rabbinate equalize the roles of men and women in the service. In Judaism, ritual life is a matter not of rights but of obligations. "We realized that if we were serious about being obligated, we had to act obligated," said Agus. Yet she had trouble finding a comfortable place to fulfill one of the most basic obligations: prayer. There was no Orthodox service where she could pray equally with men, and Reform and havurah services, she felt, deviated too far from the prescribed ritual. For ten years she chanted the prayers three times a day, every day, by herself. It was "an unbearably lonely period."

Agus also organized ground-breaking conferences on women and Judaism. She helped start prayer groups for Orthodox women where, since no men were present, they could lead and chant the Torah without violating Jewish law. This movement spread throughout the major communities of modern Orthodoxy in the United States. Agus always saw the prayer groups as a transition to full equality. She went on to help organize a traditional but egalitarian minyan, Minyan Me'at (literally "the small minyan," although it now draws eighty to one hundred members each Shabbat). Agus described it as "the first place I felt at home since I left Boro Park" (the ultra-Orthodox neighborhood in Brooklyn where she grew up).

For Agus and other members of Ezrat Nashim, challenging the exclusion of women from traditional practice was only one part of a personal search "for spiritual self-knowledge and expression."[6] They considered three paths: "to retain the traditional role [of women] and attempt to enrich it, to adopt the male rituals and hope to find spiritual satisfaction in them, or to create new or parallel rituals."[7] They were not entirely comfortable with any of the options. In their studies, however, they discovered one holiday that had traditionally been of special significance to women, and they began to celebrate it together.

Rosh Hodesh, the Festival of the New Moon, had been celebrated as a woman's holiday for many centuries, possibly since biblical times. But it had fallen into disuse. Since it followed the cycle of the moon, mirroring women's menstrual cycles, it was very congenial to women searching for a uniquely female form of spiritual expression. Since there was very little law about how it should be celebrated, Rosh Hodesh was one of the few areas where traditional women like Agus could feel free to experiment with new rituals. In a ground-breaking article she sketched one possible way of celebrating the holiday and urged women to revive it.[8] Rosh Hodesh groups began to form all around the United States, as well as around the world.

Part of the power of the feminist movement of the 1970s was its recognition that "the personal is political." Jewish feminists realized that inclusion in community leadership and spiritual enfranchisement were aspects of the same struggle.

In the fall of 1976, Susan Weidman Schneider, Aviva Cantor, and other women (ranging from secular Zionists to Orthodox) launched a new magazine, *Lilith*. They functioned as a collective, with even the student interns having a voice and a vote. In the nearly twenty years since, each issue of the magazine has kept alive for women the connection between the external world of Jewish politics and the internal world of Jewish prayer. While battling the "Jewish-American princess" stereotype and agitating for women's rabbinical ordination and their inclusion in the leadership of secular Jewish organizations, *Lilith* also published feminist prayers and blessings.

The editors recognized that it was important for women not only to see other women in positions of Jewish power but also (as "people of the Book") to see women's stories as part of the Jewish story. The very name *Lilith* was a commitment to making this happen. The thousand-year-old legend of Lilith says that there was another woman in Eden, before Eve, and that things didn't work out: "After the Holy One created the first human being Adam, the Holy One created a woman, also from the earth, and called her Lilith. Lilith said, 'We are equal because we both come from the earth.'" (*The Alphabet of Ben Sira*, 23a–b). Schneider continues the story:

> When Adam got bossy and said, "I am your superior. I will lie on top of you. You will lie beneath me" . . . Lilith fled the Garden of Eden. She refused to return, because Adam continued to insist that she be subservient. . . . Subsequently, Lilith got a very bad press. Later writers projected onto her all the evil a woman could embody. Paradoxically, she was both frigid and she seduced men who walked into dark houses alone at night. [You can still buy anti-Lilith amulets on the Lower East Side.] She was sterile, yet she gave birth to one hundred demon children a day.[9]

In the lead editorial of the first issue of *Lilith*, Schneider wrote, "In history, literature, religious practice and personal relations, Jewish women have come to accept the concepts of ourselves that others have created for us." The goal of this magazine would be to give Jewish women the information they need to "move forward and shape our own futures."[10]

The name *Lilith* was a "great consciousness-raiser," Schneider wrote on the eighteenth anniversary of the magazine's founding. "The legends of Lilith provide a window onto the paradoxical nature of the prejudices against all women, and of the stereotypes about women who speak out for their own equality."[11] (Schneider's husband, after being asked over and over why the magazine his wife edited was named after Lilith, a demon, replied, "It was either that or Shirley.")[12]

As important as it was to expose the stereotypes that shackled women, the editors recognized that they needed to give women new models, new ways to see themselves as part of the Jewish story. In *Lilith* I read about Beruriah, whose opinions on Jewish law are cited in the Talmud, and who is quoted as giving wise advice to her husband, Rabbi Meir. I read about the poet Hannah Senesh, a resistance fighter who parachuted behind enemy lines during World War II. And I read about the new generation of learned Jewish women who were challenging the Conservative rabbinate to accept the ordination of women.

Scholars and storytellers joined the journalists in unearthing and recreating what feminist theologian Judith Plaskow called "Women's Torah." Savina J. Teubal, in her books on the two wives of Abraham, *Sarah the Priestess* (Swallow Press, 1984) and *Hagar the Egyptian* (Harper and Row, 1990), used Babylonian and other sources to illuminate the hints of a prior matriarchal religion buried in the text of the Abraham story. Judith S. Antonelli, coeditor of *Neshama* ("Soul"), a newsletter "encouraging the exploration of women's spirituality in Judaism" wrote new *midrashim* about biblical women. In Plaskow's words, Jewish women had begun "hearing the silence" and filling it with their voices.

Ritual and stories are key elements of Jewish tradition. When we women could see ourselves in the classic Jewish stories, said Plaskow, we could write ourselves back into the tradition. But we would have to imagine these stories from the female point of view—which is hardly ever expressed in the traditional stories, even when they center on a woman. In doing this work of imagination, we would redeem both the tradition and ourselves, making both more whole.

When the search for spirituality and the search for female dignity converged in the early 1970s, they defined Plaskow's life work. She went to graduate school to find God and found feminism instead; she then dedicated herself to figuring out how feminism, God, and Judaism might all fit together.

Raised on Long Island in a classical Reform temple where God spoke in the sonorous voice of a rabbi raising robed arms to give a benediction, Plaskow decided at age seven that she wanted to be a prophet. From the time she was in junior high school she wanted to be a rabbi, but there weren't any woman rabbis in those days. When she eventually decided to become a theologian, her inner aim was to find a God she could believe in. But the male divinity students at Yale, instead of searching for the relevance of the religious viewpoints they studied, puffed on their pipes and picked theologies to bits.

During her second year at the program, Yale began to admit women undergraduates for the first time. The female graduate students called a meeting (Yale had admitted graduate students of both sexes for eighty years) where women began to share their experiences of being ignored and put down. Afterwards Plaskow and another grad student (Carol Christ, a Protestant) went out to dinner and talked for hours about their disenchantment with the religion department. They decided to run their own student-led courses, first on Protestant and then on contemporary Jewish theology. In their classes students shared personal responses to the reading, exploring its relevance to their lives. Reading the work of feminist theologians, Plaskow was drawn into the feminist critique of patriarchal Western religions.

For several years Plaskow had been struggling to figure out her relationship to Judaism. The Reform Judaism she'd grown up

with seemed shallow to her. "I realized how much of the tradition the Reform movement had simply truncated—large portions of the liturgy and the traditional texts." Yet after she married and began keeping a traditional home, she felt suffocated by
the restrictions of Jewish law. She began small rebellions, turning
on lights and talking on the phone on Shabbat.

Her conflict deepened as she became involved with feminism.
Though the sexism of the traditional liturgy bothered her,
Plaskow continued to go to services regularly because she found
spiritual meaning in being part of a Jewish community. Then one
Shabbat morning, she was standing outside the Yale chapel when
one of the men called to her husband, "Come in. We need a
minyan." Plaskow had been going to services there every Saturday for the last year, whereas her husband had hardly ever been
there. But her presence was irrelevant—not only to the men who
ran the service, she realized, but to Jewish tradition. Shortly afterward she stopped going to services.

Except for a few years when she and her husband lived in
Manhattan and went to the New York Havurah, Plaskow felt for
many years that she had no religious community. Her peers in
academia—other women studying religion—were her community. A spiritual turning point came when her mother was killed
by a brain tumor. Judith had commuted to her mother's home
from Kansas through five months of steady deterioration and five
more months of coma. Judith found the Reform funeral, which
was full of phrases about justice and judgment, appalling. "At another point in my life, I would have railed against God: What do
you mean, justice? My mother was only fifty-eight, and she gets a
brain tumor?"

She found herself wishing that the service had talked about
flow, about tides. She realized she had come to a new understanding of God: a sense of cycles, rebirth, energy in the universe—what some theologians called "the ground of being," the
great background force from which all things rise and to which
all things return. In that moment of crisis Plaskow saw that grad-

ually, without her being aware of it, the reading and writing and thinking she had been doing had finally led her to a God she could believe in.

In 1979 she and Carol Christ edited *Womanspirit Rising,* one of the first collections of writings about feminist spirituality. She also completed a dissertation in feminist theology. When it was done, though, she felt stuck. Jewishly she was still isolated, and professionally she didn't know what she should write about next. She thought, "What's wrong with me? I have nothing more to say."

Suddenly Plaskow's life began to come together in a new way. She was invited to teach a course on Jewish feminist theology at the first Havurah Institute in 1980. Through the New York Area Feminist Scholars in Religion—which included Carol Christ and other Christian and Jewish scholars—she had engaged in many discussions about feminist ideas of God and religion. She had taught college courses about women and religion, but she had never taught a course about women and *Jewish* religion. "It was the most exciting teaching experience I'd ever had in my life: the first time my Jewish, feminist, and work identities came together." The women who participated in the course were equally excited. They agreed that they needed to create an ongoing group of feminist Jewish women.

One of the women in the class was Martha Ackelsberg, a member of the New York Havurah whom Judith had known well for ten years. The feeling Judith had experienced since becoming involved in feminism—of a life divided into two irreconcilable parts—was one Martha had known her entire life.

Ackelsberg had gone through a lonely childhood. Growing up in Bloomfield, NJ, she was one of only two Jews in her class. In high school the isolation eased, but she still did not have close friends. Only in the summer at Camp Ramah, where it was okay to be smart, good at sports, and interested in Judaism, could she feel whole. Martha had gone to Hebrew high school at the Jewish Theological Seminary. She loved Jewish traditions and the

Hebrew liturgy, though she didn't think of herself as a spiritual person and hardly ever thought about or felt connected to God. The New York Havurah had been another island of integration in a life fragmented among graduate school and feminist activities. When she went off to Northampton, Massachusetts, in 1972 (where she taught political science at Smith College while her husband did graduate studies), Martha again began to lead a divided life, going to New York once a month for havurah retreats and Jewish holidays. After several years in Massachusetts, including a year of marriage counseling, she and her husband divorced. Ackelsberg became involved in a relationship with a woman. "I spent the next five or six years living a completely bifurcated life. I was a feminist and lesbian in Northampton, a Jew at the havurah in New York. . . . I felt they would reject me if they knew. In fact they knew, and they didn't reject me."

For five years Ackelsberg did not fully admit to herself that she was a lesbian. In 1980, wishing that she could have a child and knowing that time was short, she made one last effort to have a workable relationship with a man and finally realized that her real love was for women. She went off fearfully to the 1980 Havurah Institute, feeling that in this atmosphere where sharing of selves was encouraged, she was hiding an enormous secret.

In fact, though, the institute was a wonderful experience where all the parts of her life seemed to come together. She took Judith's course on Jewish feminist theology and loved it. Her second course focused on Jewish ideas of community. As a political scientist, Ackelsberg had written a dissertation about the theory and practice of non-authoritarian organizations—of which the havurot were an interesting example. Leading the Shabbat Torah discussion, she tried to bring her intellectual interests, her political convictions, and her love of Judaism together. She told her fellow Havurah members that "we needed to recognize that we were creating a community in and through which we could experience God. We needed to do a theology of community." She was stunned to hear these ideas coming out of her mouth. "I never thought of myself as a theologian. I was nervous even using those words." Even so, it felt "so wonderful to be there, so comfortable and whole, now that I had found this community. Except for this big secret."

And so the secret had to go. Martha decided to "come out"—to reveal that she was a lesbian—to her roommate at the Institute, Chava Weissler. Chava calmly replied, "More people know than you think."

Ackelsberg chuckles, "I felt as if I'd been carrying this huge garbage bag on my back, and all the time it had been clear plastic. It was a tremendous relief. . . . As a result of that week, I realized that it was possible for me to have some cohesion in my life. I wanted the people I was close to to know me."

She decided to come out next to Judith, who said, "I've known for years." In fact, Judith had tried to make openings for Martha to come out. Judith had talked about friends who were lesbians, and about lesbianism as a component of the feminist movement, but Martha was too anxious to pick up on the invitation.

Judith, Martha, and other women decided to try to create a spiritual community for feminist Jews. They began planning a retreat to take place Memorial Day weekend at the Grail, a retreat center run by Christian feminists.

This once-a-year gathering, which called itself B'not Esh ("Daughters of Fire"), became the primary spiritual community for both Martha and Judith. Members shared their experiences as Jewish women, talked about traditional images of God, and studied the stories of sister/wives in the Torah. But when they tried to run services together, they discovered what seemed like canyons separating the traditionalists from those who wanted to experiment with rituals. The women spent hours fiercely debating, struggling and often failing to understand each other. Many wept realizing that what they had hoped would be the perfect community—a sisterhood of women equally committed to feminism and Judaism—seemed so difficult to create. But they came

back, and over the years they slowly built trust, including an ability to experiment and to appreciate differences.

The June following the first B'not Esh retreat, Martha was invited to head the wrap-up panel for a conference sponsored by
New Jewish Agenda, called "Toward a Progressive Jewish World
View." Martha was "blown away" by the invitation, which
seemed like the final step in ending the fragmentation of her life.
It allowed her to use the insights she had developed as a political
scientist to aid the causes she was committed to as an activist and
a Jew. For some reason, though, the invitation threw her into a
turmoil. She got more and more nervous, and she couldn't write
any of her talk before she got to the conference site outside
Philadelphia.

Over the next couple of weeks, Martha's inner turmoil deepened. She feared she was having a nervous breakdown. She felt
"at sea, completely up in the air," and she couldn't talk to anybody. She only knew that something about the talk Sunday
night (which had gone perfectly well) had thrown her into a
tailspin. At some point she wrote letters to Judith and one other
friend, trying to describe what she was going through. Judith
called as soon as she got the letter, saying, "You're experiencing a
spiritual moment."

Suddenly Martha understood her crisis in a completely different way. It had something to do with finally being able to achieve
unity in her life. That powerful rush of feeling seemed to combine the overwhelming realization that it was possible to feel
whole, sadness for all those years when she'd had to live as a divided person, and fear about what it would mean to give up
those divisions. She understood now that her spirituality was not
bound up with a personal God she could pray to but with
achieving a sense of wholeness through community, friendship,
intellectual work, and political action.

Her friend, Judith, had managed to "hear me in a way I couldn't
understand myself," to look through all the confusion and understand what was going on in her soul. "That allowed me somehow

to go on with my life. I felt, 'I'm simply finding this aspect of my life I didn't know was there. Let's see where it will take me.'" Gradually she began to fall in love with Judith. "She had given me such a gift; she had seen me in a way no one else had."

In 1983, Martha and Judith planned a workshop for the Havurah Institute on gays and lesbians in the havurah movement. The Havurah Institute was very family oriented; some gays and lesbians were there, but they felt they had to remain incognito. Martha would talk about how to make the Institute a more comfortable place for gays and lesbians, and Judith would talk about how "straight" persons like herself could be allies of gays and lesbians.

That workshop crystallized their relationship. Judith realized that the quality of her friendship with Martha had changed—she, too, was falling in love. Deciding what those feelings should mean for her marriage was painful. Yet once she made the decision to choose Martha, she experienced a burst of energy and clarity that affected everything in her life. In the first two months after getting involved with Martha, she wrote the outlines for two books. Up until then she had been critiquing Judaism, and her criticisms had become a wall she couldn't get past. Suddenly, while outlining a talk for a retreat of women rabbis, she understood that she and other women could "take the power to redefine the tradition."

In her book *Standing Again at Sinai: Judaism from a Feminist Perspective* (Harper & Row, San Francisco, 1990), she named the problem in a a way that pointed to a solution. The Jewish tradition does not contain women's voices, she said. Women are the Other in Judaism; the exception to the rule, not the norm. We Jewish women must listen to the texts, so that we hear the silence, then fill in the silence with our voices. We would have to respond to the three pillars of Judaism—God, Torah, and Israel—by telling the missing stories, inventing the missing rituals, and finding the metaphors for our experience of God. Thus we would participate in creating a covenant of the entire Jewish people, a newly whole Judaism.

Martha Ackelsberg had understood that we must create feminist Jewish communities. Judith Plaskow had now given those
communities an agenda.

The question, said Judith, was "how to make women's words
Torah . . . to say through ritual that women's words and lives are
Torah." Over the years, members of B'not Esh tried various experiments: They asked the two oldest women to share "a piece of
their life's wisdom," said Plaskow. Before and after their talk, the
group said Torah blessings. Imagining themselves at Mount Sinai,
each told the story of the giving of the Torah as she envisioned it.
Each wrote about a woman who had been important in her life.
One Shabbat morning these stories were their Torah portion.
Once, instead of reading the Torah, they went looking for something to bring back as Torah. During that brief half hour, Faith
Rogow wrote a song, "As we bless the Source of Life," which is
now part of the Shabbat service in many havurot. To Judith the
goal was not to create a new sacred literature that in its turn
would be canonized and fixed. It was the process that was important: "to see Torah as living and changing."

In the twenty-odd years since Ezrat Nashim first challenged
the Conservative rabbinate to equalize women's roles, feminism
has had a profound impact on all branches of Judaism. There are
now a significant number of female rabbis, who have set a model
of less formal, more family-like relationships in the synagogue.
There is still a glass ceiling, with women rabbis receiving less pay
than men in comparable positions, and few women leading large
synagogues or major Jewish organizations. (But in 1995 Rabbi
Laura Geller became the first woman to become senior rabbi of
a congregation of more than one thousand members.) And in
the Orthodox world, there are many more bat mitzvahs and
covenant ceremonies for baby girls. Young women are studying
Talmud.

Less obvious than these external changes is the more subtle influence of activist women on Jewish spirituality, says Arlene Agus.
All branches of Judaism have become more personal. More fam-

ilies celebrating a life-cycle event feel it is important to put in their own personal and creative touches, such as their own prayers or favorite quotations.

But if the influence of feminists has been pervasive, the backlash has been fierce. When the Conservative movement voted to equalize ritual roles of women, a group of rabbis and synagogues seceded to form the Union for Traditional Judaism. Some of the more radical experiments in feminist spirituality have stirred accusations of paganism and heresy. Rabbi Jane Litman was nearly ejected from rabbinical school after a rabbi accused her in an article of engaging in pagan practices. (She filed a libel suit that was settled in her favor.)

Some men—and some women as well—have reacted with vitriol to even the most careful and traditional experiments in expanding women's role. In their prayer (*tefillah*) groups, Orthodox women were careful to omit prayers that required a minyan of ten males. But some progressive Orthodox rabbis who originally allowed tefillah groups to meet in their synagogues have had to back down after vehement objections from congregants. Since the first international conference of Jewish feminists met in Israel in 1988, a women's tefillah group has tried to pray with a Torah at the Wailing Wall every Rosh Hodesh. They have been stoned, spat on, tear-gassed, and dragged bodily from the site.

I see these reactions as a replay of a drama that recurs over and over in Jewish history. In Judaism, periods of repression by the surrounding culture have alternated with periods of acceptance and assimilation. During periods of acceptance, Jews eagerly explore the surrounding culture and eventually develop a synthesis between it and the tradition. Even our ideas about God are challenged and reformulated. This process allows Judaism to keep changing and growing, but it is also a very threatening process. It raises the question of what is essential about Judaism: what stretches the boundaries so it can contain more, and what crumbles them so that it can no longer continue as a cohesive system? When Maimonides, a medieval physician who was learned in mathematics, attempted to develop a synthesis between Aristotelian philosophy and Judaism, he was branded a heretic. But eventually his ideas became pillars of Jewish philosophy. The credo he developed never was adopted by Judaism, but as the hymn "Yigdal" it is sung every Shabbat.[13]

Jewish ideas about God have also gone through pendulum swings, from the very abstract God of Maimonides to the very personal God of Hasidism. Perhaps such a range of ideas is inevitable when people who live through their senses posit an invisible God.

What is different now is that we live in a very individualistic society. Instead of taking cues from an intellectual elite, many modern Jews have tried to imagine and encounter God for themselves. The feminist revolution has been an important part of that change, empowering both men and women to change not only the formal structures of the religion but also its rituals and even the texture of belief.

CHAPTER 7

FROM EXILE TO HOMECOMING

Jews in America, Gays and Lesbians in Judaism

The experience of exile—of being the outsider—is central to the Jewish ethical system, which is an ethics of empathy. It is central to our politics (our resistance to the tyranny of the majority) and to our intellectual life (our commitment to hearing the minority view, the other side).

Having suffered the brutality and vulnerability of exile, it is no wonder that in the America of the 1990s, with social barriers down for perhaps the first time ever, Jews are assimilating in droves, shutting the door on a past that they regard as either oppressive or irrelevant. As ethnotherapist Judith Weinstein Klein has pointed out, when a group is discriminated against, its members often take the negative stereotypes into their own self-image. It's hard for them to love each other—or themselves.[1]

In the years when opting out wasn't an option, Jews developed another answer to exile that is spiritually more enriching: identity and community. In the ghettoes of Europe and the Middle East, where Jews for centuries were forced to be outsiders, we used the experience constructively to create a nurturing inside, a tightly knit community with great sensitivity to the vulnerable and needy.

As I have traveled around the country in the course of my work, I have found many Jews expressing the sense of being an outsider. Whether or not they belong to synagogues, whether or not they are socially accepted and have a circle of friends, at some level they feel different and fundamentally alone.

Like many other Jews I experienced this exile inwardly as well, not only feeling rejected but rejecting myself and others of my group. In New Jewish Agenda's Jewish Identity group, eight of us, single men and women, explored the stereotypes we held of each other and ourselves. For five minutes during our first meeting, we scribbled furiously, writing down whatever words occurred to us in response to the phrases *Jewish man* and *Jewish woman*.[2] Then we scribbled for five minutes more, writing down our associations with the words *American man* and *American woman*. Posting the results was a revelation. Why was it that we thought of Jewish women as dark, dumpy, loud, and neurotic, while we thought of American women as leggy, slim, and athletic? Why did we picture Jewish women in aprons and American women in bathing suits? Why did we think of Jewish men as studious and nerdy, and of American men as assertive, strong Marlboro men driving race cars? Since there was almost no overlap between our two lists, did we really consider ourselves Americans? For six months we talked through the prejudices we had unearthed in ourselves. We discovered that we cared more about sensitivity than legginess, and more about intelligence than displays of macho. By the end of that process I could look around the group and feel, "I love us. I love us Jews."

While I experienced exile as a Jew in America, some of my

comrades endured a double exile as gay and lesbian men and women within Judaism. Those who reclaimed their heritage made a double homecoming: as gays and lesbians, and as Jews.

My friend David Rogoff is sitting across the dining room table, waiting to tell me his story. A psychotherapist, he has just gone into private practice after years as head of a hospice. Wearing a T-shirt with a picture of a Chagall print, he is broad-shouldered and dark-haired, with an engaging smile and outdoorsy good looks. He hugs people a lot. David has been one of the most gifted prayer leaders at our minyan, and he makes thoughtful, spiritually sensitive comments during discussions. Two years ago, when we were sitting around talking at our minyan's potluck Shabbat lunch, I asked him how he was doing. He said, "Wonderful! I just went to my first gay pride march. I've been coming out to one friend after another. I've never felt better in my life."

With that statement, he became the first gay person I know of in our minyan to come out to other people in the minyan. He has been radiating a kind of fulfillment ever since.

As a small child, David was deluged with love from a large, Yiddish-speaking, chicken-soup-making extended family. He was treated, he says, like a little Messiah. But the minute he started grade school, he went into exile from this Jewish Garden of Eden. He realized immediately that he was different from the other boys. "Other boys knew the names of cars; I didn't know cars had names. They knew baseball players; I didn't know the difference between baseball and football." By the time he was a teenager he had developed a counter-strategy. He became an intellectual, reading Russian novels and Shakespeare and listening to classical music.

Since childhood David had experienced homosexual fantasies, but in high school he began to be especially aware of them. "I had a pretty strong sense that . . . [it] would be problematic if I continued to have these feelings." College was a reprieve from his isolation. He became president of the Rutgers University Hillel group, and for the first time in his life he had friends, both men and women. He also started attending the Orthodox synagogues in New Brunswick. "Never, no matter what kind of crisis I was going through, did it ever occur to me to be anything but Jewish. Or to be nothing."

Thinking of himself as a traditional Jew helped David avoid confronting his homosexuality. Traditional Jews believe sex between men is forbidden by the Torah. Leviticus 18, which reads, "Do not lie with a male as one lies with a woman; it is an abomination," is read every year on Yom Kippur. (Leviticus 20 notes that homosexuality is punishable by death.) There were gay pride marches on television and a homophile league on the Rutgers campus, but it never occurred to David to get involved in them. When he occasionally had crushes on some of his male friends, he put aside feelings of attraction and concentrated on the friendship. He thought of himself as the only man in the world who was attracted to other men, but that didn't mean he thought of himself as a homosexual. "I thought of myself as basically like other people. Homosexuals to me were people that were really different . . . defined by society as perverts."

Thus began the split in his life. Occasionally he had opportunities for a sexual encounter with a man, but these were totally outside his ordinary life. "When I got a chance to touch a male, to be affectionate with another guy, it felt perfectly natural," but it was "on vacation from being me."

David prayed "for God to make things clear for me. I thought maybe God had a plan, was saving me for someone in particular. Once I found her, God would reward me for my patience by giving me the necessary erotic feelings to complete the relationship." Sensing that he might never marry, though, he carved out a public persona as an interesting person, a bit unconventional. He got a reputation as "the person people went to when they needed someone to talk to."

But there was no one David could talk to. Not even with his closest friends did he feel he could discuss his feelings. Gradually he came to believe that he would never be truly intimate with another person. Since the Jewish people rejected homosexuality and considered it a disgrace, he felt obligated never to speak of it. "There was a sense that I would never be known."

A few years of floundering followed college, as David started and then dropped out of a graduate program in Renaissance history at the University of California at Berkeley, and then a graduate program in clinical psychology at Rutgers. During this time, living in communal households with lots of hugging and getting involved in encounter groups helped David compensate for the lack of a partner. Eventually he found fulfilling work, developing and directing a hospice program for dying people and their families. He was mentor and good friend to two younger men, and his work relationships with women were "kind of like marriages—work wives, so to speak."

Outside of work, though, his personal life was a vacuum. Evenings were painfully lonely. David felt he was demanding too much from his friends, pushing them to play the emotional role that should have been filled by a partner or spouse. He became depressed. "I wasn't happy reading, I wasn't happy playing the piano, I wasn't happy *davening,* I wasn't happy at work. . . . Everything in my life went on strike and said, 'Until you fix this thing, or at least lay the groundwork for it, we're all going to stop.'"

Through his hospice work David met the young man he calls his guardian angel. One day in the hospice office, the phone rang: A young AIDS patient (whom I will call Mike) was being rushed to the intensive care unit in respiratory arrest. David met Mike's family in the waiting room. Sitting with them was a young black man, who was introduced as Randy. Mike's father put an arm around Randy and said, "Whatever services you make available to our family, I want you to know that Randy is also a member of our family."

David went home that night and cried. Seeing a Jewish family who loved their gay son, accepted his homosexuality, and embraced his partner, he felt, "Why can't I have this?"

For two and a half months Mike, in a coma, was kept alive on a respirator. During that time his friends came to visit, including a parade of gay men. For the first time, homosexuals were becoming visible to David. "They were real people. Some were professionals. Some were in loving relationships. They were adored by Mike's family. The nurses didn't turn around and throw up. This wasn't disgusting. My colleagues at team meetings talked about Mike and his lover as if we were talking about any family." For the first time, he realized that there were gay men who had real lives.

Then one day Mike opened his eyes and emerged from the coma. His parents told Mike that David, who was in the room, had been visiting regularly and had been a great support to the family. A few days later Mike woke up from a doze, looked at David, and said, "David, what's it like for you being gay?"

"I told him I had no idea what to do with it. It wasn't a visible part of my life. I wasn't proud of the times I had found opportunities to relate sexually. Those moments were completely outside my life. He looked at me and said, 'How can you live that way?'"

At home that night David screamed, "Why am I living this way?" He realized he was denying his homosexuality in order to avoid rejection by his parents, but that no longer seemed a good enough reason to continue crippling himself. "I knew at some level that my life was at stake. . . . I was wasting my creative energies, my life force, in creating a hiding place as the central project of my life. . . . I was wasting my life on a stupid, harmful, self-destructive project. My life was all wrong." He believed his parents wanted him to have a fulfilling life, even if they might not be able to accept the way he needed to live.

A friend suggested to David that he attend the National Havurah Institute that summer. David decided to go "with a sense of surrender, study, spiritual search. I would . . . be open to whatever answers would come."

Rabbi Lynn Gottlieb had fashioned from her experiences in New Mexico a Jewish version of the Native American vision quest. In a guided meditation, she told people to imagine themselves in a dark forest, with an animal coming out from the brush to be their guide. David imagined his beloved dog Yaffa, who had died after ten years. Your animal takes you to a place deep in the forest where you meet an ancestor who has a message for you, Lynn said. David saw a rabbi, one of the long line of Lithuanian rabbis from whom he was descended. Lynn told people to ask the ancestor a question. David asked his ancestor, "What's with this homosexuality stuff?"

The ancestor told David that on this topic, Jewish tradition was wrong. The rabbis didn't understand; they had made a mistake. "This is part of your nature," the ancestor told him. "It's divinely given. Beginning now, you need to bring it into your life, make it a visible part of your identity. You will be protected in doing this; It will be fine. And you have my blessing."

His rabbi ancestor took David to a river—the river dividing this world and the next—and introduced him to the biblical King David. King David blessed him, saying that his life would now become integrated. He would come to terms with his homosexuality, find a loving relationship, come out to people, teach, and become visible as a gay man. His visibility would help other people, as Mike had helped David.

David came home from the Institute and started making lists of people to come out to. He made lunch appointments. Some of the first people he came out to were women he knew had been interested in having a relationship with him. The people he told were touched and appreciative. Their response was a revelation to David; not until he took the risk could he be certain of the protection he had been promised by his guides in the vision quest. He was forty-three years old when he began coming out.

Within that year David was invited to join the board of the Hyacinth AIDS Foundation. He was surrounded and working with gay people who had successful careers and relationships that were affirmed by their friends. Over a period of two years David came out to his colleagues, friends, and eventually to his family. At the end of that time, Mike died. "I was able to thank him before he died for having given me my life." He hasn't yet found the intimate relationship he longs for, but "there's honesty in my life. I have a whole network of gay and lesbian friends. I have hope. Before I had none."

In March 1992 while David was coming out, the Conservative rabbinate's Committee on Law and Standards issued a ruling that homosexuals couldn't be rabbis and that homosexual relationships could not be sanctified through any ceremony. The committee left it to the discretion of local rabbis whether gay people could be called to the Torah, hired as Hebrew school teachers or camp counselors, or elected to leadership positions, but it said gay people would be welcomed as congregation members.

David was furious. Young men were dying because the community, by refusing to sanctify their relationships, pushed them out of committed relationships and into a lifestyle of casual sexual contact. The "don't ask, don't tell" policy of the Conservative movement forced gays and lesbians to be invisible, to live in hiding, he said.

His response was to try to change things. He helped organize a central New Jersey gay Jewish havurah. They met monthly. During Gay Pride Month in June, they held a "seder" celebrating their liberation as Jews and as gay men and women. Working in teams with parents of gays, David visited rabbis of local synagogues to request that they hold a program about the status of gays in the Jewish community. Through Jewish Family Service and liberal synagogues, he organized programs and workshops for gay people and their families. He told them of his conviction "that coming out and being out is a religious obligation, and the opposite is a sin against oneself and against God. . . . It's a form of suicide. It's putting stumbling blocks before the blind. It's withholding the first fruits of one's life, which one is supposed to give over. It's conspiracy to grand larceny."

He felt that being a visible, Jewishly committed gay man was as much a part of his healing mission as the work he did in hospice, that he was being guided by God to turn his experience into a blessing for others. "The stone which the builders cast away became the corner-stone," says a verse from Psalms, sung on Passover and other holidays. To David, the verse meant that Jewish communities must accept diversity, looking for the uniqueness that each person can contribute to building the sanctuary of Jewish faith. Enforced invisibility, said David, is "casting away the stone."

He resigned from the Conservative synagogue where he had been a member and wrote a letter to the board explaining why. Since that time, he says, nearly every time he comes to the synagogue, he is invited to come up to the Torah for an *aliyah*—a gentle statement that he is still welcomed as an individual, regardless of his homosexuality. After David's resignation the rabbi invited him into his office for a long and loving talk. At the end, the rabbi threw up his hands and said, "David, I know you and I know Jewish law. I don't know what to do with you."

David said, "I need to be in a community where they *do* know what to do with me. I need to affiliate under an umbrella that will celebrate my relationship, that sees me as a role model because of my visibility, because of the courage it has taken me. I knew what was right. I knew what I had to do to heal my life. And I found it in Judaism."

There are now a number of Jewish spiritual communities where homosexuals can affirm their identities. Reform Judaism has welcomed gays and lesbians as individuals, couples, and congregations and permits them to be ordained as rabbis. Reconstructionism has been welcoming. Reform Rabbi Janet Marder, a heterosexual who served as rabbi of Beth Chayim Chadashim ("House of New Life") in Los Angeles, the first gay/lesbian synagogue, wrote the following:

> The God I worship endorses loving, responsible, and committed human relationships, regardless of the sex of the persons involved. . . . My personal faith simply tells me that the duty to love my neighbor as myself is a compelling *mitzvah* [commandment],

while the duty to condemn and to kill homosexuals for committing "abominations" most certainly is not. . . . There comes a time when our deepest convictions demand that we break with *halachah* [Jewish law]. . . . Reverence for tradition is no virtue when it promotes injustice and human suffering.[3]

Dealing with Jewish law is more difficult for traditional Jews, points out Reconstructionist Rabbi Rebecca Alpert. For traditional Jews, the words of Torah

> are considered not only a record of our past, but God's explanation of God's will for the people of Israel as well. . . . According to strict interpretation of Jewish law, no law stated in the Torah can ever be nullified or abrogated. . . . The Torah contains concepts that are vital to us: that we should love our neighbors as ourselves and deal respectfully with the stranger, the poor, and the lonely in society. . . . It also contains wonderful and challenging stories of the world's beginnings and our people's journey from slavery to freedom. Those of us who choose to remain identified with the Jewish tradition do so in part because of the foundation laid by Torah. We cannot simply excise what we do not like; it is our heritage and the primary text of our people.[4]

But, says Alpert (who was ordained as a rabbi, married, and had children before coming out as a lesbian), "How do we live as Jews when the same text that tells us we were created in God's image also tells us that our sacred loving acts are punishable by death by decree of that same God?"[5] She suggests three responses. We can interpret the text in ways that permit us to live with it, see it as a historical record of attitudes at a certain time, or confront it— argue with it emotionally in our Torah discussion and take action to change its effects in our communities.

Alpert and others have suggested that if the traditional communities were prepared to recognize the current situation as a violation of the precept that all people are created in God's image, it would be possible to interpret the Torah in ways that did not make pariahs of gay people. For example, Rashi, the best-known medieval commentator on the Bible, says that the phrase "as with a woman" refers to a specific sexual act, so the text could be interpreted as prohibiting only one specific sexual act between men.[6]

Confronting the text, said Alpert, means acknowledging "the pain and terror and anger" that gay people feel reading the words of Leviticus and the damage these words have caused in their lives. Gay activists have designated the two weeks in the spring during which these passages are read as Jewish Lesbian and Gay Awareness weeks. They urge synagogues to hold study sessions where gay and lesbian Jews can "tell our stories—of our alienation from the community, and of our desire to return. . . . [and] of what this prohibition has meant in our lives."[7]

Gay and lesbian Jews have also created their own synagogues, where they can be affirmed in both their gay and Jewish identities. New York's gay and lesbian synagogue, Congregation Beth Simhat Torah ("House of Joy in the Torah"), has created a sanctuary—in both meanings of the word—in an old Greenwich Village factory building. In some ways, the congregation is very similar to many other liberal synagogues, says Rabbi Sharon Kleinbaum. In the chapel is a memorial wall with metal plaques and lights denoting the anniversaries of the deaths of congregation members. There is a Sunday school where kids learn Bible stories and Hebrew. In addition, though, special attention is given to helping children cope with the stresses society puts on a child who has a gay parent.

This community lives with extraordinary pressures. The blue padded chairs in the chapel were given in a bequest from a member who died of AIDS; as he got thinner and thinner, he could no longer sit comfortably in the folding chairs that were used before. In a congregation that now has between nine hundred and one thousand members, there have been a hundred deaths in the last twenty years, many of them men under fifty. Kleinbaum is inspired by the quiet determination of her congregants with AIDS to go on with day-to-day living in the face of gradual deterioration and certain death. "There are incredible heroes here," she says, "fantastic stories of human courage and strength."

The committee to visit the sick is bigger and more active than in most synagogues. The ultimate questions of religion are encountered every day. When the community moves its services to the Jacob Javits Center to accommodate the 2,000 to 2,500 people who show up for High Holiday services, the memorial wall comes along on a movable partition. Their dead are still considered part of this community.

It is also, said Kleinbaum, a community of extraordinary joy, where the spiritual meaning of Judaism is lived with great intensity. "Judaism is about experiencing God in moments of vulnerability," said Kleinbaum. "The basic Jewish themes [are themes] a gay person lives every day. It's not a literary metaphor to talk about not being at home, being an outsider. It's the way a gay person experiences their life. If they can experience their Mt. Sinai, they will experience something very deep." Simply having the synagogue, a place where people can joyfully affirm themselves as gay Jews, is an antidote to exile: "Just creating an environment where people are accepted and welcomed for who they are is revolutionary."

"I think everybody is on a spiritual journey," said Kleinbaum, "trying to achieve some level of integration in life, some sense of wholeness. But many people lead blind lives; they're not forced to ask questions about what it means to be a human being connected with the transcendent. . . . Being an insider, ironically, can be deadening to spiritual life. There has always been a tension in Judaism between *galut* [exile] and home. The Torah was given in exile, in the desert, not in the promised land. There's a perspective that people have in exile. You're open to what you can hear in the desert that you can't hear in the city. Exile can happen anywhere."

Of course, not everybody who treks the wilderness of establishing a gay identity makes it to Mt. Sinai. Some people cope with the pain of rejection by becoming alcoholics or drug abusers. "The sense of worthlessness can be profound. . . . The problem is, if you don't have a vision of what the promised land looks like, exile can kill."

One member of the congregation committed suicide last year; he simply could not cope with being gay. The community cannot provide employment for people who lose their jobs when it is discovered they are gay, and it cannot make up for the estrangement from family. One woman's liberal Conservative family did not speak to her for seven years after she came out. "A synagogue does not make it all better," said Kleinbaum. "When a person walks in this door, we might be the only space in the whole week where that person can be out. It takes a tremendous spiritual toll."

Last year, one congregant's lover had to have a serious operation. The congregant could not take time off work the way she might have if it had been her husband. When she called the hospital, she had to go to a pay phone because she couldn't risk talking from work.

Some members of the congregation grew up in Jewish homes and came out in their teens or twenties—at a time in life when many young people, gay or straight, turn away from religion as part of establishing their own identity. At that age they saw Judaism as part of the problem; their focus was on establishing their gay identity. When they were a little older, though, they began to miss their Jewish identity and struggled to integrate the two.

Another group of members married and raised their children as Jews before coming to terms with their homosexuality. As a result, some who were Orthodox had to cope with their children rejecting them. There is a special support group for gay Orthodox Jews.

People coming out now are at a very different time in history, said Kleinbaum. One member first came to Congregation Beth Simhat Torah as an eighteen-year-old, and its safe environment was where he came out. Nevertheless, he assumed he couldn't go to rabbinical school because he was gay. Now, eighteen years later, he is just entering rabbinical school.

The work of integrating gay and Jewish identities goes on at many levels. When they retell the Purim story in this community, they notice that Queen Esther had to deal with the issue of when it was safe to "come out" as a Jew. There have been numerous times in Jewish history, such as the Inquisition, when coming out as a Jew would have been literally deadly, says Kleinbaum. At Yom HaShoah, the day of remembering those who died in the Holocaust, members of Beth Simhat Torah also remember the gays who were forced to wear pink triangles and were gassed by the Nazis.

Judaism "has much to speak to the pain that gays and lesbians feel, even when it has sometimes been a cause of that pain," said Kleinbaum. "Sometimes they need a rabbi to be a witness to their anger. It's an ancient Jewish tradition to be angry at God. I think it's a healthy thing."

Coming out, David Rogoff says, has deepened his experience of Judaism. Jewish prayer for him now has "more joy, more liberation, more of a sense that God belongs to me, not the rabbis." Coming out has also helped clarify for him the deepest Jewish values. In the Jewish story of the creation of the world, "Before God says 'Be fruitful and multiply,' God looks at Adam and says, 'It's not good for a person to be alone.' That's before anything."

CHAPTER 8

CELEBRATING

Creating New Traditions

When people come to a turning point in their lives, some inner gyroscope calls out for ceremony. Such a turning point happened to me in 1980, when I was thirty-six. Midway through my first year with the Germantown minyan, I met a man at a retreat, became engaged, and went off to Canada to live with him. Six months later, I was back.

Once again I found myself changing jobs, cities, and boyfriends. But this time was different. No longer was I anonymous and alone; instead, I returned to a community. My Jewish women's group helped me to work through my anger and sorrow and figure out what I wanted to do next. I realized that in addition to my distress over the failure of the relationship, I was disappointed not to have had a wedding. A wedding was not only the consecration of a relationship but a ceremony of adulthood. In the Jewish community, it was the formal acknowledgment that you had begun to create your own Jewish household, to create the building blocks from which the community is made. Well, I hadn't gotten married, but I had begun to create my own Jewish household: I was keeping kosher, lighting Sabbath candles, and observing the holidays. I wanted to celebrate the new commitment I felt to be part of the building of the Jewish people. And so I hit on the idea of having an adult bat mitzvah.

My women's group helped me to reach that goal. One member, Linda Cherkas, taught me the *trope* (notes) for the chapters of Torah and haftarah to be chanted on my special Shabbos. The women's group agreed to serve as a catering team, helping me prepare food for the reception. (Rivka, the artist, created the only sexy salmon mold I have ever seen, with black olive slices for the salmon's long eyelashes and red pepper slices for the seductive wiggle of its tail.) When I began to study the Torah portion for my birthday, my heart leaped. It contained the Ten Commandments and the Sh'ma, the Jewish affirmation of faith. What could be more appropriate for my declaration of commitment to my heritage?

New twists on traditional celebrations get a lot of support in the havurah movement. As part of their zesty pursuit of a living Judaism, the havurot embrace all the concrete rituals, from sniffing sweet spices at Havdalah (the close of the Sabbath) to wearing sneakers on Yom Kippur (on the Day of Judgment one should not wear leather, which has been fashioned by killing an animal). The havurot are serious about celebrating. Holidays give focus, purpose, excitement, and beauty to the community. Simhat Torah, the giving of the law, is observed with dancing as wild and joyous as in the most traditional Hasidic community (but men and women dance together here).

Havurahniks revived a long-forgotten kabbalist custom of holding a special seder of fruits and nuts at Tu B'Shvat, the birthday of the trees. They revived an even more obscure thousand-year-old custom of dressing in white and dancing outdoors on Tu B'av (the fifteenth day of Av), after the close of the Tisha B'Av

mourning period. One year, havurahniks revived an ancient lit-
tle-known holiday of the sun's cycle: Once every twenty-eight
years, the sun is believed to cross the exact spot in the sky where
it was at the moment of creation. We gathered at dawn in someone's backyard, with a booklet of prayers written especially for
the occasion.

Many baby-boom Jews, whether Orthodox or nontraditional,
sensing that homogenized, postindustrial American culture
lacked texture, began reviving East European folk ceremonies
that their parents had abandoned. Newly Orthodox Jews held
ceremonial haircuttings at a baby boy's third birthday. Instead of
having bridal showers, women in the Germantown minyan gathered for a traditional "Shabbos Kallah," offering blessings and
prayers for the bride. Some havurah Jews held weaning ceremonies; smashing the baby bottle was the highlight of the weaning ceremony for Fern Amper and Eli Schaap's daughter Yona.
The parents read biblical passages about weaning ceremonies
held by Sarah and Hannah and revived the custom of donating an
amount of money to charity equal to the baby's birth weight.[1]

A ritual is a spiritual ballet. It captures in symbols the emotions
that go with an important life transition. Think of the cheer that
goes up when the glass is broken at the wedding, or the moment
of finality when the mourner shovels dirt onto the coffin at a funeral. Passing from one stage of life to another can be frighten-
ing; rituals ease the transition by affirming the sacredness of the
moment and helping people feel a connection to their community and heritage.

Even when celebrating a passage acknowledged by the tradition, havurahniks feel impelled in some way to make it their own.
In the Germantown minyan community, parents would insert
their own special readings and poems into the traditional bris, the
circumcision ceremony for a baby boy. Since they see Jewish tradition as accumulated wisdom rather than absolute law, where the
tradition seems to have neglected an important life transition,
haverim feel free to invent a Jewish-style ritual to fit.

I felt a need for ritual because I had hit a turning point in my life. But it was a turning point—acceptance of my life as a single adult woman—that the tradition had not anticipated. Many of us in the havurah movement, though, are living lives not anticipated by the tradition. Ceremony, we have learned from our tradition, is a powerful tool for dealing with the change points in our lives. Sometimes, though, we have to use this heritage in radically new ways to make it address the lives we live.

In writing the Freedom Seder, Arthur Waskow had discovered both the power of ceremony and its adaptability to new times. In the years that followed he adapted one ceremony after another. Building a sukkah (the traditional harvest hut) on the lawn across the street from the White House, he transformed it into a powerful symbol for the anti-nuclear movement. In dealing with the hydrogen bomb, he said, we were all as vulnerable as people camping out under the lacy latticework of the sukkah's branches. Our houses, our fallout shelters, and our Cold War diplomacy were all illusory protections. Borrowing a phrase from the traditional liturgy, he argued that nothing could save us but Sukkat Shlomecha ("The Shelter of Your Peace"). And the holiday of Sukkot, whose theme was hospitality and universality, would teach us how to arrive at that peace, by a mutual respect among all nations of the world.

Waskow soon began exploring another dimension beyond political theater: the power of rituals and symbols to help people achieve emotional and spiritual change. He explored some of these transformative rituals and symbols in the "new approaches" sections of his book *Seasons of Our Joy,* a guide to the Jewish holidays. One of the passages in the Bible that most fascinated him was Sotah, the ritual for the jealous husband (Numbers 5:11–31). If a man suspected his wife of adultery but couldn't prove or disprove it, he was to bring her to the priest, who would sprinkle dust from the floor of the tabernacle into holy water and have her drink it. The priest would tell her that if she were innocent the water would have no effect, but if she were guilty drinking it would cause her belly to swell up, and she would be cursed. If the water had no effect, the case was closed—and when she went home, the priest told her, she would conceive a child. Feminists have generally been outraged that the *woman* should have to go through an ordeal to purge the man's jealousy. But Waskow was fascinated (and I am, too) by the power of the symbolism to exorcise something as stubborn and irrational as baseless jealousy.

The High Holidays are another time when we try to transcend grievances and guilt, whether justified or unjustified. Waskow adapted the *sotah* ritual to aid in this emotional task. During the Slichot service that prepares for the High Holidays, Waskow and other members of Fabrangen would write out their worst thoughts and actions of the previous year in water-soluble ink, plunge the papers into salt water, and watch the words dissolve. Then each member would wash another's hands by pouring sweet, fresh water over them.[2]

As Waskow implies, there is a deep connection between the emotional and the spiritual. A loving relationship is one of the most powerful ways to experience the presence of the holy; conversely, its rending can drain all sense of holiness from life. And the restoration of trust to a wounded relationship is no less a miracle than the knitting together of a fractured limb.

During my engagement, living in a faraway community where I had few obligations or friendships to structure my life, I began davening from the prayerbook daily at dawn. Wrapping myself in the towel that served as my prayer shawl, I felt as if I began each morning with a hug from God. All day, going about the chores of the household, I kept up a running dialogue with God. When I ended the relationship, however, I stopped praying. The problem was not that I didn't believe anymore in whatever God I had found; I was simply so angry that I hung up the phone. I was angry and depressed for months.

Finally, feeling that I was suffering a spiritual as well as an emotional crisis, I asked Rabbi Zalman Schachter-Shalomi, my main spiritual mentor at the time, what I should do. At first he suggested some kind of Native American purging ritual with smudging sticks. The deeply skeptical look in my eyes made him realize that a New Age–style ritual wouldn't be healing for me. So then he told me, "You need to write your fiancé a *get*"—the paper of divorce, which in traditional Judaism can only be given by the man to the woman. Though no American court of law would recognize our six months of living together as a marriage, according to Talmudic law a couple who have a sexual relationship and state their intention to wed are in fact married. I wrote my fiancé a letter, declaring the relationship over and explaining why; he wrote back to tell me that he was engaged again to someone else. With that exchange of letters, that symbolic act rooted in Jewish tradition, I was free. I began to pray again. Soon I entered a new relationship with the man who became my life partner.

New rituals have been especially important for women, since established Jewish tradition ignores many of the key emotional events in women's lives. The most common new tradition developed since the 1960s is the naming ceremony for girls. As havurah families began to have children, they struggled to find ceremonies for bringing infant daughters into the covenant that would match the primitive power and authority of the *brit milah* (covenant of circumcision) for boys. People dug out readings, wrote their own poetry, or tried to adapt symbols and rituals from the tradition. Among those suggested in various articles by havurahniks were planting a tree, washing the girl's feet, and even a ritual rupturing of the infant girl's hymen.

We usually assume that traditions take hundreds of years to develop. But *bat mitzvah,* initiated in 1922 by Rabbi Mordecai Kaplan, became widespread among Conservative and Reform Jews in the late 1950s and now occurs in various formats in many modern Orthodox communities. Although traditional among Sephardi Jews, ceremonies welcoming the baby daughter were out of fashion in Ashkenazi communities until havurahniks and feminists developed their own in the late 1960s.[3] Such ceremonies are now common even in modern Orthodox communities, although they are still so new that there's no standard name for them. (*Simchat bat,* "rejoicing in a daughter," and *brit b'not Yisrael,* "covenant of the daughters of Israel," are among the names used.[4]) Rabbi Nancy Fuchs of the Reconstructionist Rabbinical College in Philadelphia was a guest at a baby-naming ceremony where the main symbolic action was washing the feet. The grandmother explained to her that this was an ancient Jewish custom. Nancy chuckled. It is true that foot washing occurs in the Bible, but its use in a baby-naming ceremony had first been suggested only a few years before—in an article coauthored by Rabbi Fuchs![5]

Gradually women began to develop ceremonies for other events in their lives not acknowledged by Jewish tradition. To purge the horror of rape, Laura Levitt immersed herself in the mikveh.[6] To share with friends the bitterness of her divorce, one woman served a meal of burned toast. Various mothers and daughters developed ceremonies to mark the onset of a girl's menstruation. In Boston a woman convened friends for a ceremony on the tenth anniversary of her mastectomy, celebrating her survival of cancer. A woman in central New Jersey organized "a ceremony of letting go" to help her resolve her grief for a baby who was stillborn twenty-one years before.

During labors for her five children, Rabbi Nina Beth Cardin used some of the medieval Italian women's prayers collected in her book *Out of the Depths I Call to You: A Book of Prayers for the Married Jewish Woman.* Cardin, the petite, dark-haired editor of *Sh'ma,* went further by creating her own simple ritual for the months of pregnancy. After the birth of Cardin's first child, she had followed an old custom of lighting an additional candle at Shabbat for each child. Then she lost two successive pregnancies, one in the fifth month. In each subsequent pregnancy she placed an additional candle on the table but did not light it. On the first Shabbat after the new baby was born, the whole family rejoiced together as the new candle was finally lit. The unlit candle "praises God for the promise" and stands mutely as "a prayer to God to keep the promise," Cardin said.

Some new rituals celebrate moments unanticipated by the tradition, such as adoption, the commitment ceremony of a lesbian couple, or the reunion of a birth mother and the child she gave up for adoption many years before. Other new rituals permit grieving or healing for losses Jewish tradition didn't acknowledge or anticipate: miscarriage, abortion, hysterectomy, sexual abuse, or loss of a love. After an abortion, one woman, surrounded by a small group of friends in the darkened chapel of her synagogue, cradled the Torah in her arms, speaking to it as if it were the child she had lost. She explained why she had made this difficult decision and how much she hoped someday to raise a child to adulthood. Then she replaced the Torah/child in the ark.

Many women find the traditional Jewish divorce ritual demeaning rather than healing because the woman remains entirely passive, receiving the document of divorce from her husband. Rabbi Cardin helped some women develop a ritual for the moment when the reality of separation hits: the day when the partner moves out of the house. As friends encircle the woman and hug her, they read a biblical passage in which Abraham separates from Lot because their herdsmen have been fighting:

> And Abram said unto Lot: "Let there be no strife, I pray thee, between me and thee . . . ; for we are brethren. Is not the whole land before thee? Separate thyself, I pray thee, from me; if thou wilt take the left hand, then I will go to the right; or if thou take the right hand, then I will go to the left." (Genesis 13:8)

Then, as at a funeral, the woman tears a cloth (in this case, a bedsheet or pillow). "The ceremony says that there are times when members of a family can't live together and must separate, but they can separate in a civil way," said Cardin.

Most new rituals use traditional Jewish symbols and stories in new contexts. Candle lighting, blessing of wine, symbolic foods like eggs or honey, the canopy and seven blessings borrowed from the Jewish wedding appear frequently in new rituals. Bathing, hand washing, and foot washing have been used in many new ceremonies—the naming of babies, coming of age, and healing— because mikveh—immersion after the menstrual period—is one of only three commandments that traditional Jewish law designates specifically for women.[7]

In the twenty years since the first woman rabbi was ordained, many female rabbis (including Fuchs, Cardin, and Rabbi Jane Litman of the Continuing Education Department of the University of Judaism in Los Angeles) have become mentors, helping women find in Jewish tradition the stories and symbols they need to create a ritual that serves a new purpose yet helps them feel connected to the tradition at a key moment in their lives. For many life transitions Judaism provides wise, powerful, and healing rituals, of which weddings and funerals are the best examples, said Rabbi Litman. But in facing some of the new crises of modern life, "women are cut adrift" at the moment when they most need the solace and anchor of tradition. "Our task is to take the wisdom of Judaism and apply it to our lives."

Litman was brought up in a consummately secular home. Her father was a psychoanalyst, and both parents were political activists who fought the Red-baiting hate campaign of Senator Joseph McCarthy. Their Los Angeles home was intellectually and culturally very Jewish, but nonetheless deeply hostile to religion. Her father would read Bible stories like the story of Samson and say, "This is what religion is about—superstition and violence." Her parents were even opposed to Jane going to the bar and bat mitzvahs of friends. When as a teenager she started going to synagogue on her own, her parents were appalled.

Jane started attending the University of California at Berkeley as a pre-med student, but she soon switched to Jewish studies. She began fasting on Yom Kippur and became a vegetarian as a way of keeping kosher in the dorms. By the end of her second year she was active in the emerging Jewish feminist movement, lobbying to get a course on Jewish women offered as part of the

Jewish studies major. After a year of rabbinical school at the Reform movement's Hebrew Union College Jane went off to Israel,
became involved in promoting Jewish-Arab dialogue, and finally
returned five years later to complete rabbinical training at the
Reconstructionist Rabbinical School in Philadelphia.

Her initial attraction to Judaism was intellectual; she found
Buber and Heschel too exciting to put down. Then Jane came to
realize the value of community. She had married young and divorced young. When she felt like a failure at marriage and at life,
"the love and caring of community pulled me through. When I
fell, I was caught and held tightly. So many people live alone, not
just physically, but profoundly—all these unconnected, unraveled
people. I was woven tightly into a loving net."

Ritual was the last piece of Judaism to fall into place for Jane.
Very much her parents' daughter, she still thinks of herself as "a
very committed rationalist," and ritual seemed alien to her. But
eventually she came to feel that "it's irrational not to see that people have a mythic nature," a spiritual dimension that does not get
enough nurturing in secular America. "Ritual," she says now, "is
the unspoken language of myth."

Ritual embodies certain values and helps people live those values, Litman adds. For example, rituals in which men's and
women's roles are equal teach equality. Rituals in which rape, in-
cest, or abuse are named bring these horrors out into the air
where they can be healed. Ritual is a bridge "connecting people
to other people, to the right path, to God."

It seemed natural, then, that if "for historical and political reasons, some rituals don't exist yet," Litman would help people create them. She began to do research on women's folk traditions in
Judaism and the matriarchal pre-Judaic Middle Eastern traditions, searching for rituals and symbols that could be revived or
transmuted to meet modern needs. When she became pregnant,
she turned one of these folk customs into a ritual. Traditional
women wrap a red thread around Rachel's tomb in Israel to ensure a healthy pregnancy. Litman took the traditional red thread

to her women's group and had them wrap it around her while they blessed her.[8] She has helped other people create rituals about surviving rape, accepting infertility, and sending a child off to college. At the college sendoff, those present told leaving-home stories from their own lives, said the prayer that begins "Blessed be you in your comings and in your goings," and sang songs. Creating new rituals empowers people and helps them to feel closer and more committed to the tradition, Litman said. "It's like riding a bike," she added. "Could you imagine if you never got on unless the rabbi held you?"

Although God warns the Israelites in the Bible that "you shall not add anything to what I command you or take anything away from it" (Deuteronomy 4:2), Judaism in fact has evolved, and Jews have always created new rituals. The synagogue and the worship service were necessary innovations after the destruction of the first Temple. The sixteenth-century Kabbalists created the Tu B'Shvat seder, modeled on the Passover seder but celebrating the birthday of the trees and incorporating their own mystic theology. Medieval rabbis were troubled about what to do with the ritual of Shabbat candle lighting, because it is not prescribed by the Torah or the Talmud. The rabbis incorporated change by ruling that when a ritual grows up among the people and becomes deeply rooted, it eventually takes on the status of a commandment. In our own time, Israel's Independence Day, Yom HaShoah (Holocaust Memorial Day), Yom HaZikaron (Memorial Day for Israeli soldiers), and Yom Yerushalayim (the anniversary of when Jews recaptured Jerusalem in the Six-Day War) are all celebrated not only as secular but as religious holidays, with prayers borrowed from other festivals.

Nevertheless, some people feel that any experimental ritual, even if constructed entirely from building blocks of tradition, is a threat to the integrity of the tradition. When *Jewish Catalog* authors Sharon and Michael Strassfeld described the *brit* ceremony for their infant daughter, which involved immersing the baby in a water bath, one woman wrote that their ritual used elements of Christianity. The Strassfelds countered that it was Christians who modeled their ceremony of baptism on mikvah, which has always been the Jewish way of bringing adult converts into the covenant.[9]

Rabbi Susan Schnur, editor of *Lilith* magazine, told feminist poet and liturgist Marcia Falk during an interview, "As you know, you've got detractors within Judaism who would claim that what you're doing is not Jewish." Falk replied, "Why should I let *them* define what Judaism is and place myself outside of it? I use Jewish sources, Jewish language, Jewish experience. I call myself a Jew."[10]

The Reconstructionist movement, which sees Judaism as an evolving civilization rather than a fixed system of law, has been an important source of new ritual. The archive of new ritual at the Reconstructionist Rabbinical College contains ceremonies for all sorts of occasions—even a ritual to sanctify blood donation. Contemporary American Jews especially need ritual in our lives, said Margot Stein Azen, a student at the Reconstructionist Rabbinical College, because in our society, "everything is broken down into bits and bytes. . . . Judaism connects us to the generations. . . . If you can find what you need in Judaism, you will truly have come home." But, added Azen, who is the coauthor/performer of *Guarding the Garden,* a musical about Judaism and ecology, we need to contribute our own special insights and flavors if we are to connect to tradition: "We are tired of buying Judaism off the rack."

All the traditional Jewish life-cycle rituals except the funeral are focused on the first third of life: birth, coming of age, and getting married. But Jews are living longer. Some new rituals focus on consecrating transitions typical of the latter two-thirds of life. Working with Rabbi Fuchs, members of an adult education class on life-cycle passages created a retirement ceremony far more meaningful than the standard dinner and a gold watch. Beginning with candle lighting, the ceremony compares retirement to the Jubilee, the Sabbatical of Sabbaticals; freed from the workday struggle, one can concentrate on spiritual life.

Many Jewish women feel a need for rituals for maturity and aging because we are living lives not dreamed of by the tradition. Some, like me, are staying single into maturity. Others pursue new careers after their children are grown, so that the transition points in our lives are not simply defined by children's birth ceremonies, bar or bat mitzvahs, and weddings.

For her fiftieth birthday, Phyllis Berman, program director of the Elat Chayyim Jewish retreat center, held a woman's seder, with four cups representing the four stages of life: one filled with sangria, for the onset of menstruation; one with champagne, for love and sexuality; one with milk, for pregnancy, childbirth, and child rearing; and one with clear spring water, for menopause. As they drank from the cup, women who had experienced that stage shared their stories.[11] Adapting that ceremony to celebrate my own fiftieth birthday, I found gathered around me raising that cup of sparkling water a group of men and women whose vitality and wisdom inspired me. I was happy to become part of their company. I could see the next phase of life not as deterioration and withdrawal but as an opportunity to consolidate, use, and share the learning and strength I had been gathering in all the years so far.

More and more women in the havurah movement, and increasingly also in synagogues, have chosen to celebrate their maturity by having adult bat mitzvahs. Carol Levin, chairperson of the Hadassah study group in Highland Park, New Jersey, had her bat mitzvah at age sixty-four in the Highland Park Conservative Temple. When she was growing up, she said, her Conservative synagogue didn't even provide Jewish education for girls. She has avidly pursued Jewish education throughout her adulthood, taking courses at her synagogue, at local universities, and even at Hebrew University in Israel. Publicly affirming her commitment to Judaism by chanting the haftarah and leading part of the service was a moment of elation that she will never forget, she said.

On the special Shabbos of my bat mitzvah, when I gave my *d'var Torah,* my friends Dan and Debbie were called to the Torah for the *aufruf* before their wedding. The three of us were showered with candies (and all the little children scrambled to retrieve them from the floor). The entire community rose, singing "Siman Tov, Mazel Tov" and dancing and clapping around us, pulling us in a weaving snake-dance in and out of the rows of folding chairs. Grabbing my hands, Dan and Deb hugged me and each other. In sharing this peak event, I had discovered something special: the important times in my life, and in Dan and Debbie's life, were also important times in the life of the community. The coming together of a community and an individual life—the acknowledgment at a key moment of transition that what happens in your life matters to your community—is part of what gives rituals such power. As I have celebrated life transitions with them, I have become more deeply connected to the havurah communities in which I have lived, to Judaism, and to the Jewish people.

The cliche at bat mitzvahs and graduations is that the ceremony is a commencement, a beginning. It's certainly true at weddings (though no one ever says it) that the ceremony is the beginning of new concerns that one will grapple with for the rest of one's life. I don't know if it would have been the same when I was thirteen, but my bat mitzvah at thirty-six really was a beginning. It launched me on a lifelong struggle to define my relationship to Jewish tradition, Jewish observance, and to God.

CHAPTER 9

PATH OR DWELLING PLACE

Living by Jewish Law

Jewish tradition talks about "accepting the yoke of the commandments." For me, deciding my relationship to the commandments, to Jewish law, has been as hard as searching for God.

A guest at a wedding ceremony told Rabbi Ephraim Buchwald, director of the National Jewish Outreach Center, that she
was "a good Jew in her heart." He snapped, "Lady, feeling like a
good Jew in your heart doesn't make you any more a good Jew
than feeling like an astronaut in your heart puts you on the
moon."

When I had my mountaintop revelation and started talking to
God, I felt immediately that if this search were going to go anywhere, I needed to know what it meant to be Jewish. I couldn't
know that until I did Jewish things.

I had been brought up on the idea of Judaism as ethics, but

there didn't seem to be much difference between Jewish ethics and everybody else's. I would have to put flesh on the elegant bare bones of Judaism I had learned in my parents' Reform synagogue. I would have to find people to teach me how to live a Jewish life.

As has happened so often since, once I brought these questions into my daily dialogue with God, an answer began to take shape in my experience. I was offered a job in the middle-sized city of Dayton, Ohio. I called the local Conservative rabbi, Jack Riemer,[1] and asked if there was a class for people like me, who were Jewish but ignorant of many of the basic elements of traditional Judaism. At the time, there was not. (Now, however, there are many.) There was a class for people converting to Judaism, but I was already Jewish. There was a Bible class, but I thought I knew the Bible stories. I wanted to know what Jews *do*.

I said to God, if You want me to follow a Jewish path to You, why don't You provide me with teachers? I now realize that the thirst to learn more about Judaism was the first and most profound answer to my prayers.

The lowest job on the journalistic totem pole at the *Dayton Daily News* was religion writer; as a newcomer, that's where I started out. The Conservative movement had just voted to count women in the minyan. I was assigned to write a story about it. Rabbi Riemer suggested I interview Goldie Kopmar, the petite, gentle, dark-haired wife of the Conservative cantor. I sat perched on the edge of a chair in her living room, scribbling away in my notebook, glancing at the clock so I wouldn't miss my deadline. But I heard her with my heart. Judaism is a way of life of profound psychological and spiritual wisdom, she said. All its parts are interconnected, and one shouldn't thoughtlessly tamper with any part. As an example, she talked about *niddah,* the laws requiring a husband and wife to refrain from sexual intercourse during and for one week after the woman's menstrual period. The periods of restriction helped her and her husband to keep coming back to each other with new excitement and appreciation, she said. The times when sex was forbidden ensured that they would see each other as full human beings, not just as sexual partners.

Pursuing my career as a reporter, I had bounced from city to city and boyfriend to boyfriend. I felt powerfully drawn to the idea of a way of life that bound families together in a stable, respectful, and loving relationship. That Shabbat, when I heard Rabbi Riemer say from the pulpit, "Judaism is a religion of law," I was ready to hear. Law, boundaries, structure, I thought—that's what I need in my life.

In a very informal way, Goldie was my teacher. At a Jewish book fair, she handed me a copy of the *Jewish Catalog*. It had what I was looking for: easy-to-follow, informal directions on how to be Jewish. The catalog assumed that one didn't have to adopt the whole system, explicitly saying, "You can plug in wherever you want."[2]

Along with the details, the authors gave the emotional flavor of each observance. Even more important, the Catalog had an idea—the idea of havurah, a group of companions doing Jewish things together. Of course! To live a Jewish life, I needed other Jews to do it with. Our little Dayton havurah rarely scraped together a minyan, even counting women, men, and the cat. But from that very first Saturday service—singing, talking, eating, and hanging out together from morning till nearly dark—we breathed in the blend of rest and companionship that creates the holiness of Shabbat. On Friday nights we lit candles together, sang songs, and had potluck dinners (which were truly potluck; one week we all brought noodle puddings).

As I spent weekends with the havurah, I began to discard things that were intrusions on my Shabbat peace. It was not a day to do laundry or shop; it was a day to take it easy, to appreciate and be appreciated. As the magic of the day worked its spell on all of us, havurah members with more Jewish education than I began to recall what they had learned, but never practiced, about Shabbat. One woman said that she would no longer write on

Shabbat. A man announced that he was going to stop answering his phone. I thought they were being a little pretentious, since we all had to drive (violating at least one Shabbat law) to get to our havurah services. Gradually, though, I came to understand that the peace of Shabbat is built from many little bits of "not doing." Each bit of not-doing is a brick in the wall between one's family (or, in my case, the havurah) and the world—the wall that for one day transforms home into a castle.

"More than the Jews have kept the Sabbath, the Sabbath has preserved the Jews," said Ahad Ha-Am, a European writer of the last generation.[3] Blu Greenberg, a feminist who grew up in and maintains an Orthodox Jewish household, says, "I couldn't live without Shabbat." She writes that Shabbat is the central, orienting framework of her life:

> On Shabbat, I can almost feel the difference in the air I breathe, in the way the incandescent lamps give off light in my living room, in the way the children's skins glow. . . . Immediately after I light my candles, it is as if I flicked a switch that turned Shabbat on all over the world, even though I know very well the world is not turned on to Shabbat.[4]

On Shabbat I began to experience extraordinary rushes of joy and creativity. When I was blocked on a story, on Shabbat my mind would teem with ideas. (I knew I couldn't write them down, though, because it was precisely my withdrawal from the problems I was struggling with that made it possible for me to see solutions.) For nearly every returnee to Judaism I've talked to, the transformative experience of Shabbat has been central. Maybe one can learn from books how to be Jewish (although I think it's better to learn from a mentor); observing Shabbat, however, teaches us *why* to be Jewish.

Natalie Richman, a medical librarian with long, curly dark hair, had grown up in East Orange, New Jersey, in a Conservative home where candles were lit each Shabbat. She had learned the laws of the Sabbath in Hebrew school, but she can't recall anyone suggesting that people ought to follow them. After Saturday morning services, her family often went to the mall to shop. In college and afterward, Richman had largely abandoned Judaism and explored other spiritual paths, such as Wicca, an earth-centered feminist religion based on traditional Celtic witchcraft. In her late twenties, however, she became seriously involved with a Jewish man and began to go to services with him. When the relationship ended, she found herself almost physically missing the Shabbat service. The singing especially had touched and comforted her. In the new community she had moved to, Richman began going to services by herself. For two summers she spent a week at a New Age Jewish retreat center, Elat Chayyim, and found herself making a vow to begin observing Shabbat "not strictly according to Jewish law, but in my own way."

By herself, in the quiet of her own kitchen, she lit candles. She unplugged the phone, turned down the answering machine, and decided she would not clean, do dishes, shop, or handle money. She spent the day quietly reading, studying, and praying—going to services if she felt like it, sleeping late if she felt like it. She didn't want to feel bound by the full set of Shabbat laws, because she knew too many people who had been raised Orthodox and felt trapped by the rules. So she made distinctions: she might drive to visit friends, but not to do business. She might write a letter to a friend, but she would not make grocery lists or do any writing for her job.

Shabbat became a very different day from the rest of the week. "I'm always trying to do too many things. I get burned out. I have a hard time balancing," Richman said. "Shabbat has given me a real tool for balancing my time and my life. It's really a holy day for me. It's a gift. When I thought of it as a sacrifice, as a rule, it was hard—I thought, 'If I can't go shopping, it'll make the rest of the week that much busier.' When I thought of it as a gift, I was ready. I don't *have* to do anything. I'm there for myself, and I'm there for God."

Many people I talked to were drawn toward the Jewish way of

life because of the extraordinary experience of spending Shabbat with an Orthodox family or an Orthodox community. For Nancy Edelman, a freshman at the University of Buffalo, the first step came when she crossed a campus courtyard to munch honeycake from a table set up by the Lubavitch movement at Rosh Hashana. Having come from an assimilated family, she was at first annoyed by the spate of follow-up calls urging her to attend a Shabbat program at the Chabad House, the Lubavitch movement's college outreach program. But when she finally went, her life was transformed. She followed the speaker, Rabbi Manis Friedman, back to Minneapolis to attend Bais Chana, an Orthodox study program for women. She came back with a new name—Sarah—and a new set of commitments. "I just found myself saying, 'This is really true. There really is a God, and He's really working out the world.' Then I didn't have a choice. I had to keep kosher; it was God's law. God is good, He created me, this is what I was created for—it's my obligation because I'm a Jewish person. And I was very excited to enter a holy world, to feel that what I was doing was right."

Her boyfriend, Bruce (now Baruch), made the journey with her into Orthodoxy. He is now the Chabad House rabbi at Rutgers University. Sarah, who had spent her senior year of high school working as a short-skirted hostess in a lobster house, was wearing a long-sleeved flowered dress with a lace collar and a brown pageboy wig on the day I interviewed her, and was very pregnant with her and Baruch's sixth child. Over their front door hangs a sign: "Welcome, *Mashiach* [Messiah]."

Jay Rovner, a brown-bearded Talmud scholar who wears professorial sweater-vests and tweed caps, was also drawn to Orthodox observance—though not to Orthodox belief—by his exposure to the warmth of an Orthodox Shabbat. Jay grew up attending a Conservative synagogue in Minneapolis, learning about laws his family did not practice. One of his Hebrew school teachers took Jewish law seriously and tried to get his students to do so. Jay began spending Shabbat at his teacher's small Orthodox

synagogue, and he loved it. Unlike the large, impersonal synagogue where his parents went, this place was warm and informal.
Children ran in and out. There was a comforting, musical buzz of
voices as each person said the prayers at his own pace, catching
up with the prayer leader at major stopping points.

Jay was at the point in his life when he was ready to pull away
from parents and establish his own identity. He didn't do it by
staying out all night, though, or running around with people his
parents didn't approve of; he did it by following Jewish law. Since
his parents refused to start keeping kosher for his benefit, he did
his best while living in his parents' house to follow the laws: not
mixing meat and milk, passing up the bacon and the family's special treat, lobster. To avoid driving on Shabbat, he stopped going
on fishing trips with his father.

Jay enrolled in a joint program of Jewish studies at Columbia
University and the Jewish Theological Seminary. Living in a
dorm with observant students and taking meals at the seminary, it
was easy to sustain an Orthodox lifestyle. But college for Jay was
a time of questioning. Because he didn't believe in a God who
gave commandments at Mt. Sinai, he began to vacillate in his observance. But on an emotional level he still felt Judaism was right
for him. While in graduate school he met Helen, who was also a
midwesterner raised in a Conservative home. Realizing she was
someone he could marry and make a life with, he began to wrestle with what kind of Jewish life he wanted. He liked the way the
mitzvot, the laws, gave structure and meaning to life. After he and
Helen married, they moved to Minneapolis and began attending
the Orthodox synagogue he had loved as a teenager. Out of respect for the community, their religious practice became more
and more Orthodox. For example, they began to follow Orthodox (rather than Conservative) standards for keeping kosher, because they wanted all members of their community to feel comfortable eating in their home.

In addition, the more Jay thought about some of the revisions
in the law made by Conservative Judaism, the more troubled he

was by them. Their reasoning seemed superficial. For example, the Conservative rabbinate permitted the use of electricity on the grounds that it wasn't really fire, but to Jay it was obvious that electricity did everything fire did.[5] The more he studied the traditional texts, the more he felt that Judaism was a cohesive, integrated system of great beauty and wisdom. On an intellectual level he couldn't believe that the commandments were given at Sinai, but he felt that the Orthodox community he lived in—by committing itself to the observance of those laws—helped to make them holy. The community was God's partner in creating a holy world.

After years of living with Orthodox observance, Jay cannot imagine taking it piecemeal. It works for him spiritually because it has become second nature; he doesn't have to struggle with each decision. "It's like when I make pancakes with my son, Ben," he explains. "We get the flour, the sugar, cinnamon, milk, eggs. But the pancakes are not the ingredients. You might say, wouldn't they taste the same if we left out salt, or put in more flour? Maybe. But what we're looking for is pancakes, not the ingredients. It's wrong to tally up the mitzvot and say, this is too heavy a burden. It's how it's integrated and experienced in life."

For my part, I approached the commandments in an experimental way: I began from a base of nothing and added on one at a time. Having tasted the wisdom and richness of Shabbat, now I wanted to seek the wisdom in other Jewish commandments. I decided I would begin keeping kosher when I left Dayton to begin my sabbatical year in Washington, D.C. Arthur Waskow, who was renting me a room in his house, said, "Maybe we'll all start keeping kosher."

Arthur and his son and daughter discussed it at a family meeting, and the kids agreed. We set up an assembly line: dip the silverware in boiling water; dry it; then mark the meat silverware with a drop of red model-airplane paint, and the milk silverware with blue. There was a sense of palpable transformation in this ritual. We were exhilarated. We were making a new beginning.

It was harder for me to sustain a sense of meaning about keeping kosher, though, as I lived with it day to day. When I moved to Philadelphia, I met kosher vegetarians. They told me that some commentators say God intended the Jews to be vegetarians.

> Moses goes up to Mt. Sinai to get the Ten Commandments, and God says, "Thou shalt not kill. . . . that means no more meat."
>
> Moses says, "God, I don't think the people will go for this."
>
> So God says, "OK. Tell them if they want to eat meat, they can only eat animals that have cloven hooves and chew the cud. They can eat fish with scales but not shellfish, fowl but not birds of prey. If I make it complicated enough, they'll find it's simpler to do without it."

They're still waiting, said the vegetarians, for other Jews to figure this out. I had agreed philosophically with the idea of vegetarianism for years, but keeping kosher didn't seem to raise my consciousness to the point where I was ready to give up meat. Instead of being lifted up to a higher moral plane, in fact, at first I found the opposite happening. I was drowning in a sea of petty detail: Every time I dropped a fork into the wrong dishpan, I thought I had to throw out the dishpan. I couldn't seem to turn around in my kitchen without messing up my kosher system. At one point I had thrown away three dishpans in a week. Then I chanced to visit the home of a Lubavitch rabbi while his fifteen-month-old daughter was picking up handfuls of gooey spaghetti with tomato sauce from the chrome tray of her high chair. I asked his wife, "Do you have two trays for the high chair?" She laughed, saying, "Are you kidding?"

I realized that even for the strictest families, the rules had to have limits and loopholes. For this to be a way of life, after all, people had to be able to live it. Then, one day, I was standing in front of a food vending machine at work, peering through the glass trying to see if the bag of corn chips had a kosher label. It suddenly hit me that here I was at work, in an environment which in no way supported my Jewishness, but I was still feeling connected to my community because of my efforts to keep kosher. The almost paralyzing loneliness that had dogged my first years of working as a reporter was gone. During my workdays, constantly performing and risking failure, I remained connected to a Jewish world where I was simply loved. And when I shopped, cooked, or washed dishes, I was sustaining not only myself but my community.

Unlike the Orthodox world, the havurah community had a live-and-let-live attitude about how people interpreted the rules of keeping kosher outside their homes. The woman across the hall from me had a rule she called "specialties of the place and the season," which meant that she would permit herself to eat lobster in Maine but not Philadelphia. I applied this rule liberally until my daughter was two and a half. I was eating lobster in Maine when she asked for a taste; she loved it. I then realized that if I wanted my daughter to keep the Jewish way of life I had come to cherish, I had to be more consistent. At this writing my daughter has just turned eight, and she has never forgotten that incident. She has, however, reinterpreted it. "Mommy and I tried eating shellfish once," she says. "But we didn't like it." Now I try (not completely consistently) to steer the family toward pizza, fish, or vegetarian restaurants when we eat out.

When I got married, I took on the third major mitzvah, or commandment, around which my life is oriented—*mikveh,* the ritual bath. In traditional Judaism a woman immerses herself in the mikveh just before her wedding, and every month thereafter, seven days after the end of her menstrual period, at which time she resumes sexual relations with her husband. (During the intervening time, in Orthodox families, the wife sleeps separately from the husband and they do not touch at all, not even to pass a plate of food at the table.) The mikveh ritual dates from the earliest days of Judaism: the days of the Temple, when many of our practices were concerned with ritual impurity and purification. "Living water" (from a flowing stream, or rainwater from a cistern on the roof) must make up part of the volume of the mikveh.

When I was about to get married, I talked with Malka Goodman, who was known as something of a mikveh expert in our community. A dark-haired preschool teacher with an expansive lap, she was married to a former Lubavitch rabbi who had followed Reb Zalman Schachter out of Orthodoxy into a more mystical mode. She had given a lot of thought to the mystical possibilities for women contained in this very traditional mitzvah. She suggested I take plenty of time in the mikveh pool, allowing myself fully to let go of my life as a single woman and to prepare myself emotionally for the new stage of life I was entering.

When I came to the mikveh, my nervousness was dispelled by the attendant, Mrs. Goldhirsch, a gentle, grandmotherly woman with an eastern European accent and her hair in a frizzy gray-brown bun. Women in my community called the attendants "mikveh ladies," but the Hebrew *shomeret* ("guardian") seemed more appropriate for Mrs. Goldhirsch; she was to me a guardian angel. After letting me and the friend who came with me into the suite of rooms containing the mikveh, Mrs. Goldhirsch gave me a little hug and a kiss on the cheek, explaining, "I kiss all my brides." I undressed in a little booth and came out wrapped in a big white towel. Leaving the towel behind, I descended the steps into the small blue-tiled pool, dipped once under the water, and tried to let my old life—the pain of it—flow away and dissolve in the water. I came up weeping and stood there, still crying, saying goodbye to a certain version of myself. Goodbye to the loneliness, the uncertainties, and the long struggle to become myself, which had culminated in this moment of finally feeling ready to share myself with someone else. As I cried and cried and cried, Mrs. Goldhirsch said, "It's all right. Take as much time as you need."

When at last the tears slackened, I dipped below the surface again. Underwater, I tried to let hope and openness flow into me, to create in myself the space for good new things to happen. Finally I said the blessing and dipped under once more, thanking God with all my heart for the gift of this moment.

That experience was the model of what for me would become a monthly transformation. Every month, descending under the water, I would let the old month flow out of me, with its angers, tensions, pains, and self-judgments. Immersing again, I would re-open myself to optimism, joy, gratitude, and purpose. Mikveh required an elaborate physical preparation: a half-hour soak in the tub, hair shampooed and combed, nails cut to the finger's edge. Even belly-button lint and grit in the holes of pierced ears had to be removed. My friends joked about that preparation time; one said the tradition was indeed wise, because this was the only half-hour in the month that a woman with children had entirely to herself.

Part of the function of the mikveh attendant is to inspect the woman's hands, feet, and back to be sure that her nails are clean and closely trimmed; that she's taken off her wedding ring, makeup, and jewelry; and that there are no stray hairs clinging to her body. Many women are put off by this inspection. But Mrs. Goldhirsch was always so gentle about it—murmuring apologet-ically, "Oh, there's just a little hair," if she found one—that I al-ways felt taken care of rather than violated. Over time, even when I had exacting mikveh attendants who made me dig bits of soil from the crevice alongside the nail, I came to appreciate their re-ligious conviction. I came to feel that they were my helpers in presenting myself to the waters as naked as a child in the womb, with not even a speck of the world's dirt intervening between me and God, so that I could truly emerge reborn.

I learned that I had to prepare not only physically but emo-tionally. The first few times I went to mikveh, I found it so extra-ordinarily powerful that I cried the whole way home (a risky re-action when you have to drive forty-five minutes on highways in the dark). The month flooded in on me, and I couldn't handle it. Then I developed a ritual of emotional preparation. Just before I got in the tub, I would look over my calendar; while I soaked, I would review the month. What were the blessings I needed to acknowledge? What were the pains I needed to let go of? What were the strengths I needed to take in to deal with the new month? Tucking all those meanings into the few brief moments of my dip, I would come out of the waters feeling almost bathed in light.

The rabbis extended the biblical prohibition on intercourse during the menstrual period for an extra "clean" week after menstruation ends. Many women have noticed that the laws of *niddah* engineer the couple's sex life so that they will come together at the time when they are most likely to conceive. One woman, who often accompanied brides to the mikveh but had never come herself, said Mrs. Goldhirsch told her, "Are you trying to get pregnant?" (She was.) "Come to mikveh and you'll get pregnant immediately." (She did.)

But it wasn't working that way for me and Steve. We were well into our thirties when we married, and for two years we tried to conceive. Eventually I confided my disappointment to Mrs. Goldhirsch. Month after month, she encouraged me, "All we can do is accept God's will. It will happen in God's own time. Have faith."

Then we lost a baby in the fifth month of pregnancy. Mrs. Goldhirsch had noticed my absence from the mikveh. She hugged me and patted my hand. "All we can do is accept God's will. It will happen in God's own time. Have faith."

When I came back after losing another baby in the sixth month of pregnancy, she said, "Get a different doctor."

After the emotional turmoil of those losses, it meant a great deal to me to find myself back in the mikveh, going one more time through a ritual of renewal. It told me that life was going on, that I was going on, despite the pain.

Gradually the mikveh came to be not just water but a transformative element for me. I have never felt myself more truly praying than while standing chest-deep in the mikveh. Sometimes I feel that my prayer is flowing directly from my heart to God, with not even my conscious mind intervening. Those are moments of extraordinary blessing.

In the havurah and feminist Jewish worlds I inhabit, many people have reinterpreted or adapted the traditional mitzvot. Arthur Waskow, who is now part of the Germantown community, has just completed a book about new approaches to the mitzvot called *Down-to-Earth Judaism: Food, Money, Sex, and the Rest of Life.*[6]

Innovation and adaptation in Jewish law are nothing new. As I later learned in my Talmud class, the law has changed throughout Jewish history, both through evolution (as people dropped some observances and created new customs) and by rabbinical decree. When a practice no longer met the needs of the community, rabbis created legal fictions to allow the law to adapt. For example, biblical law decrees that all debts must be canceled in the sabbatical year. As Israel became a more urban, commercial society, this law was strangling commerce; no one was willing to give loans in the years close to the sabbatical. So the great scholar Hillel issued a ruling that while individuals could not collect debts, they could turn their debts over to the court, which was not a person and therefore could collect them. The Orthodox rabbinate has been amazingly adaptable in issuing rulings to accommodate modern technology, such as automatic timers for lights and electrical devices on Shabbat.[7] But the havurah idea that individuals—not rabbis and scholars, but average Joes and Judys—are entitled to change and adapt the tradition is something new.

Our havurah community in Philadelphia contained a spectrum of observance, from very experimental to egalitarian Orthodox. My husband and I were solidly in the center of the spectrum. Each High Holiday season we would discuss where we were Jewishly, and generally we would decide to take on one more sliver of observance. Steve and I never considered becoming fully Orthodox, but we wanted to keep enriching our Jewish life and deepening our commitment. One year we bought a crockpot so we could have hot meals in winter without cooking on Shabbat. We started more regularly ending Shabbat with the spices, wine, and candles of Havdalah. Basically, though, our observance was stable, and I felt a bit stagnant. I had finally become comfortably embedded in Jewish observance—and it no longer felt quite as alive as when I was struggling to achieve it.

Then we moved to Highland Park, New Jersey, and my complacency was given a jolt. In or adjacent to this town of thirteen thousand people were five Orthodox synagogues (ranging from black-coated to modern Orthodox), one right-wing Conservative synagogue, and our small, not particularly experimental havurah. On the fifteen-block-long main street, there were two Jewish bookstores and three or four kosher restaurants, including Jerusalem Pizza and a kosher Dunkin' Donuts. The supermarkets were stocked with lots of kosher brands. Suddenly Jewish observance was both easier and a lot more problematic for me.

Every Shabbat, as we walked bareheaded to our havurah, Orthodox men in yarmulkes and women in large hats pushing baby carriages would stream down our sidewalk. I began internally arguing with Orthodoxy, justifying my style of observance against the implicit criticism of the Orthodox world. I had to ask myself: Was it legitimate to be a pick-and-choose Jew? If it was, then my current practice of taking on a mitzvah a year was fine. But if the mitzvot were an integral system—a fabric that would unravel if taken in pieces—then I had better pick up my pace; with 613 mitzvot, it would take me 613 years to observe the complete set. (My friend Rabbi Nancy Fuchs points out that almost half of the 613 had to do with the ancient Temple and are unobservable today, "so you are closer than you think!") Nevertheless, a person who decides to become Orthodox at some point has to make a "leap of observance" analogous to Kierkegaard's leap of faith. Feeling pressure to take on new practices, I felt a corresponding resistance.

I learned more about the details of Shabbat observance, and there were so many details that I felt smothered. One should use liquid soap rather than bar soap on Shabbat, because tanning and smoothing of leather were among the thirty-nine forbidden categories of work, and you would be smoothing the bar of soap when you wash. One should tear toilet paper ahead of time, since tearing during Shabbat is forbidden. One should not use hot water for dishes or bathing, because it would cause the hot water heater to turn on, violating the prohibition against kindling fire. Highland Park had an *eruv* (a fictional border within which one could carry items), but in other communities you weren't allowed to carry anything outside of your house on Shabbat—not even your baby. And things whose use was forbidden on Shabbat couldn't even be touched. I loved seeing the Shabbat candles lighting up a glistening white tablecloth, but Orthodox families wouldn't place them on the table because you couldn't move them to put on a fresh tablecloth for the next meal.

Many of my Orthodox friends seemed to find comfort from living within this structure of rules, and a few seemed to radiate a sense of wholeness. But I also encountered a number who seemed obsessed with the details in a way that to me seemed the antithesis of spirituality. Haym Soloveitchik, who teaches Jewish history and thought at Yeshiva University, an Orthodox college, says that today's Orthodox Jews are more intent on adhering to the exact letter of the legal texts than their own grandparents who lived nestled in the traditional culture of eastern Europe. Having lost the intimate sense of God's presence that pervaded that culture, they have substituted an attempt to live according to God's will as revealed by Jewish texts, he said: "Having lost the touch of His presence, they seek now solace in the pressure of His yoke."[8]

Even in Europe, as the traditional world collided with the modern one, the demands of Jewish law had been stifling for many. Thinking of all these prohibitions reminded me of my grandmother, who had run away as a teenager from the home of her rabbi father in Poland and shunned religion until she was in her seventies. My grandmother remembered Shabbat as "dark, cold, and boring."

I wanted whatever Shabbat I created for myself and my family to be warm, exciting, and full of light. I liked the idea of Shabbat as a journey, with everything prepared ahead of time so that all I had to do was get on board. In order to take on the mitzvah of not turning lights on and off on Shabbat, I bought a bunch of automatic timers. But I could never seem to get the timers to work—a failing I attributed to my deep ambivalence about going any further with this project of observance of Jewish law. My brain seemed to be populated with highly sensitive anti-authoritarian nerve cells, which had proliferated during years of postadolescent battles with my father and the U.S. government during the Vietnam War era. If I even began to consider taking on a fully traditional lifestyle, they all seemed to begin firing at once.

I don't write on Shabbat. Remembering my grandmother, though, I have been reluctant to tell my daughter not to draw— her favorite and most peaceful leisure activity. I am uncomfortably aware that I and other pick-and-choose Jews often make choices based on convenience rather than conviction, and that this doesn't seem to be the foundation for a strong spiritual life. Sometimes I long to have the comfort with the idea of being commanded that Blu Greenberg describes in her lovely, homey book, *How to Run a Traditional Jewish Household:*

> I don't for a moment believe that God said at Sinai, "Do not carry money in your pockets on Shabbat," or "Do not mow thy front lawn," or even, "Go to synagogue to pray," but the cumulative experience of Revelation, plus the way that experience was defined and redefined in History for a hundred generations of my ancestors, carries great weight with me.
>
> I never have to think about picking and choosing. I am committed to traditional Judaism. It has chosen me and I have chosen it back. And just as I am commanded to observe the laws on a Shabbat that rewards, pleases, heals, or nurtures me, so I am commanded on a Shabbat when it doesn't strike my fancy. . . . I go to *shul,* which might even happen to be tedious that particular Shabbat, but which offers me that which I could not buy for a bid of a hundred million dollars anywhere—community, family, faith, history, and a strong

sense of myself. . . . the possibility of investing time with special meaning, . . . life with a moment of transcendence.[9]

For the rabbis of the Talmud, the mitzvot were the expression of God's will, and the highest form of faith is obedience to them. I am touched by the faith of people who obey the commandments as God's will, but I'm convinced neither that there is such a thing as God's will nor, if such a thing exists or is ascertainable, that the mitzvot are an expression of it. The very idea of obedience is to some extent anathema to me. That resistance stems partly from my particular personality and family history but also, I think, from a basic human drive for autonomy. Although the drive for autonomy may have gone to extremes in our society, it is an important part of the dignity of the human being and ought to be respected. People like Blu Greenberg are able to combine a comfort with commandment with the ability to challenge the tradition and make it grow, but I think they are rare.

Working on this chapter gave me an opportunity to genuinely rethink the idea of mitzvot. To each interview, each source I read, I brought a question: What is the meaning of the mitzvot? Must you accept all of it, live it as an integral system to encounter that meaning?

The Bible contains some clues to the purpose of the laws. For example, it introduces keeping kosher as a way of being holy. After listing the permitted and forbidden foods, God says, "You shall be holy, for I am holy" (Leviticus 11:43). The idea of a practice that brings holiness into daily life appeals to me. But what does holiness mean? The root of the Hebrew word *kadosh* (holy) means separation. Reminding the Hebrew people to "separate between the clean beast and the unclean," God says in Leviticus, "I am the Lord your God, who have set you apart from other peoples. . . . You shall be holy unto Me; for I the Lord am holy, and have set you apart from the peoples, that you should be Mine."

Keeping kosher and observing the other Jewish laws *does* set us

apart from other peoples, a fact that has both positive and negative consequences. If holiness is a matter of maintaining an independent moral stance—that is, being able to remain aloof from
the immorality of a surrounding society—then it helps to have
practices which set one apart. I think Jewish differentness is valuable; part of what we have to offer the world is the critical perspective of the outsider. Especially in America, it is a good thing
to have a certain distance from what Herb Levine, former chair
of the National Havurah Committee, calls "the McDonaldization
of world culture."[10] I like being special, and I think it's worth taking extra effort to maintain our distinctiveness. But I also treasure
the pluralism and universalism of America. One's moral vision
must connect one enough to people outside one's group to feel
their pain and care about what happens to them. Does living the
whole system of mitzvot separate us too much?

Jewish law isn't solely concerned with ritual or lifestyle
mitzvot like keeping kosher and Shabbat. In the Torah, ritual and
ethical commandments are given equal weight, and they are
often intermingled. The same phrase that is used to introduce the
idea of keeping kosher ("You shall be holy, for I the Lord your
God am holy"; Leviticus 19:2) is used to introduce a whole section about social morality: leaving the corners of the field for the
poor, not exploiting the laborer, judging fairly, not gossiping, and
not putting a stumbling block before the blind. The lofty phrase
"You shall not hate your brother in your heart . . . but you shall
love your neighbor as yourself" (Leviticus 17:18) comes immediately before a seemingly petty and inexplicable set of laws forbid-
ding cross-breeding of cattle, sowing two different crops in one
field, or wearing garments with two different kinds of thread.

While the rabbis of the Talmud spelled out in great detail the
ritual laws hinted at in the Torah, they also elaborated and expanded the ethical laws, giving birth to a whole Jewish way of
thinking about caring and responsibility. In order to love your
neighbor as yourself, you have to be able to imagine how your
neighbor sees the world. In their drive to figure out how the

righteous person should act in every situation, the rabbis therefore cultivated the ethical imagination. Not putting a stumbling
block before the blind, they said, also means not doing something
that might cause another person to sin. It is forbidden to sell
weapons to a nation or individual who might use them for ag-
gression, to give alcohol to a person who should not drink, and
to lend money without a witness or receipt (since the person
might be tempted not to pay you back). It is forbidden for a father to strike his adult son, since the son might be tempted to hit
back, and if he did he would be guilty of a capital offense.

In my havurah, as in many other communities, Jews are still
using this heritage of ethical law and ethical imagination to help
them think about how to be good people. One Shabbos, when
the Highland Park minyan was meeting at our house, I peeked
into my daughter's bedroom while JoAnne Rosenberg was leading a service for the little kids. It was one of those boring Torah
portions with dozens of seemingly picayune laws, and I couldn't
imagine how she would help five-year-olds get something out of
it. She focused on just one of the laws: You shall build a parapet
(fence) around the roof. She explained that houses in Israel had
flat roofs and people used to treat them like an extra room, going
up there for various purposes. If there was no parapet, someone
might fall off. This one rule was meant, she said, to teach us to be
careful that no one should be injured because of something we
didn't take care of. The kids could think of lots of examples: trip-
ping over toys that weren't picked up, or getting hit by a swing or
ball because no one looked to see if someone was in the way.

During the frigid winter of 1993–1994, the street in front of
my house became a sheet of ice. When I was slipping and sliding
while dragging our trash cans to the curb, it occurred to me that
I should probably sprinkle sand so that the garbagemen wouldn't
have as much trouble picking up the trash as I'd had setting it out.
But it was cold, dark, and late, so I decided against it. Then, back
in my warm house and pulling off my boots, I remembered the
"parapet principle." As I pulled my boots back on, hefted the bag

of sand from the garage, and slipped and slid out to the street again, I prayed, "Please, God, let no one be injured because of something I failed to do." Laws like this in the Bible and Talmud make me realize that in very important ways, God *is* in the details. An accumulation of small decencies add up to a decent person, a *mensch*.

I couldn't help asking, as the rabbis had asked before me: Is there any true spiritual relationship between these ethical mitzvot and lifestyle mitzvot, such as keeping kosher? The great medieval philosopher Maimonides believed that every single mitzvah had a purpose, and to do them blindly without being conscious of the purpose was to miss the point. "Every one of the six hundred and thirteen precepts serves to inculcate some truth, to remove some erroneous opinion, to establish proper relations in society, to diminish evil, to train in good manners, or to warn against bad habits," he said.[11] He thought of the whole system of mitzvot as a discipline, meant to purify us and help us achieve the self-control to be better people. The mitzvot, he said, are designed to teach us to "strive after perfection."

One Shabbat I was feeling frustrated with the minutiae of keeping kosher, and I asked myself why I bothered with this practice I hadn't grown up with. Fortunately, Rabbi Yakov Hilsenrath's sermon at the Highland Park Conservative Temple that day was about the importance of developing a spiritual discipline—that it was easier to keep the very abstract ethical commandments if you knew you were in control of your mouth and your body.

The idea struck home. I'm a fairly undisciplined person: I hate housework, let unfolded laundry and unsorted papers pile up in mounds, and gain weight every time I go on a diet. But the words that fly out of my mouth when I am angry are what I'm most concerned about.

I knew after years of self-assessment every Yom Kippur how hard it is to change. I told myself that perhaps God, knowing we would get discouraged at trying to become better people, gave us concrete mitzvot so we could feel that we had achieved some interim success in living up to divine standards. It wasn't a terribly ethereal or truly spiritual reason for observance, but I was excited about the idea of the mitzvot as back-door entryways to self-control. So I resolved to think of the laws relating to the mouth as an input/output system: Each time I exercised more discipline over what went into my mouth, I would dedicate that restraint to ensuring that what came out of my mouth was also kosher.

A nice strategy, with only one drawback: I can't see it working. I probably haven't thought about the connection between kosher food and kosher speech from the day I made the resolution last year until today when I wrote about it!

In living my Jewish life I tend to follow the pattern described by Rabbi Mordecai Kaplan, founder of the Reconstructionist movement. I choose to observe the mitzvot that I find fulfilling and meaningful—those that help me to feel connected to the Jewish people, to feel or express the significance of the events of my life, or to be a better person. The rest, says Kaplan, "may be relegated to archaeology."[12] As Kaplan suggests, I do not hesitate to invent new ways to make the mitzvot more vivid or satisfying. I tend not to follow many of the "thou shalt nots" that cut me off from experiences outside the Jewish world that I find satisfying. But when I saw what I do spelled out in black and white in Kaplan's words, I found myself wanting to rethink this approach. It seemed like a very shallow foundation for a spiritual life. Bernie Novick, a member of the Highland Park Conservative Temple who is quite committed to Jewish law, commented to me that he couldn't respect a Judaism based solely on observing "what feels good" to a particular person.

Kaplan reduces the mitzvot to "folkways," cultural artifacts of Jewish history. But I continue exploring the mitzvot because I suspect that there is some deeper spiritual teaching that one can only hear by doing. The Jewish thinkers whose ideas about mitzvot touched me most deeply were Martin Buber and Franz Rosenzweig. Both believed that Jews in our time must be builders of the law, not just its inheritors. Buber declared that he would follow only those mitzvot which he felt personally commanded to do; to take on all the rest of the law would simply interpose a barrier between him and the direct experience of relationship to God.[13] Rosenzweig countered that to presume to be builders of the thirty-five-century-old Jewish tradition, "we need stronger safeguards than our instincts"; we need a genuine love, knowledge and respect for the tradition, "the feeling of being our fathers' children, our grandchildren's ancestors."

Rosenzweig reminded Buber that the Jewish people, committing themselves to the covenant at Mt. Sinai in the Bible, say in unison, "We shall do and we shall hear." The connection between commandments and God is only realized, Rosenzweig asserted, "when we cause it to come alive by fulfilling individual commandments. . . . We know it only when we *do*. . . . Not that doing necessarily results in hearing and understanding. But one hears differently when one hears in the doing."[14]

The Passover seder is vivid, but I heard the Passover story at a different level after I started observing the laws for making the house kosher for the holiday. Growing up with the story of the Exodus from Egypt, I always knew that oppression is wrong and freedom is necessary. After covering the countertops with foil, scalding the stove top and silverware, and bringing out a completely different set of dishes, however, I rediscover each year in my gut that transformation is possible.

When I started reading contemporary theology and interviewing contemporary thinkers about the meaning of the mitzvot, both Orthodox and unorthodox individuals spoke of meanings that emerge in living with the mitzvot. Blu Greenberg writes:

One of the most remarkable qualities of the Jewish religion is its ability to sanctify everyday life—the routine, the mundane, the necessary bits and pieces of daily existence. . . . What Judaism says in effect is this: Yes, commemorating a unique event in history is a holy experience, but so is the experience of waking up alive each morning, or eating to nourish the body, or having sex with one's mate.[15]

Having commandments, rituals, and blessings associated with these humble daily activities, she says, "transforms [each] into something beyond itself. . . . It is not one great big leap or one awesome encounter with the Holy, but rather just so many small steps, like parts of a pattern pieced together."[16]

Rabbi Zalman Shmotkin, director of the Lubavitch Chabad House of the Upper East Side in New York City, points out that the root of the word *mitzvot* is a word meaning "connect." Potentially, each mitzvah is a connecting point to God. I wondered: How is that connection made?

Reb Zalman Schachter-Shalomi, who was originally ordained by Lubavitch but has become one of the most unorthodox of contemporary rabbis, suggests approaching the commandments in a Zen manner: just trying really to be there in the moment of lighting the candles or tasting the wine.

Theologian David Hartman, a Jew who is Orthodox in his observance but less traditional in his theology, points out that *halakhah,* which is usually translated as "law" or "path," actually means "walking." The mitzvot help us to continue walking with God. The rabbis of the Talmud, Hartman points out, did not think of God only as a king but also as a lover taking the people of Israel (seen collectively as female!) as his bride. In this image, the relationship is one of mutual respect, affection, and partnership. The mitzvot are signs of God's love for us; our performance of them is visible evidence of our love for God.[17]

Reading this, I had a sudden image of the mitzvot as wedding ring: a sign of commitment that you voluntarily wear, a sign that you have sanctified yourself and set yourself off in a special relationship that provides for your growth, but voluntarily excludes other relationships; as in a marriage, this commitment and focus is part of what allows you to blossom.

Rabbi Ephraim Buchwald, founder-director of the National

Jewish Outreach Program, agrees with Maimonides that every one of the mitzvot, looked at from a proper perspective, has something to teach us—usually something about values. He says that God wants humans to be partners in perfecting the world. The task of the Jewish people is to model the kind of behavior that would allow humans to create this perfect world; and the purpose of the mitzvot is to raise our consciousness so we can accomplish our mission. For example, the law says to put on the right shoe first, but tie the left shoe first, so as not to favor one part of the body over another. If we have to remember every morning when we get dressed to avoid favoritism in dealing with parts of the body, how much more so with human beings! Similarly, some Orthodox Jews tithe food as in Temple days, leaving a portion of every meal at the side of the plate—a physical reminder to provide for the poor.

Rabbi Manis Friedman, director of Bais Chana Lubavitch women's study and retreat center in Minneapolis, says the mitzvot teach us how to relate to each other and to God. Friedman says that humans need limits and rules, both to behave appropriately and to feel secure. Our boundaries tell us who we are. Submitting to the yoke of the commandments, however, teaches us something more—how to surrender:

> In saying, "Surrender to me totally, submit to me completely, but be accountable and responsible for your morality," God was telling us how to be married, because surrender and responsibility are essential to every intimate relationship. . . . The surrender in a relationship never means a surrender of responsibility, but a surrender of ego and self-satisfaction.[18]

Surrender, says Friedman, is necessary both for knowing your partner and for knowing God.

At Ruach, a summer retreat led by a group of New Age Orthodox rabbis, my bunkmate, Elisa, was trying to explain to me why she felt comforted by and comfortable with the system of mitzvot. Her reasons were in some ways like Friedman's.

"Do you make rules for your kids?" she said.

"Of course."

"Why?"

"Usually because I think the rules are necessary for their health and safety."

"Do you insist on their following your rules even when their health and safety aren't at stake?"

"Yes, or at least even if I don't always do it, I think I should. I think children feel more secure knowing that there are limits and that the limits are enforced. I think children who don't have limits don't develop self-discipline."

"Those are exactly the reasons why I think God makes rules for us. Knowing what the boundaries are makes me feel more secure, and more loved."

For Rabbi Michael Paley, the mitzvot are both anchors in reality and connections to a level that transcends the mundane world. All through the day, as he orders lunch and does other things connected with the mitzvot, he catches glimpses of these larger meanings. "I don't have boring days," said the sandy-haired rabbi.

Paley teaches at Bard College and at the Wexner Heritage Foundation, which gives scholarships to adult Jews to take time off to study their religion. He came from a family that was very involved with Jewish ethics and causes such as the civil rights movement, but dismissed kosher and other ritual laws as silly. Paley started keeping the mitzvot, all in one day, after hearing a lecture on the laws of keeping kosher by Rabbi Saul Berman, a modern Orthodox teacher. "All of a sudden, I understood that *kashrut* [dietary laws] was a whole system to bring holiness and meaning to the everyday act of eating. I came home and said to my mother, 'I won't eat this. I'm keeping kosher.'"

Before he became a vegetarian, he raised his own chickens and slaughtered them himself according to the kosher rules. "I was studying the book of Leviticus and wanted to know what that felt like, what the priests did," Paley explained.

That spring he began walking eight miles to Havurat Shalom on Shabbat, leaving at eight o'clock in the morning to get there at ten o'clock. He was seventeen years old, an "adventuresome and somewhat chaotic" youngster. "I suppose I was always in search of some sense of higher order; I was dissatisfied by the order granted to me by my suburban life." He had experimented with all sorts of 1960s "lifestyle stuff . . . I needed some boundaries."

It was not just a sense of structure that he sought and found. It was "a connection to something enduring. . . . Where most people were struggling with commitment, I had this whole set of commitments, which were very liberating to me." (He jokes that he has two real commitments: the mitzvot and baseball.) "Obligations are precious," explains Paley. The mitzvot helped lift him above a world where there seemed to be no fixed value except what people enjoy or feel like doing, and into a realm of more permanent values.

The mitzvot also help him have clear boundaries in relation to other people. When he was chaplain of Columbia University, a meeting of the deans was called for a Friday afternoon. At five minutes till four, Paley got up to leave. The senior vice president, who was leading the meeting, said, as Paley recalls, "'Where are you going? We're not done yet. We need your input.'"

"I said, 'The Sabbath is coming.'

"The vice president said, 'I'm not letting you leave.'

"I said, 'Shabbos is coming. This is my higher commitment. Right after Shabbos, I'll write you a memo.'

"'What are you leaving to do?'

"'I'm leaving to do nothing. I'm not going to turn the light on, I'm not going to take a car ride.'

"'In that case, you certainly can't leave.'

"'I'd rather die than stay in this meeting. And people in my tradition have died for this, rather than violate Shabbos.'

"So I left. He was stunned. Later he told me it had been a real education for him."

If the mitzvot are to teach us about Jewish values (as Buchwald suggests) or our relationship with God (as Hartman, Paley, and Friedman suggest), I figured it must be important to think about inner meanings when you do them. Some parts of the Jewish tradition, such as Hasidism, stress intention (*kavannah*) in performing the mitzvot. Although I can't do it all the time, often I find this approach helpful. One year, for the first time, I followed the commandment to count the *omer,* numbering the forty-nine days between the holidays of Passover and Shavuos. I saw counting the omer as God's gift to show us we could move from one place to another, from the slavery of Egypt to the revelation of Sinai, one day at a time. My intention for observing the commandment of the omer was to be more self-controlled in handling kids' bedtimes. For forty-nine nights I said the omer blessings, and each night I got the kids to bed on time without yelling. One day at a time.

Blu Greenberg says it's not necessary to "engage in a lot of God-talk or God-think;" simply living with the mitzvot "anchors and connects you" to God, to community, and to yourself. "Every time I say a *bracha* [blessing] and put something in my mouth, do I think about God? No, but sometimes I do. For the one out of ten times it does connect me to God, it's worth it." Just taking care, day after day, to live according to the law means that under the surface you will be aware of the sense of "the commanding voice, the source," she says. The laws constantly connect you to community, and community gives you a spiritual base, "a sense of being part of a people who are partners in the covenant." And living within the law "anchors you to yourself. It helps you to organize and frame your life, to create an identity as a Jew. . . . The mitzvot, the ways of living as a Jew . . . have been transported through the generations; they tie the generations together."

As hard as I found it to live fully within the system, I found it empty to live without it. As Rabbi Edward Feld has written, "A Judaism that has given up on *halakha* ceases to be interesting, for it no longer thinks of Judaism as making a difference."[19]

Adin Steinsaltz, an elfin white-bearded man from a secular family who became one of Israel's leading Orthodox rabbis, had anticipated my doubts and ambivalence in his book *Teshuvah: A Guide for the Newly Observant Jew.* With relief, I read the following:

> It is not unusual for the ba'al teshuvah [the one returning to tradition] to find himself in a state of spiritual crisis. . . . Taking upon oneself the yoke of the Torah and the mitzvot is by no means an easy task. It means the adoption of a distinct and all-pervasive way of life. . . . Faith is not a package one receives all neatly wrapped and sealed. . . . A person who confronts the necessity of making a change in his life . . . must also reckon with internal resistance.[20]

Reading Steinsaltz I realize I am in one of those destabilized periods, and that I am growing again. Steinsaltz suggests that people who are feeling "stuck" should take one small step in some area of observance they are particularly attracted to, as a way of moving forward in the search. My husband, Steve, always my best and most sensitive advisor, reminded me that the saying of blessings was also a mitzvah; the rabbis suggested that people should be saying one hundred blessings a day. Rather than despairing over my inability to achieve the discipline of the mitzvot, I would concentrate for a while on prayer, the connecting point with which I had begun my search into Judaism.

Steinsaltz also advised returnees to Judaism: "It is important to remember that each positive precept fulfilled, each transgression avoided, is in itself an achievement. The first step is never sufficient, but even the longest journey must begin somewhere."[21]

After I finished writing the first draft of this chapter on mitzvot, I undertook three small experiments with expanding my Shabbat observance. I put Kleenex boxes in each bathroom, so I wouldn't have to tear toilet paper; I committed myself to using liquid soap rather than bar soap; and I tried to light candles on time. The first week was a disaster. I was so tense about getting everything done so I could light on time that I yelled at the kids, causing my son to throw a tantrum that lasted an hour and a half. We spent the first half-hour at the Shabbat dinner table with him sobbing, and my daughter and I resolutely trying to sing louder than he sobbed. But the second week was better. I managed to get done before lighting the candles all the things that were not permitted on Shabbat, such as driving and cooking. After they were lit I did a couple of permitted things, such as setting the table and putting on pretty clothes. I ended up lighting the candles five minutes after I was supposed to, and I congratulated myself on coming close.

But the rest of Shabbat held a nice surprise. The two easy mitzvot I had chosen, not tearing toilet paper and using liquid soap, served as gentle reminders throughout the day that it was a special, sacred day. The following day, reverting back to my normal practice, I was very aware that it wasn't Shabbat, but that Shabbat would be coming again. Rabbi Art Green, the founder of Havurat Shalom, says that the essence of Jewish spirituality is to live life "in the presence of God" so that embedded in the ordinary day is a sense of holiness as profound as once was associated with the Holy Temple.[22] Like keeping kosher when I was at work, these two little mitzvot, which had seemed so petty to me, helped me to feel more connected to the sacred time, the meeting time with God that is an anchor for my life.

After I had lit the candles on time for five weeks in a row, I noticed something interesting. On a Tuesday, I shut off my computer just a half-hour earlier than usual and took a few minutes to straighten up the living room and put the refried beans into a pan to warm. When my daughter and son came home, we had a mini-Shabbat. I was able to spend a half-hour of time really paying attention to each of them individually. The discipline of Shabbat, even if just for a moment, was helping me bring more order and peace to the rest of my life.

Maybe it's time to take Steinsaltz's advice, I told myself, to look at how far I have come rather than fretting about how far I want to go. My friend Jerry Langer points out that the Bible gives two commandments about Shabbat: to observe or guard it (*shomer*), and to remember it (*zachor*). My family and I are not among those who are strictly observant, or *shomer Shabbat,* but we are not among those who forget it. Jerry calls himself "Zachor Shabbat," a rememberer of Shabbat. In remembering and practicing many of the mitzvot, we remember that daily life is holy—and that we, by our actions, participate in making it holy.

"Jewish ritual is very good at explicitly recognizing the blessing in life, the goodness in life, the specialness of it," said Jerry. "The existentialists were right, that there is no inherent meaning in a lot of things, including life. Given that fact, and that we're here, what does one create? Judaism says one can create meaning, and a high level of meaning, a moral meaning, and can turn mundane things into holiness."

Yes, I need to express my Jewishness, to participate in the richness of the Jewish experiment with life. I think about my journey. I was drawn toward exploring the mitzvot by Goldie's remarks about how *niddah* and other Jewish laws provided a stable context for her marriage. I have moved from that time of chaos and loneliness to a stable, loving, nurturing marriage grounded in the Jewish way of life. Jewish observance doesn't work for me when I'm constantly criticizing myself for the standards I don't meet, but it works beautifully for me when I see every small bit of observance as a gift of connection from God.

At a community level, I hope the mitzvot can teach us, as Herb Levine says, "how to remain a separate people yet convey through our way of life a universal theological idea . . . redemption for our planet and all its living creatures."[23] At the level of my one small individual life, I can taste that redemption: mitzvot, holidays, and community form a fabric into which I am woven. They are the context of my life. Without in any way losing my individuality, I have lost the atomization that plagued me at the beginning of this journey. The blessing after the meal speaks of the covenant sealed in our flesh. People usually take that to mean circumcision, but I think it can refer more broadly to all the mitzvot. They are signposts, reminders; it is through them that our relationship to God becomes embedded in our everyday flesh-and-blood life. Within this structure, I have found my identity. I have become myself—a Jewish woman at the dawn of the twenty-first century.

PART II

BEING

*M*y journey, and this book, began with an experiment in prayer—an experiment in imagining how I would live life if I thought there was a God. But I've postponed the chapters on prayer and God to the end of the book. There is a reason for this: Many people in our time, however much we may yearn for a spiritual life, are uncomfortable talking about God. Caught between old ideas and new sensibilities, we don't have a language to describe what we experience.

In the 1960s, Time *magazine announced the "death of God." Reb Zalman Schachter-Shalomi says what really died, for Jews, was rabbinic Judaism: the culture slaughtered by the Nazis, and the idea of God it cherished. The idea of the fatherly God, stern but kindly, taking a close personal interest in his beloved children—for many people, especially many Jews, that idea was dead. New ideas about God are being born: God not as noun, but as verb, says Reb Zalman, not as being but as process. Rabbi Yitz Greenberg says that in Jewish history, cataclysm has triggered transformation. The destruction of the Temple propelled us out of the biblical era into the second great era in Jewish history, the rabbinic era. The Holocaust has forced us to the dawn of the third great era. We cannot predict the shape of the new Judaism that will emerge, but it will likely involve a sweeping change in how we experience and express our relationship to the holy.*

CHAPTER 10

PRAYING

Ancient Words, New Reasons

How do we even find God and when we do, what do we say?
—Ellen M. Umansky[1]

Let them pray to be able to pray and if they do not succeed, if they
have no tears to shed, let them yearn for tears . . . let them take
strength from the certainty that this too is a high form of prayer.
—Abraham J. Heschel[2]

My return to Judaism (and to religion per se) began with the
need to pray, to pray even though I didn't have any clear
belief in Someone or Something to pray to. I began to talk with
God; to say this is what I'm angry about, what I'm puzzled about,
what I yearn for. I listened very hard for a response. And I began
to feel I was finding it—not in an actual voice in my head, which
would have terrified me and gotten me to drop the whole enterprise, but in answers that formed in my mind and in my experi-

189

ences. Sometimes, chuckling apologetically toward Heaven, I would take God's part in the dialogue as well as my own, and I would find myself looking at things in ways that hadn't occurred to me before. When I came back to the East Coast and got involved in the havurah movement, I began to realize—only slowly and through years of doing it—that my personal prayers were only part of the reaching toward God I needed to do. When I prayed alone, I felt like an insignificant atom reaching toward a distant God. But when I prayed in community, infusing my own meanings into the traditional prayers, I felt as if my heart traveled a well-worn path toward holiness, one that had been smoothed by many journeyers. The service gave me a framework, a spiritual moment, when I could allow all the longing in my heart to peak and pour out toward God.

Prayer is the central activity of many havurot, but it is also the most problematic.[3] From their beginnings in the 1960s, havurah-niks lived in a religious milieu where only Doubt was King. In their meetings, in their services, and in their magazines, they struggled to define why and how to pray. Like Heschel, who complained that most contemporary congregations "recite the prayer book as if it were last week's newspaper,"[4] havurahniks were deeply critical of contemporary Jewish congregations, which they found sterile and hypocritical.

Heschel had complained that most congregations try to "pray by proxy. . . . vicariously,"[5] getting the rabbi to do their praying for them. The havurahniks wanted to pray for themselves. But for many of the haverim there was a major obstacle. For two millennia, Jewish prayer had been *avodah*—service of God. People may have mumbled the prayers, but they said all of them, every day, because this was what God wanted. In the 1960s it was no longer evident what God wanted; in fact, it was no longer evident what God was or even *if* God was. Heschel had written, "Unless God is at least as real as my own self; unless I am sure that God has at least as much life as I do, how can I pray? . . . If God is unable to listen to us, then we are insane in talking to Him."[6] Unlike Heschel, most havurahniks weren't sure whether God existed, and if so, whether God was listening. And yet they wanted passionately to pray. Heschel says prayer is "our humble answer to the inconceivable surprise of living."[7] With all its problems, havurahniks found life amazing, and they needed to express that wonder in prayer.

Intellectually many of them were closer to Mordecai Kaplan, who identified the divine with that force in human beings which impels them to seek the good. But the havurahniks wanted prayer that was more personal, more passionate than one could drum up for an abstract distillation of human goodness. The people attracted to Havurat Shalom felt there was such a thing as holiness, that the ancient sages were "onto something," and they wanted to know it.

Art Green wrote about their dilemma in a symposium in *Response* magazine, the independent journal where Jewish students and members of the havurah movement worked out many of their ideas:

> I want to be able to *daven* [pray]; I want to be able to love and allow myself to enter the religious world of Rabbi Akiva, who sees the central spiritual metaphor as that of loving embrace. But how do you love God in a post-holocaust mental set? . . . at times, in the midst of prayer, [I] feel myself to be a liar, trying to deny evil in order to go on praying. I look around, in such *moments,* with a kind of horror: "My God, after all that are we crazy Jews still sitting here praising Him?" And that praise seems to be both blasphemy and madness. But somehow that moment is overcome, and I find myself again able to pray in joy.[8]

Green was a scholar and "in part" a follower of Reb Nahman of Bratzlav. As he explained, Reb Nahman

> seems to glimpse the total absurdity of the life of faith, and . . . yet knows, through endless struggle, that the assertion of faith is his only goal. A God who can be totally present and totally absent, who can

fill the soul and yet make one cry out to overcome the distance, who can be spoken of only in the language of absolute paradox: that face of God . . . I can somehow make my own. Only that sense of movement in transcending paradox and confronting paradox can keep me from that most dangerous of sins, despair.[9]

Just as they hoped to refashion the world rather than accepting the one they had inherited from their parents, havurahniks felt they would have to reinvent or rediscover how and why to pray. Alan Mintz, editor of *Response,* called in the spring 1969 issue for "small groups of highly motivated religious experimenters who might peel off layers of inhibition" and approach prayer as "experiments in thought." Havurahniks could seek three goals in prayer, he said: personal integration or wholeness, transcendence or mystery, and "moral reassessment or recommitment."

Meaning the words, and finding meaning through them, became one of the ongoing goals of the havurah service. Rabbi Michael Paley remembers vividly his first visit to Havurat Shalom. The group, led by Reb Zalman Schachter, sang one prayer for fifteen minutes, then skipped ahead—bypassing about a third of the traditional service—to the Sh'ma, the Jewish affirmation of the oneness of God. They focused on the six key words for five minutes, breathing them in yogic style. "The order of the service was completely obliterated for the sake of this unbelievable *kavannah* [meaning]," recalled Paley. "It went on and on like that for two hours."

When Paley moved to the neighborhood and joined the havurah, members "used to get up every morning and pray for two hours, meditating, screaming the prayers. We used to shout at each other," recalled Paley. "[One of our members] would say, if our prayer really means anything we should stand up right now and go march against the war."

A twofold ethic toward prayer evolved, of confronting on the one hand, and experiencing with all the senses on the other. They would struggle with the texts, argue with the prayers. Paley remembers one person shouting, "How could you believe in a religion that talks about 'the abominations' of other religions? That's so narrow and parochial!" At the same time people would try to respond fully and sensually to the emotions and images of the prayer, and would share their responses. "A psalm would hit you, and you'd talk about it awhile," recalled Paley. "There would be long periods of silence."

Zestful singing was vital to the havurah service. It helped these very intellectual characters transcend the busy brain and open the heart. They rediscovered energetic or mournful Hasidic melodies. They enthusiastically adopted melodies for the liturgy composed by the bearded singer, guru, and Orthodox rabbi Shlomo Carlebach. And they clapped, swayed, and sang the traditional prayers to rhythmic American folk melodies, especially Negro spirituals.

For many havurahniks prayer remained a form of groping, of sifting through the traditional liturgy and trying to find phrases, ideas, and images they could connect to; what made it work was that they did it together. In the winter of 1981–1982, *Response* magazine published a nearly two-hundred-page double issue on prayer. As Michael Swartz wrote, though there often seemed to be little or no fit between the ancient words and their modern world, havurah members had outgrown their "Joan Baez and Bob Dylan" days, when they thought they could make services meaningful by writing new prayers keyed to current events. They had begun to realize that like the ancient scholars and seekers whose poems are contained in the liturgy, their services would have to confront basic human dilemmas that don't change from generation to generation. Now havurahniks often used *kavannot,* interpreting old prayers in new ways. Struggling to find meaning in the *kedusha* (the holiness prayer, which depicts choirs of angels praising God) at one service, Swartz read a poem that began with the line, "God fired the angels." Human beings, the poem suggested, have now been given the angels' job: to sing with one voice despite our differences. Near the beginning of most services in the Germantown minyan, the leader would suggest a *ka-vannah,* which might connect the prayers to some tragic or joyous world event, or to the changing seasons. Sometimes there was a suggestion about a way to reinterpret: "What would *we* mean by the restoration of Zion?"[10] *Kavannot,* explained Rabbi Hershel Matt in the *Response* issue on prayer, were "prayerful preparations for prayer; not directions to the congregation, but directions to the heart."

As one of Rabbi Matt's students would discover, life itself over time would train our hearts to respond to the traditional prayers. Though Herb Levine and Ellen Frankel had come from actively Jewish families and both had been whiz kids in their afternoon Hebrew programs, neither as a youngster had made a connection of the heart to the Jewish liturgy. When she was growing up in Rabbi Matt's Conservative synagogue, Ellen's parents worked hard at raising funds for the Jewish community and were active in the synagogue; her mother was the rabbi's secretary, and her father chairman of the ritual committee. But, she said, "I remember no conversations about God, and no questions from me about God."

Ellen connected with Judaism not through its teachings about God but through its stories. When she got bored with synagogue services, she used to sneak into the synagogue library and curl up with a book of *midrash* (explanatory tales based on scripture).

Ellen loved Hebrew school, too—not as a source of spirituality, but as a kind of linguistic and cultural detective work. She was good at languages. There was the challenge of first mastering the vocabulary and grammar, then unraveling the meanings of more and more complicated texts. Traditional Jewish prayer was a skill to be mastered, and she quickly became an expert. By the time she was eleven she was leading the junior congregation service and chanting the Torah portion for the week.

In those years of leading services, it had never occurred to Ellen to pray personally. God was a word on paper, a phrase the community agreed on, not a Reality toward which her heart yearned. When she outgrew the religious school, Rabbi Matt took her on for a year as his personal student. About once a month she went home with Rabbi Matt for Shabbat with his family. Unlike Ellen's home and those of her friends, there was no decorator furniture here, no rugs on the floors—only walls lined with books, the simplest of furnishings, and passionate, fascinating conversation. Matt was a quiet man, almost saintly in his faith and humility. Rabbinical students and Jewish leaders, including Heschel (with whom Matt had remained friends after graduating from the seminary), came to share the peace of Shabbat at his table. There were trilingual puns in Hebrew, Yiddish, and English, and always lots of joyful singing. It was an entirely different experience of the Sabbath. When there were no guests, Matt's sons would go outside to play basketball. (They went to a yeshiva and got their fill of Jewish subjects all week.) Ellen and Rabbi Matt would sit and study Torah together, going over the portion of the week and discussing what it meant. It wasn't until Matt's death, some twenty years later, that she understood how those years of study had awakened an "undercurrent of spirituality" that would shape her life from then on. "At his house," Ellen said, "I felt whole."

Suddenly, when she was thirteen, Ellen was "banished from the *bimah*" (the platform from which the Torah is read). After her bat mitzvah, she was no longer permitted to read the Torah or lead the prayers. In the grown-up world of Conservative Judaism at that time, the leadership roles she had enjoyed were reserved for men. Ellen was so outraged at her sudden demotion that on Simhat Torah, the holiday celebrating the completion of a year's cycle of study, she picketed the synagogue with a sign saying "Equal Rites for Women." Rabbi Matt was ardently in favor of equality of religious rights for women and fought to change the policy at her synagogue. As chairman of the ritual committee, however, Ellen's father fought to preserve the traditional policy, and won. Ellen did not chant the Torah portion again until she encountered the havurah movement ten years later.

Ironically, at the moment her religious rights ended, Ellen's inner religious life was just beginning. Entering the teenage whirl of expensive bar mitzvah parties, she felt alienated, awkward, and self-conscious. She found a haven in Jewish studies. Discovering that she was more comfortable with the texts than with her peers, she devoted herself to the Jewish Theological Seminary's Prozdor program, commuting nine hours a week to New York by bus for five hours a week of classes. In Talmud she could decode a blueprint of the rabbinic mind. "It was like a detective adventure" to figure out the reasoning of these scholars who had lived some fifteen centuries ago. As a small rebellion against her parents, she became more religiously observant than they: On the Sabbath, she refused to ride in a car or do homework or write.

Despite her immersion in Jewish texts, Ellen had never connected with the idea of a personal God-father-king as depicted in much of Jewish prayer. She began picking up ideas of God from science fiction, imagining an ultimate power beyond human comprehension.

In 1969, during the height of the youth culture, Ellen went off to the University of Michigan. There she severed her connection with Judaism. Wanting to eat kosher food, she had signed up to eat at Hillel for a semester, but she didn't like the students there. They were conservative, stable graduate students; she was a radical. She resolved the dilemma of keeping kosher by becoming a vegetarian. She channeled her spirituality into the political movements of the day (until she was arrested in a demonstration and got scared). She didn't go home for the holidays and did not even attend services for Rosh Hashana and Yom Kippur, the holiest days of the Jewish year. She began a spiritual search. She read about Zen Buddhism. Though she read the works of Martin Buber and Heschel as well, because she considered them spiritual teachers, for the most part "I just kind of checked out of Judaism for three years and checked into Eastern religions." She felt a great inner peace, a sense of being precious and worthy.

When she met Herb Levine, the man who is now her husband, she began the next phase of her spiritual journey: integrating her college spiritual search with the Judaism she had learned
by rote as a child. Ellen and Herb discovered the havurah movement as they were discovering each other in English literature in
graduate school at Princeton. When Ellen read a Hebrew note
Herb had scrawled in the margin of a text on Romanticism, and
laughed, Herb knew he had found a woman who was his intellectual match in both his worlds—the cosmopolitan world of literature and the (to him) homier world of Jewish thought.

Herb clearly was excited by their common bond in Judaism.
Their second date was for Friday night dinner. He made the meal
for her: chopped liver prepared by hand. (Unfortunately, she
hated chopped liver.)

Ellen and Herb began to celebrate Friday night Shabbat together. They lit candles, had dinner at home, and spent the
evening reading aloud to each other. On Saturday afternoons,
they joined another couple to discuss *The Ethics of the Fathers.*
Their study partners—Princeton's Hillel rabbi, Eddie Feld, and
his wife, Merle, a poet—had been among the founding haverim
at Havurat Shalom. From Merle and Eddie, Ellen and Herb
learned for the first time to take Torah personally—to ask what
all this Jewish tradition they had learned about meant to them,
emotionally, in their lives as modern Jews. They started leading
services at the Hillel, and Ellen unrolled the parchment scroll to
chant the Torah for the first time since her bat mitzvah. "We
knew we were home," she said. "That was the real beginning of
exploring spirituality for me. I finally put it together with Judaism." Ellen and Herb were moved to write about their experience in an article, "Havurah in the Ivory Tower."[11]

Herb got a job teaching English at Franklin and Marshall College in Lancaster, Pennsylvania. Being knowledgeable and skilled,
they were enthusiastically welcomed into the Conservative synagogue and soon were leaders of the community. But they needed
to continue the spiritual exploration they had begun in Prince-

ton, and that was more difficult to accomplish. They tried several times to form a havurah, but each time it soon fell apart. In a small town, it seemed to take all the energy of the few committed Jews to maintain the established organizations; alternatives were too threatening.

In the summer of 1980 Ellen and Herb attended the first Havurah Institute, where they connected with havurah members from all over the country. For both of them, the Institutes gradually came to mean a change in career and life direction. Judaism in the family Herb came from was a very intellectual, historically oriented brand. In the joyful heart-singing of the havurah Herb discovered a new dimension of himself: the Levite, the descendant of those who had danced in the courts of the Temple in praise of God.

He also saw the vocation of teaching in a new way. The rule at Havurah Institutes was that each teacher must also be a learner, taking classes from other teachers. There was a high level of give-and-take in the classes, and learners were encouraged to become teachers as well. Herb discovered that he could bring the tools of literary analysis that he'd learned in graduate school together with the Jewish texts he'd studied as a kid, coming up with insights that were exciting both to him and to his students. Gradually he realized that he would rather delve more deeply into his own Jewish heritage than be a scholar of English literature. He took a sabbatical and began working up a course on Bible as literature. He completed a book on Psalms, became editor of the *Reconstructionist* magazine, and after leaving his college teaching position entered rabbinical school.

The Havurah Institute was a turning point for Ellen in a different way. In 1977, at age twenty-six, she had to have a hysterectomy. For the next few years, Rosh Hashana, the New Year, had been nearly unbearable: The liturgy for the holiday includes two texts about barren women of the Bible, Sarah and Hannah, whose prayers are eventually answered with children who become leaders of the Jewish people (Isaac and the prophet Samuel). "I knew it wasn't going to happen to me," said Ellen. "I didn't turn to God; I felt as if I didn't have any spiritual resource."

Her time at the Institute had been so exciting that Ellen decided to go to a Yom Kippur retreat led by Reb Zalman Schachter at Fellowship Farm, near Philadelphia. Zalman used the traditional service like a kaleidoscope, keeping many of the traditional pieces but turning them to mirror and refract against each other in a dozen different ways. He had people sit in pairs, gazing into each other's eyes, confessing as if each were a priest and could absolve the other. He had them think about sins that weren't in the prayerbook—the subtle sins that modern people commit against each other. Ellen felt her heart opening up. "It was the first time in my whole life that Yom Kippur meant anything to me," she recalled. "I connected personally. I really thought about atonement. I did *heshbon ha-nefesh* [an examination of one's soul]."

As she studied with Zalman, Ellen began to understand that every Jewish service had a shape whose purpose was to open the praying individual's heart to God. "Herb and I could do the service cold," she said, "but this was the first time we understood that there is an emotional process in davening, a gradual rising in spiritual intensity."

Zalman introduced them to the mystical Kabbalistic concept of four worlds: the physical world of doing, the world of emotions and creativity, the world of the intellect, and finally the world of pure being. The order of the prayers, he said, could help them to gradually open to each of these levels in succession. When it came time for the Torah reading, Ellen asked to be called to the Torah for an *aliyah* and to receive a special blessing. There, in front of her peers, she prayed to be given a child. Three months later, she and Herb adopted a daughter.

Back in Lancaster, Ellen and Herb took over the volunteer advisorship of the college Hillel. Although they couldn't seem to find a critical mass of adults to maintain a havurah for study and exploration, they found college students who were searching. In talking with the students, they were able to continue exploring themselves; however, they were at a different life stage than their students and were asking different questions. They began to import havurah-world speakers to talk to their students ("We wanted the kids to realize that they didn't have to have the same Judaism as their parents"). They would then stay up late into the night talking with their guests.

"It allowed me to see that I had been involved in an 'us versus them' relationship to Judaism," Ellen said of what she learned. "If I found spirituality in Zen, in folk music, that was okay. I wasn't betraying my Judaism if I respected other people's faith and learned from them. It was liberating: I didn't have to be parochial." She could integrate all she had learned into her Jewish life and into her prayer.

As she experimented with feminism, psychodrama, and some of Zalman's New Age syncretism, Ellen discovered that liturgically she was fairly conservative. She needed to hear the traditional words in the traditional order, to feel an uninterrupted connection with the long, long past of Judaism. But her encounters with those who were experimenting helped to infuse new meaning into the traditional words. She could understand some phrases as metaphors, and she could find *kavannot* that would add layers of meaning to the traditional texts.

Over time, Ellen's career and her deepening investment in Judaism began to converge. Since graduate school she had been working devotedly on a novel, closeting herself to write for hours every day. When the novel didn't sell, she revised and revised it. Meanwhile she'd been writing articles about the Jewish world—a book review or occasional commentary here or there. Gradually more of her writing focused on Judaism. In 1985 she wrote *Choosing to Be Chosen,* a novel for Jewish youngsters on identity issues. In 1989 she completed a massive collection of traditional Jewish tales. She was working on a book on Jewish symbolism in 1990 when the Jewish Publication Society asked her to become editor-in-chief.

When I first met Ellen at a Havurah Institute in 1989, she was leading a "beginners' service" for people who knew little Hebrew and would have trouble participating in a regular service. I had been attending havurah services for many years, had picked up a fair amount of Hebrew, and had found my own ways of entering into and being nourished by the prayers; in fact, I'd been at the same 1980 retreat as Ellen and had taken classes with Zalman. But as Ellen gently explained the unfolding of the service through the four worlds, I found myself entering the emotional flow of the service as I had rarely done before.

In 1987 Rabbi Hershel Matt, her first teacher, died suddenly of a heart attack. As memories of him flooded through her during the funeral and in the days following, she began to understand in a new way her own opening to the power of traditional prayer. "I realized that Hershel was really my spiritual father. It wasn't Zalman who had opened up the *siddur* for me, it wasn't the havurah leaders, it wasn't the feminists, it was Hershel, with his example of quiet faith."

She remembered his humility. When his sons went through their hippie stage and came home from college for the holidays with wild, flying hair, he would call them up to the pulpit for the Torah reading without worrying about what the congregation would think. He would pray quietly to himself in a corner, rather than standing at the lectern. "His sermons were all about God. My father complained that they were boring; a rabbi's supposed to talk about current events."

Most of all, Ellen remembered a time when her mother had come home outraged from the synagogue office. A family in the congregation had come to the rabbi asking for a reduction in their synagogue dues, and the rabbi had immediately granted it. Ellen's mother, who was Hershel's secretary, pointed out afterward that the family was about to go on an expensive Caribbean vacation. Hershel said simply, "They must need the vacation."

Her mother used the anecdote to prove that Rabbi Matt was, in Ellen's words, "hopelessly naive." To Ellen, it meant quite the opposite: that he had the wisdom and faith and humility to trust.

Although Ellen gained strength from using the words of the prayerbook, she still had trouble believing in a personal God who would help her in times of trouble. But by cherishing Hershel's example, she has come to have greater faith in the world and in other human beings. "If you really don't have too much faith in people, you can't have much faith in God either. It's as hard to believe in people as to believe in God," she said.

Her favorite prayer today is "Ahavah Rabah" ("Great Love"), which talks about the reciprocity of love between God and human beings. When it's sung to a beautiful melody, she tries to let go and allow herself to believe in the possibility of love and reciprocity. Sometimes, in spite of her own inner tensions and the pressures upon her, she comes to a place of peace or wholeness. In the outside world as well as in prayer, the example of her teacher's faith sustains her. "I carry Hershel inside me all the time. Often I will ask myself, what would Hershel say or think or do in a certain situation. Abraham Heschel says, 'We live and act according to the image of man we cherish.' My spirituality is involved in really meaning that, trying to live that every day. I try to see the world through Hershel's eyes. When my father's voice would say, 'Don't trust people's motivations, be on guard, the world is corrupt,' I try to hear Hershel's voice saying, 'Assume you can trust.'"

When Ellen and Herb were ready to adopt a second child, they decided to take a child with special needs. They did not know that the child they chose, a bright but volatile three-year-old who was the product of an abusive home, would tax their emotional and spiritual resources to the very limit. Small as he was, he was already suffering rages, deep depressions, periods when he thought everyone (including his parents) was against him, and times when he couldn't cope with even the simplest demand. Optimistically, Ellen and Herb believed that pouring enough love into this child could heal the wounds of his first chaotic years. But after three years they began to realize that their son had lifelong problems with which they would have to cope every day. They began to feel the need for a sustaining spiritual community where they could draw in love and concern to recharge the wells that were constantly being drained.

They threw themselves into Jewish community activities in Lancaster, where Ellen was a leader in building a Jewish day school. But they didn't have the intimacy of a havurah community where they could share Shabbos in the way they wanted to: as guests in each other's homes, singing, studying, and immersing themselves in a Jewish world. Once a year they would go to the Havurah Institute, where, said Ellen, "For one week a year I could be whole." Finally they decided to put their spiritual life before their work life. Even though it meant an hour and forty minutes of commuting each way to Herb's teaching job, they would move to Philadelphia, where they could be part of the Germantown minyan.[12] Within a year, Herb was chairman of the National Havurah Committee, and the Germantown minyan had become a spiritual center for their lives.

As their son grew older his problems worsened, and he needed increasing professional attention. In the face of this constant emotional stress Ellen never abandoned God, but she compartmentalized: Her family struggles were one world, her religious life another. She didn't pray for healing for her son, or for her own hurt soul as a mother. Even so the beauty of the liturgy comforted her, and from the community itself she felt she received a kind of healing. The Shabbat service, the holiday and life cycle celebrations, and the Sabbath dinners with friends lifted her out of the claustrophobic world of family and renewed her strength. "I live from Shabbos to Shabbos," said Ellen. Shabbat, community, and prayer had become her sanctuaries.

As they worked with the liturgy and made it their own through their comments, amendments, and experiments, some havurahniks began to think of prayer as an important and very human need, rather than an approach to the divine. Prayer, wrote Reconstructionist rabbi Rebecca Alpert in *Response* magazine, is "a framework" in which people can "affirm life as meaningful and purposeful," feel connected to Jews around the world and over centuries past, and find a vision of holiness to guide their lives.

The feeling of belonging became an important source of spiritual nurturance in the havurah world. Just being in a room of people searching their hearts, sharing their inmost thoughts, and probing the texts for hope and strength helped members feel they transcended to some degree the barriers that normally separate people from one another.

Every now and then an iconoclast would raise the issue the havurahniks had started with: Why do we bother? Rita Poretsky was one of these. For the *Response* double issue on prayer, Rita (an artist who had explored Eastern religions) took the question to various friends at Fabrangen, then wrote an article summarizing their answers. Chava Weissler, who kept her long thick hair coiled in a bun and had a wry sense of humor, had a humanist approach similar to the Reconstructionists. She thought of prayer as a catalyst for personal growth. "A meaningful time of prayer," she told Rita, "is when I integrate something in myself which I previously hadn't integrated. I come in touch with some feelings which I couldn't get before."

Pam Hoffman, who eventually became a rabbi, had taken upon herself the obligations traditionally reserved for men, including the obligation to pray three times daily. These prayers had given her life a structure, she said, in which holiness was constantly being reasserted. Shaharit, the morning prayer, "is a spiritual cup of coffee with which to start the day," said Hoffman. "Maariv, the evening prayer, ends the day." Minchah, the afternoon prayer, was the hardest and by its very difficulty presented its own special rewards. "Minchah brings a halt to whatever you are doing. If a busdriver or a shopkeeper, you stop and say, '*ashre yoshva betecha*—happy are those who dwell in Your house.' . . .

Minchah . . . says stop and bring your gift to God, the *karbon,* the sacrifice to draw nearer to God."

Pip Mandelkorn, who had experimented with yoga and Eastern traditions, thought of prayer as part of a larger spiritual discipline. "With practice," he told Rita, "we can wash away pride and egoism, if only for awhile, long enough to do the job [of prayer] in a good and even humble state of mind."

After interviewing all these people, though, Rita still found herself deeply ambivalent toward prayer. "When I attempt to chant the daily [fixed] prayers, I discover that I am quickly bored, perhaps because I am not willing to allow what is holy to intervene in my already established daily activities."

Rita traveled to India, trying to find her truth in meditation, then moved to Philadelphia, where she sometimes put in an appearance at the Germantown minyan. She learned that both she and her mother had terminal cancer. In the three years until her death in 1989, as she braved radiation treatments, sat *shiva* for her mother, and sought alternative therapies for herself, she struggled to come to terms with family, community, God, and prayer.

I, too, was often impatient with the liturgy and its traditional metaphors for God. But as I used this framework for my own personal prayer week after week, it began to acquire patches of special meaning. Phrase by phrase, I began to see connections between my own life and what at first had seemed like an elaborate and distant language. Once, when I was embroiled in an investigative series that had engendered many enemies, I found myself fervently praying a line that I had once considered embarrassing and rather paranoid: "Save me from vicious people . . . from ruthless opponents and harsh judgments." I was discovering that one's best intentions can be distorted. I was learning how disturbing it is to be hated.

At one point I participated in a discussion about what kinds of prayers were permissible in Judaism. I learned that it was considered blasphemous—a prayer in vain—to ask God to bring back to life someone who had died; you could not ask God to reverse the laws of the universe for your sake. But you could ask God to give you the strength to deal with your losses, and you could ask God to help you find words that would comfort the bereaved. This is the kind of prayer I began to pray, and for me it worked.

As a medical reporter in Dayton, Ohio, my beat included mental hospitals. One day, walking down an alley, I heard a voice call my name. I confronted a vision in rags: a pale, lined face, wild eyes, unkempt hair, and trembling hands. Buried in that face I recognized a lovely young woman who, some months before, had helped me expose the horrifying conditions of the mental hospital where she had been locked up against her will. Now out of the hospital and off her psychiatric medication, she had become a pathetic, starving creature of the streets. Not knowing what to do, I said a quick silent prayer asking God to help me guide her toward the treatment she needed in a humane setting. I took a deep breath and began to speak with her. Crying, "Friend, friend," she took my hand and agreed to meet with me and a nurse I thought could help her. I don't know what happened to her in the long run, but I know that in dealing with her I found a strength, calm, and ability to act that seemed far beyond anything I was able to summon on my own.

I stopped praying for my life to change and started praying for the ability to change it. The strength I could find through prayer was quite different from anything I could achieve by exhorting myself; it seemed to function on a different level. Maybe prayer was just a neurological bypass around some of my psychological blocks, but it was such a powerful, transcendent, and renewing experience that I felt it would be ingratitude and blasphemy to try to rationalize it away. In prayer I seemed to gain access to the pool of the world's strength, drawing up what I needed for myself. I began to ask what I wanted to do with my life, eventually making a number of changes that resulted in a happier, richer, and more sustaining way of life.

Over the years, I learned more ways that Jewish prayer could help me achieve inner wholeness and healing. When I became engaged and moved to Canada to live with my fiancé, I found myself in a region where I knew no one, had no job, and had heavy new responsibilities in caring for his small children. I began to get up early every morning to say the daily prayers. Rising as dawn melted the dark, praising God who is "veiled in light as in a garment," I could almost sense the arm of God resting lightly on my shoulder, steadying and supporting me. The daily prayers were very different from the Sabbath service that had been my only exposure to Judaism. The daily prayers mirrored my daily concerns about having enough money to run our household, trying to act wisely in perplexing situations, and not taking offense when I felt wrongly accused. Sabbath became a day for praise only, a day when I gave both God and myself a rest from the struggle.

The dialogue with God continued throughout my day. As I would later learn Heschel counsels us to do, I instinctively brought my whole self to prayer. I opened myself before God, with all my hopes, fears, and questions. For six months, morning prayer and impromptu prayers throughout the day helped me to stay strong as my relationship with my fiancé began to crumble.

When the relationship ended, I felt as if I was experiencing a sickness of soul. I knew that I had to heal my anger at God as well as my anger at my former fiancé. I had met my fiancé on a retreat led by Rabbi Zalman Schachter, and I decided to talk to Zalman about what I could do to heal myself. "Praise God every day" was Zalman's prescription. I began praying as I jogged in the morning. Looking around, praising God for everything I saw and sensed, I became attuned to the multitudes of patterns of leaves and the way the wind moved them; and to the layers of sound, from the distant drone of an airplane or an insect to the nearby thud of my own feet. I began to realize in how many ways I was surrounded, supported by, cradled in blessings.

God began to exist again for me, not just as the remote and silent object of my entreaties but as the Presence who had breathed beauty and meaning into the world. I continued to argue with God (I, of course, having to supply the rejoinders as well as the complaints), but it was in a different context. Once again my heart began to thaw along with the weather, and I could see the butterflies that had been waiting to emerge all along.

Another few lines of the traditional prayers took on meaning for me: "With great mercy You bring the dead to life again. You support the fallen, heal the sick, free the captives." I had experienced what felt like a spiritual death and a resurrection. I had been a captive, bound in my depression as if in coils of rope, and now I felt free again. I no longer worried about whether I believed literally in the resurrection of the dead. I knew that in some important way the words were true, and that it was important for my spiritual health to affirm that every day.

CHAPTER 11

BEYOND FATHER AND KING

Reimagining God

When I began talking to God, I stumbled into a paradox. I believed the theology I had been taught in my Reform Jewish Sunday school: If there was a God, that God was beyond human imagination. But I could not continue the conversation without giving God a face. And that was a problem. The faces of God that I had inherited from my childhood—stern King or Judge, or even kindly Shepherd and Father—were not faces I could pray to. They were faces that made me feel trapped, paralyzed, and inadequate rather than capable, joyful, and blossoming. As a feminist living in post-Holocaust America, I would have to imagine a face of God that would affirm me as a woman, and empower me as a citizen rather than make me feel like a helpless subject. And I had to imagine a face of God that would somehow explain the enormous scale of suffering and injustice in the world. Jogging along the frozen highway early in the morning, with apologies to the actual God (whom I imagined not judging me, but looking on with tender sympathy), I put my imagination to work creating a God-face I could pray to.

From the beginning I assumed a loving God, perhaps because the glimmerings of God's Presence I had felt were loving glimmerings. Or perhaps it was because my parents (my first gods, I suppose) had been loving parents. Or perhaps it was because without the goal of encountering a loving God, I could not imagine embarking on this project. The first question I asked myself was this: How could a loving God not intervene in the world? How could God love and yet maintain a distance from the ones cared for? I answered from my own experience. My own mother was surely one of the most loving people I had ever known, yet here I was on the other side of the continent from her. Only in traveling this distance had I been able to find my career and become my own person. So perhaps the most loving, unselfish thing a parent could do was let the child go. A wise mother would know that it is impossible to develop the strengths you need for living unless you are responsible for yourself. It seemed to me that I could see that wisdom operating in the world. Muscles used become strong; character facing adversity learns to cope. Must the mighty Mother of the world therefore give her children freedom even to the point of allowing them to kill each other, to destroy as well as to create?

As soon as I asked the question, I felt my imagined God's pain. She must know us as intimately as herself. We were indeed parts of her; these winding mountains and valleys Her nerves and sinews. For one nation to slaughter another, even for one person to shame another, must be as if her hand chopped off its own finger. Yet in her wisdom, she knew that only the wounded hand could staunch its own blood. We could only become ourselves if we learned to govern ourselves, to heal ourselves.

From the gift of these thoughts and imaginings, almost like visions without shape, came the gift of being able to pray. A door opened through which I could pour my heart and feel that I was pouring it not into a void, or against an impenetrable wall, but into a receiving and sympathetic and responding Presence. I didn't always pray to that image of an infinite Mother, but when I was stuck, when I felt that prayer was absurd, a one-way shout, I could conjure her up and proceed again. Since that beginning, as my life has taken new turns and my relationship to Judaism has broadened and deepened, I have adopted from tradition and evolved from my experience new images, new names, new ways of sensing, opening, and feeling connected to God. The ability to imagine God, and so to reach for connection, is a gift God has given to human beings.

Having opened the door to prayer, I could search for the whole world of the sacred. That search quickly brought me back to Judaism, and to a dilemma. I needed a tradition, a familiar language of sacredness, a firm soil in which to root my growing relationship to God. But how could I say the familiar words *Melekh Ha-Olam* ("King of the World") without blocking out the maternal face that made it possible for me to pray?

I was fortunate that at the moment I was encountering Judaism, Judaism was encountering two movements—feminism and 1960s participatory democracy—that would enrich this traditional soil and make it a medium in which I, a barely sprouted seed of a twentieth-century Jew, could flourish.

When I moved to Washington, D.C., to participate in Fabrangen, I found a whole community that was actively struggling with how to imagine and relate to God. One focus of concern was names for God. Judaism has always known the power of names. Jews traditionally are forbidden to say the four-letter name of God, YHVH (made up of the Hebrew letters י, ה, ו, and ה), which is a form of the word meaning "to be." When God speaks from a burning bush and tells Moses to lead the children of Israel out of slavery in Egypt, Moses asks what name he should give for the God who has sent him. God tells Moses to say he has been sent by "I Am." In prayers the word *Adonai* ("Lord") is said whenever YHVH appears in the text.

The English word *Lord* and the Hebrew *Adonai* were troubling to members of Fabrangen. We saw equality between men and women as a matter of simple justice, a moral commitment. When we said, "Blessed be You, the God of Abraham, God of Isaac, and God of Jacob" (the three patriarchs regarded as founders of Judaism), we added the names of their wives: Sarah, Rebecca, Rachel and Leah. When we translated references to God, we tried to find gender-neutral names: Ruler instead of King, Parent instead of Father. For some of us, though, these changes weren't enough.

A small group of women began meeting to discuss the issue. We quickly realized that neutral translations weren't going to be sufficient to change the old-man-with-a-white-beard image of God we had all grown up with, an image that was jarring to us when we prayed. One member of our group wrote a short paper suggesting alternative names or ways to imagine God.

We were not the only ones struggling with the language of prayer. Two members of a women's prayer group at Brown University, Naomi Janowitz and Margaret Wenig (who later became a Reform rabbi), had written a prayerbook for women that transformed the male imagery in often surprising ways:

- "The Lord is my Mother, my Strength"
- "You alone, our Sovereign, will be exalted . . . in Your great womb we find love for us"
- "Lord our G-d, lay us down in peace. . . . Shelter us in the soft folds of Your skirt"[1]

Our ad hoc women's group talked about the idea of God as Queen. Though exhilarated by the imagery of a powerful female, we felt that simple female equivalents for male language wouldn't do. Within two years, however, a poet would dedicate herself to creating the new models of prayer that I and my friends were seeking.

The poet, Marcia Falk, was quite young (perhaps four years old) the first time she was told that God was neither male nor female, "that *he* had no body at all: *he* was beyond the limitations of gender." In Bible stories, prayers, and rabbinic commentaries or tales, "God was a character always referred to as 'he.'....As a child praying, I never envisioned a female God; that was unthinkable. . . . I would not have said, in so many words, 'God is a man,' because I knew that this was *conceptually* incorrect. Jews did not believe this. But I talked to him as though he were. . . . God was an extremely knowledgeable, very intelligent old man."[2]

As a young teenager Falk tried hard to really pray, but her attempt to have a personal, intense relationship with God was in a sense the beginning of the problem. "I was supposed to be like God, created in God's image, but He was always He and I was always she."

Her Jewish education had taught her to question and interpret. By her mid-teens Falk had rejected the traditional notion of God. She was searching for some other way to talk about the moments of holiness she felt walking in the woods or working at her art.

In the 1970s she did a new translation of the biblical book Song of Songs. The Song of Songs spoke in women's voices, "not reported by a male narrator, not filtered through a patriarchal lens." This work helped her find her voice as a poet "while reclaiming my history as a woman and as a Jew."[3]

But when she tried to translate the Psalms, Falk realized sadly that the Song of Songs was unique. Nowhere else in the Bible or any of the other ancient sources did women speak in their own voices. She decided she would have to contribute her own voice to the tradition. She began writing a unique kind of poetry— new blessings.

Falk says she was fortunate that at the moment she decided to embark on this project, there was a whole group of women writing and debating about how a feminist might address God in prayer. Many of the first people to try to alter God-language did so for political reasons. As feminist Judith Plaskow had written, having only male names for God subtly legitimates the idea that males are, and should be, in charge of the world. Falk felt that "if we are all created in the image of divinity, the images with which we point toward divinity must reflect us all."[4]

The words that begin the standard Hebrew blessings, *Adonai elohaynu melekh ha-olam* ("Lord our God, king of the world"), and the English word *God* have become "verbal idols," Falk said; they "have ceased to remind us that divinity is not really male, not really human at all."[5] She decided that the way to avoid such idolatry is to have a great many different images and names for God, and to remember that every name humans can invent is only a metaphor, a partial image rather than a literal truth.

Choosing the right language was tricky. God as Queen still suggested domination.[6] Shekhina ("the in-dwelling Presence of God"), which the Kabbalists had evoked as the feminine aspect of God, had connotations of being the consort or lesser aspect of God. But traditional Jewish sources were full of nonhuman, non-gendered metaphors for God, such as Rock of Israel and Tree of Life. Falk dreamed those metaphors into new blessings.

She worked for thirteen years on her *Book of Blessings*.[7] As she completed the blessings they circulated through the Jewish world, becoming part of the prayer life of many women and men. Gradually she stopped focusing on what she called "smashing the icons." Her new goal was to create alternative metaphors that express the sense of holiness of a person who does not believe in the traditional male God. Sometimes she even worries about using God-language at all. "So many people I know and respect have no use for God."

What is spirituality? muses Falk. "It's not a *what* out there. It's when you realize you're part of the greater whole. . . . When you really feel that, it just sweeps you off your feet. It's the source of compassion, ethics, justice—it's the insight that we really all are one. That if it hurts you, it hurts me, because I really am you, you really are me. We are one."

New language about God met with a lot of resistance at first. It sounded foreign, un-Jewish, to those familiar with the liturgy.

But within ten years, in many parts of the Jewish community, language that included women had come to seem like a matter of simple justice. Individual congregations rewrote the prayerbook, as did the Reconstructionist movement, whose new version lists a variety of options for addressing God.[8] The Reform movement re-issued its Haggadah with gender-neutral substitutions such as *Sovereign* for *King.*

Changes made for the sake of justice would end up having spiritual implications. They provided options for how people of the late twentieth century might credibly imagine God. Men as well as women came to new insights as a result of the questions raised about God-language. Arthur Waskow suggested using the name *Yah,* the first syllable of YHVH, to express the breath coursing through all of us, the sense that our being is part of the great I-Am.

The burgeoning numbers of monthly Rosh Hodesh groups helped put flesh on the bare bones of Jewish feminist theory. I met Lynn Gottlieb in Philadelphia at an unforgettable evening celebration of Rosh Hodesh Nisan, the beginning of the month in which Passover falls. Chanting in a penetrating voice with her flowing dress, bare supple arms, and long hair whipping back and forth like so many flags in a bracing breeze, Gottlieb, a student at the Jewish Theological Seminary, recreated the dance of triumph of Miriam and the Hebrew women after the escape from Egypt and crossing of the Red Sea.[9]

Andrea Cohen-Kiener, the hostess and organizer of the group, talked about Passover as the birthing of the Jewish people: coming out of Egypt, *mitzrayim,* the narrow place. The twelve or so women then formed two lines. Each of us in turn crawled through this symbolic birth canal, being massaged and helped along by all the women in the line—each woman reliving her birth as a Jew, and all of us together birthing our people.

That Rosh Hodesh group symbolizes to me the other side of the movement away from the male, personal God with which many of us had grown up. While some people, like Judith

Plaskow, were drawn to a very abstract idea of God as ground-of-being, others felt God as embodied in the world. Feeling the world as pulsing, alive with God, we created ritual on Rosh Hodesh to celebrate—to embody—that embodied God.

Because the Bible refers to God's dwelling with the Hebrew people in the wilderness, the later tradition gives the name *Shekhina*—from the root "to dwell"—to God's presence. Shekhina, says Gottlieb, is "She Who Dwells Within": God in each of us, God in and shining through the world.

If we wanted to nurture a Jewish women's spiritual idiom, to begin growing replacements for all the womanly flowers that had been weeded from the garden of our tradition, Rosh Hodesh groups gave us permission and opportunity to do so. At many Rosh Hodesh groups, there was a guided meditation or visualization. We began with a central symbol, rooted in the Jewish calendar. Each woman saw it in her own way, unfolded its meaning in her own way, and (if she wished) shared what she had seen. At Tu B'shvat, the birthday of the trees, we closed our eyes while each of us imagined herself as a tree. Our leader asked, "What kind of tree are you? Do birds sing in your branches? . . . How does your bark feel to the touch? What shape are your leaves? What kinds of fruits and flowers do you bear? As a tree . . . as a woman . . . what nourishment do your roots seek in the earth? What do you need to sustain you?"[10]

I found such exercises healing and centering. I experienced my life not as that of one isolated and transient individual, but as connected to the deep and timeless myths of the Jewish people and through them to the Source of All. Rosh Hodesh groups began creating rituals and ceremonies celebrating turning points in their lives as women (for example, a blessing for menstruation, and a celebration of weaning a child). Penina Adelman, one of the organizers of the Philadelphia group, gathered new rituals for the seasons and the life cycle into a book, *Miriam's Well,* that became a resource for the Rosh Hodesh movement. Rabbi Lynn Gottlieb, privately ordained by Reb Zalman Schachter-Shalomi and others, uses dance, chanting, drumming, and Shekhina-language to bring a mythic dimension to her congregation of artists and free spirits in Albuquerque, New Mexico.

From one small experiment, I learned what a powerful effect changing the language of prayer can have on one's spiritual life. In the Germantown minyan I heard my friend Susan Leviton using Marcia Falk's phrase *M'kor Khaim* ("Fountain of Life") in place of *Melekh Ha-Olam* ("King of the World"). As I incorporated this image of source or fountain into my prayer, I began to visualize power, life, light, and goodness flowing into the world and into me. Many times every day I return to that image of holy life flowing through me, and I am sustained by it. Why is the God-language we use important? In prayer, the name is a doorway: open if it's the right name, slammed shut if it's not. Calling a name of God (when I'm conscious of it, when I slow down enough so it's not on automatic, or when I use something other than the standard formula) is an act of reaching, at least for me.

Paradoxically, though, I have become less dependent on particular names. Over the years I am finding that every name of God is a word of prayer, and every word of prayer is a name of God.

My experience with prayers of praise has been so healing that I try most mornings to say the daily blessings for waking up, going to the bathroom, and washing my hands and face. When my son gives his clarion morning call from his bed, just before he jumps on me, I say the blessing thanking God for the rooster who knows the difference between night and day. I have come to feel that each story in Judaism and each blessing is a name of God. Each tells something about the ways we encounter or imagine God. God is the source of potential miracles—the one who, our story says, split the Red Sea. As I live with the miracles of a nurturing marriage after so many years of being alone, and bouncy children after so many years of infertility, I can understand that name. When I say the blessing for washing my hands in the morning, I have a very different image: of God as Mother, nagging me to wash my hands so I won't get sick. (Do I participate in God now that I do the same thing for my children? I think I do.)

When I say the blessing for the first steps of the day, the words of the blessing ("Who guides the steps of man") help me to see the steps of this day, and every day, as part of the larger pattern of my life. They help me to feel how much I have been guided, and to have faith that I will continue to be guided.

When I say the blessing for going to the bathroom, the words of the blessing teach me about the God of intricacy and design, the creator of "all the tubes and ducts of my body, for if even one of them should fail to function," I would die. And when I shiver with fear at that thought, the blessing teaches me reassuringly about God "the healer of all flesh."

When I say the blessing over the bread, I am aware that God does not literally draw the bread from the earth, as the blessing says. I try not to say the blessing automatically, but to slow myself down so that I see the process: the planting of the seeds; the rains; the first pale green sprouts; the grain growing tall and waving in the breeze; the kernels swelling; the giant combines scything it down, combing out the kernels, and spitting out the chaff; the milling and the powdery flour becoming dough; the rising and the baking; and the trucks on the highway bringing it to market. I see all those people, sweating in fields and bakeries, living their own struggling lives, linked in a chain of which they are hardly aware.

Recently, when I read how Arthur Waskow thinks about blessings in his book *Down to Earth Judaism: Food, Money, Sex and the Rest of Life,* I began to visualize the rest of the process: the food coming into me, being broken down and parceled out to my body, and becoming part of me in a process of miraculous complexity over which I exercise no control.[11] And then I visualized the energy, flowing in my blood to my brain, allowing me to dream these words, followed by the symphony of muscles, bone, and nerve signals—of which I am surely not the conductor—allowing my fingers to type them. After that it occurred to me to

think about the miracle of history that led to the planting, to humans discovering (how on earth could they imagine it?) that
hard-hulled grain could be milled and moistened and cooked
and eaten. Over the years of this mini-meditation, my name for
God is all these things, from the rain to the rolling trucks, from
the long-ago women with their grinding stones to my hands
typing on the keyboard—all are miracles. And that is only one of
my blessings, only one of my names for God.

CHAPTER 12

UNBINDING THE BOUNDARIES

Mysticism, Music, Moving, and Mixtures

S ome people never encounter holiness—or if they do, they don't notice. Or perhaps they are scared and look the other way. Holiness sneaks up on some people. That's how it's been for me: holding a hand of someone I love and finding holiness there, in my palm. For some people, though, holiness bursts over the head like a shower of light, saying, "Follow me."

As a teenager, Zalman Schachter lived with miracles. When the Vichy government took over Belgium and began collaborating with the Nazis, Zalman's family was sent to an internment camp. As Rosh Hashana approached, some people planned to hold a secret service in the bunker. Just before the holiday, young Zalman risked his life to sneak out of the camp about five in the morning and persuade a local butcher to give him two ram's horns. He drilled each with a wire hanger to make it into a *shofar*.

They were holding a secret service in their bunker, and Zalman had just blown the *shofar,* when the commander of the camp came in with his whip and an automatic. Reb Zalman tells the story, switching back and forth between the French he used then and the English he uses today:

> "What's this noise?" said [the commander].
>
> I said, "*C'est le cornet de notre liberation, monsieur le commandant.*"
>
> He said, "*Notre liberation?* Tootle it again." So I gave another blow. On the spot he pulls out a letter and reads the names of the people whose visas were waiting for them in the American embassy in Marseilles. Our family was on the list. . . . By Yom Kippur we were in Marseilles.[1]

When he got to New York and entered the Lubavitch yeshiva, Zalman quickly became notorious among his classmates. He was the one in the longest and whitest caftan on Shabbat, always sneaking off to a corner to meditate, trying to go the deepest, the farthest into the unknowable.

Years later Shefa Gold (then called Sherry Pelicrow) was sitting in the dark heat of a Native American sweatlodge, red glowing rocks in front of her and snow piled deep outside, with nine other people, all of them Jews by birth and none with a "living connection" to Judaism. After three hours of chanting and prayer, the dark and heat were so intense that she felt she would die. Suddenly, from her own mouth (and the mouths of the others) came a chant she hadn't heard in years: the Sh'ma, the affirmation of God's oneness. She realized how deeply she had buried her Jewishness, "and how much beauty it contained."[2]

In other eras and cultures, mystical experiences were signs of heavenly grace. But in materialist America, the only world accepted as real is the world of the senses. For insight into unseen worlds we turn to the priests of science, to electron microscopes, radio telescopes, and cyclotrons.

Like many Americans I had tended to dismiss most mystical claims as gimmickry or self-deception. When I began to interview modern mystics and their followers, I found people who were generally intelligent and thoughtful, but with a special thirst—a thirst for a direct experience of divinity. I didn't know what to make of them. I was drawn toward what they had experienced, but also scared, and very skeptical. To research this chapter, I had to experiment with mysticism. My experiments freshened my dusty spirit in a very extraordinary way; but they didn't erase my fear. I felt keenly that every crossing of the mystical boundary walks a thin edge between foolishness on one side and madness on the other.

Jewish tradition shares the same ambivalence. In the eighteenth century, when a wave of mystical enthusiasm—known as Hasidism—swept the common working Jews of eastern Europe, the rabbinic elite reacted with horror. These *Mitnagdim* ("opponents") won the day. In the Orthodox world of today, many of the descendants of the Hasidim look a lot like Mitnagdim, clinging to law and study and looking skeptically at those who press the boundaries of consciousness. There have been great mystics who were also great legal scholars. Joseph Karo (1488–1575), author of the *Shulkhan Arukh* ("Set Table"), the authoritative summary of Jewish law, was one of them. There has also been a great deal of concern to keep mysticism in its place. Referring to great sages exploring mystical practices, the Talmud says that four went into the garden: one died, one went mad, one became a heretic, and only one returned. The one who returned was the greatest of the scholars, Rabbi Akiva (Babylonian Talmud, tractate Hagigah, p. 14b). To be taught the Kabbalah, the medieval mystical Jewish tradition, you had to be male, a scholar, over forty, and married—established enough that you weren't likely to go off the deep end.

Because Judaism is a religion of law as well as of faith, perhaps more than any other religion it lives in the tension between fences and oceans—that is, between commandment and mystery. I wanted both. I was drawn toward the structure of rules, of prescribed daily, weekly, and monthly rituals, as an antidote to the chaos of unguided freedom in which I lived. But I had also sought religion because I needed an opening out of the material and rational into the realm of possibility. James Fowler, a Protestant scholar of the psychology of religion, says that young people go through a stage of debunking their parents' faith, but as they grow older they come to acknowledge that life is full of mystery and not everything can be rationally explained.[3] I had reached that point in my life. Jewish mysticism provided ways to express those feelings.

In dealing with mystics, I had three questions: First, how can one become open to holiness, and remain open despite the pressure of the mundane? Second, can one live with mystical openness, yet be grounded enough to know the difference between nonsense and greater sense? Third, can mystical experience nurture one's ability to fulfill the covenant, to be a better person, to bring a better world?

The havurah generation read about the passion and joy of the Hasidic movement in books like Heschel's *The Earth is the Lord's*. They wanted the joy, the passion, the transcending of the mundane, the direct connection to God—but not necessarily the strict adherence to law which anchored the Hasidim. The two most influential teachers of the new generation of Jewish mystics, Reb Zalman Schachter and Reb Shlomo Carlebach, were both European-born and well-marinated (as Zalman would put it) in the flavor of the Hasidic world. Their models were the charismatic rebbes, leaders of the various Hasidic sects. Though he appealed to young people with his trademark guitar and his joyful melodies composed in the Hasidic tradition, Shlomo remained committed till the end of his life (in 1994) to an Orthodox interpretation of Jewish law. Zalman in contrast, became an eclectic synthesizer. Both brought to a spiritually thirsting generation of young Jews what Zalman calls the "spiritual technology" of Hasidic tradition: the Hasidic story, with an aha! punch line that speaks to the heart; ecstatic singing and dancing; meditation; and the special counseling relationship of rabbi and disciple. Thus we learned to break the boundary of the mundane to glimpse the holy.

I learned the uncanny power of the Hasidic-type tale from Rabbi Jonathan Omer-Man, a British-born rabbi working at the Los Angeles Hillel Foundation to reach young Jews who had been involved in Eastern religion. The first thing I did when I started research for this book was attend a Shabbat retreat at which Omer-Man was to be the featured speaker. He came in very late and very rattled. There was an engine fire on his plane coming out of Los Angeles. The plane had limped back to Los Angeles on only one engine. He literally reviewed his life as smoke streamed by the window, and he had never prayed more fervently. Finally they landed. He caught another plane and came East. He grinned wearily and said, "You know us human beings. Once the crisis is over. . . ." And he told this story.

> Yankel, about to have a date with a wonderful woman, can't find his cufflinks. Hearing the honk of the car that is to pick him up for his date, he raises his arms—sleeves flapping—to heaven and cries out, "God, please help me find my cufflinks."
> He looks down, and there they are, right in front of him. He looks up to heaven and says, "Never mind, God, I found them myself."

From living with that story, I understand that the best Hasidic tales reverberate in one's consciousness. Dozens of times since that Shabbat retreat, I have found myself praying for something, having things turn out all right, and saying with a sheepish grin, "Let me give you the credit, God. Don't let me assume the cufflinks were right under my nose all along."

The grilled cheese sandwich I left under the broiler while I went out for an hour became a glowing ember and flakes of soot settled over the kitchen. But the house was still standing; the computer had not melted, and my notes and tapes for this book had not gone up in flames. Remembering the cufflink story, I thanked God and acknowledged that a minor miracle had taken place.

Shlomo's stories were often about reconciliation, said a man who participated in Shlomo's House of Love and Prayer in San

Francisco in the late 1960s. Twenty-five years later, in 1993, I came to Ruach, a June retreat in the Catskills led by Shlomo, with rabbis Meir Fund, David Zeller, and others. First there was Shabbos prayer with lots of singing. Then supper, very late, with more singing. We sang grace and cleared away the dishes. The singing grew more and more ecstatic until it erupted into dancing, which grew more and more spirited until people—arm in arm in boisterous, joyful chains—were leaping from one tabletop to another. Past midnight, a smaller group sat around a table while Shlomo, beaming in his silver vest and cloud of white curls, told story after story until nearly dawn. Because it was Shabbos, I couldn't write down the eight or ten stories he told that night: of reconciliations in the Soviet Union, in South America, of a son of a wronged man being repaid by the son of the sinner. But the story of "Reb Moishele Good Shabbos," from Shlomo's childhood in Europe, is typical.[4]

The story began in 1939, a year after the Germans had come into Austria. It was dangerous for Jews to walk on the streets—especially for Shlomo's father, the chief rabbi of Baden bei Wien, on the outskirts of Vienna. Early on Shabbos morning, Jews would slip to the Carlebach house to pray, racing through the prayers between 6:00 and 7:30 A.M. with the windows shut. Then along came Moishele Good Shabbos, singing "Good Shabbos, Good Shabbos" in a wonderful *niggun,* a melody no one could forget.

"He throws open the windows," recalled Shlomo, "saying, 'How can you tell the whole world "Remember the Sabbath Day" when the windows are closed?'

"So we say, 'Moishe, the people on the street want to kill us.' He says, 'You know, they're all our cousins—the children of uncle Esav [twin brother of Jacob, biblical patriarch from whom the Jews are descended]. Maybe if I would remind them of Shabbos, maybe they will stop killing us.'"

Moishele Good Shabbos was on Hitler's enemy list. There were posters all over to arrest him because he spent every night carrying food to the wives and children of men who had been arrested by the Nazis. But he promised Shlomo and his brother that he would visit them again. At four o'clock the next Wednesday morning he knocked seven times, said "Good Shabbos," took Shlomo and his brother by the hands, sang "*Tsur Yisrael*" ("Rock of Israel"), and left. That was the last Shlomo heard from Moishele Good Shabbos.

Many years later, Shlomo was in Israel, walking near the beach in Tel Aviv, when a man called out to him, "Aren't you Shlomo Carlebach from Baden bei Wien?"

This man was the neighbor of Moishele Good Shabbos. He told Shlomo that Moishe got false papers and was sitting on the train leaving Vienna when he said, "I just have to sing 'Good Shabbos' one more time, because I lived so long in this city." Some Nazis recognized him, took him off the train, and beat him to death in front of his two little children. "I swear to you that he didn't stop singing 'Good Shabbos' till the last moment of his life," the man told Shlomo.

Many more years later, in 1977, Shlomo was supposed to play at a bar mitzvah in Manchester, England, on a Sunday. As they were flying from Israel to London, the pilot suddenly announced that there was an airport workers' strike in London and the plane would land in Zurich, Switzerland, instead. It was Friday afternoon, not long before Shabbos; Shlomo, an Orthodox Jew, couldn't travel on Shabbos. Someone suggested he spend Shabbos in Antwerp, Belgium, where he could catch a boat across the channel to England early Sunday morning. He managed to get to Antwerp just before Shabbos. Walking down the street, he saw a young man who looked familiar. He invited the young man to come to his host's home the following evening for the singing and storytelling that end the Sabbath. In the midst of the singing, someone called out to the young man, "Hey, Lazer, do you remember your father's *niggun?*"

The young man turned out to be Moishele Good Shabbos's son. He was so tiny when his father was killed that he didn't even know his father had a special melody. So Shlomo was able to give this man his father's legacy, the beautiful Shabbos melody, and with it the story of his father's unquenchable spirit. He said to the young man, "You know something, I'm sure the whole airport strike was only so that I should come here and give you over your father's *niggun*."

As wonderful as Shlomo's stories were, it was through his music that he brought the passion and joy of Hasidism to our generation. Shlomo would start a story with a little melody, a refrain that would weave through the story, popping up between the sections until it burst forth at the very end, as in the story of Moishele Good Shabbos. The very essence of the story was there in that tune. In the introduction to his Shabbos songbook, Shlomo said, "The head reaches very high, but not as high as I want to reach, where every Jew wants to reach, where even the entire world wants to reach. Only music reaches there."

In our havurot, Shlomo's melodies, more than any others, were the ones that helped us bring our prayers alive. When I read in the newspaper that Shlomo had died, I went to the Jewish bookstore in our town and bought his Shabbos songbook. That Shabbos I sang the melodies to my children. In the introduction to the songbook, Shlomo says, "Please, sing with your children Friday night. Sing at home, sing in the street, sing under a tree, sing under the sky, and sing under the roof where your children are sleeping."

Some members of the havurah generation became disciples of Shlomo or another charismatic teacher. I was always wary of such a relationship. But I came closest with Reb Zalman.

Shortly after I came to Philadelphia in 1979, I walked into the crowded Hebrew-school classroom that served as the home of the Germantown minyan one Shabbat morning to find a man in a long, flowing robe conducting the minyan as if it were an orchestra. The 1960s were recent enough that the leather Birkenstock sandals and the thick gray beard curling over a cotton embroidered Indian caftan were nothing new to me. But I wasn't used to seeing these paired with the trappings of traditional Judaism: the long sidecurls (*payes*), prayer shawl (*tallis*), and skullcap (*yarmulke*). As we sat in a circle in our classroom chairs, he divided us up into three sections and had each sing one phrase—melody line, harmony, or bass—from a Beethoven sonata. He told us that we were to imagine our prayer group as a pipe organ, with all of us being pipes. While we breathed out our tune, he prayed the traditional wailing chant as a descant set against it. It was gimmicky, but breathtaking. For just a moment, I did feel that all of us were praying as one instrument, praying not from our talky heads or our needy psyches but straight from our joyful hearts. As we sang our phrase over and over, the music seemed to go on by itself, with me inside it. The moment was like a Zalman signature: beautiful, creative, eclectic, and definitely beyond the boundary of what one would expect to find in a Jewish service.

Zalman had been fascinated by mysticism since his youth. As a young teenager before World War II, Zalman sneered at religion. One day in Belgium when he was fourteen he walked into a storefront synagogue prepared to mock the service. Instead he was swept up into a community of young followers of Chabad, a mystical tradition founded by the first Lubavitcher Rebbe, Shneur Zalman of Lyady (1745–1813). In their workshop these young diamond-cutters shut out the whine of their drills by discussing Jewish mystical texts and existential novels with the aid of a microphone and earphones. When they decreed that Zalman wasn't mature enough to be introduced to the Lubavitch mystical text, the Tanya, he hid in the bathroom trying to overhear their discussion. He got caught and whacked, but it was worth it, he said. His goal became to live—and to teach others to live—like the diamond-cutters, fully and zestfully at the intersection between ancient mystery and modern life.

At the Lubavitch seminary in New York, Zalman became a passionate youthful missionary for Chabad. He would lure unaffiliated Brooklyn youngsters to Hebrew school with cakes, candies, and fascinating stories. Having come from the wreckage of Europe, it seemed to Zalman that in America only the Lubavitcher Rebbe, Joseph I. Schneerson, was aware of and talking about what was going on under Hitler. In 1943 the Rebbe hinted that the Messiah might come by the end of the year. The nineteen-year-old Zalman fully believed that the Messiah would come; indeed, he thought it likely that the Messiah would turn out to be the Lubavitcher Rebbe. When 1943 ended and Europe's ghettos continued to burn with no Messiah in sight, a small chink opened in Zalman's faith. But there was no dramatic renunciation. Instead he threw himself with renewed fervor into reclaiming what the Rebbe called the real diamonds: the young, unaffiliated Jews of the New York streets.

In 1945, at the age of twenty-one, Zalman was sent into the field to open up Lubavitch yeshivas in the outlying cities of Bridgeport, New Haven, and Rochester. He was married the next year, received his Lubavitch ordination the following year, and within four years had three children. His trajectory was that of a model young Orthodox rabbi.

But Zalman's move to the hinterlands (by Lubavitch standards) turned out to be an outward movement religiously and emotionally as well. He began reading psychological literature, which he felt would increase his effectiveness as a teacher. One day in the library in New Haven, Connecticut, he stumbled across a book about prayer by an Irish monk and discovered to his shock that it had insights and techniques that helped to deepen his own prayer life. He had thrown himself into the Lubavitch world with all the intensity of his nature, and for years it hadn't occurred to him that there could possibly be any valid spiritual insights outside Judaism. Now he remembered that what had originally attracted him to Chabad and Lubavitch was their ability to integrate mysticism and science, ancient and modern. When Rabbi Menachem Mendel Schneerson, a former teacher of Zalman's with an engineering degree from the Sorbonne, took over as Rebbe Zalman had had high hopes. But instead of opening out, the movement and the Rebbe seemed to him to be getting more conservative and turning more away from the world.

Just as passionately as he'd thrown himself into Orthodoxy, Zalman now began to read voraciously about other religions. His life moved into a new stage, one that might be called "the search for the cosmic keys." He was attempting to fuse technology and mysticism by discovering what he calls the technology of prayer, or "davenology." Zalman believes the techniques that help one connect to God are found in many different cultures. For example, Hasidim used *schnapps* (hard liquor) to loosen up and "get the spirit" during their *farbrangen* (a combination of study, party, and prayer meeting with their rebbe). Some Native Americans used mind-altering drugs like peyote as part of their "sacred technology" for connecting with God. When he went to a *farbrangen* and the Rebbe teasingly urged him to drink up so he would have a good meditation, Zalman took it as an omen that he was correct in pursuing his interest in psychedelics as an expander of the possibilities of prayer.

During the late 1950s and early 1960s, while serving as Hillel rabbi and professor of religion at the University of Manitoba in Canada, Zalman began exploring all sorts of spiritual paths and looking for peers and companions among the leading mystics in a wide variety of religions. He visited with Trappist monk Thomas Merton and accompanied the Latin mass at Gethsemane monastery with his own Hebrew prayers. In 1962, wearing his prayer shawl and *tefillin* (the leather straps and boxes containing Bible verses used by Orthodox men in weekday prayer), he prayed his way through an ecstatic LSD trip with Timothy Leary. The Lubavitch movement distanced itself from him after a reporter, seeing that he had given a talk on "the Kabbalah and LSD," called Lubavitch headquarters to see if the Rebbe had given Zalman permission to take LSD.[5]

Zalman has been inducted as a sheikh with the Sufis (New Age Moslems), sat in meditation with Zen masters, and smoked the peace pipe with Native American elders. He was invited to talk about Jewish mysticism at SwamiRama's Himalayan Institute. The Dalai Lama invited him to come to India (with a delegation of other rabbis and Jewish spiritual leaders, including Yitz and Blu Greenberg) to talk with Tibetan Buddhists about how a religious community might survive in exile. "I see myself as a Jewish practitioner of generic religion," he told an interviewer in 1983.[6]

This universalism, Zalman says, is a necessary development in Judaism. "People are afraid, sometimes, when I speak about a 'permeable Judaism' that we're going to be swallowed up. We're not going to be swallowed up! We're going to be healthy. Good membranes let stuff through both ways. I sweat and I breathe: Oxygen comes in and sweat comes out, and that's how I manage to survive."[7]

Sharing his synthesis with young Jewish searchers, he says, is like planting seeds and giving tools, empowering people to grow their own Jewish spiritual life. For his young college students in Canada and elsewhere, Zalman wrote *The First Step*, translating some of the techniques of Jewish mysticism into popular language. He began attending programs in group dynamics and incorporating the techniques of the transpersonal and humanistic psychology movements into his workshops for Jewish college students. He was invited to lead retreats at colleges throughout the United States.

In 1975 his workshop in Berkeley, California, gave birth to the Aquarian Minyan. Some of these young seekers, through psychedelic drugs or Eastern religion, had found a vision of a great unity underlying the world and wanted to connect that vision with their Jewish pasts. Zalman gave them a mystical skeleton of a Jewish service and invited them to put flesh and clothes on it. Each part of the service, he told them, represents a mode of worship: The first part, the Borchu ("Blessed is He," the call to prayer), is in the mode of creation; the second part, the Sh'ma ("Hear O Israel," the prayer affirming God's unity), is in the mode of revelation; and the third part, the standing prayer or Amidah, is in the redemptive mode. Then in each phase of the service, he invited them to share their experiences of creation, revelation, and redemption. All the experiences they had gathered could be brought home to Judaism and expressed in whatever way felt appropriate—through song, dance or movement, or meditation. They tried out each of these modes, then talked about their experience.

After the five-day workshop, a group of participants got together to talk about creating their own alternative Jewish community. Zalman came back and did a second workshop, five nights a week for four weeks, helping them solidify the tools they would need to create their own very special community of prayer. Though they were from the beginning (as Barry Barkin, one of the founding members, put it) "about the least organized an organization can be and still function," they have lasted for twenty years. Their all-day Shabbat service, which started with exercise-davening in the crystalline morning air of a mountainside park and ended at dusk around a warm fireplace in someone's living room, was among the least traditional and loveliest I attended while doing research for this book. One of their members, Yehudit Goldfarb, inspired by the Chinese spiritual exercise called t'ai chi, developed a series of movements in the shape of the Hebrew letters. I stretched through the fluid and stately gestures with her, our shadows etching the Hebrew letters on a sunny sidewalk.

In 1975 Zalman moved to Philadelphia to become a professor of religion at Temple University. He began the third phase of his evolution: consolidating his explorations, and attempting to create a New Age Jewish religious community. When he first began dreaming of and writing about this new type of community, while at the University of Manitoba, Zalman conceived of a kind of Jewish ashram where people would come together to work out the techniques for a twentieth-century Jewish mystical life. Envisioning it as a monastic community (in the days before women's liberation) he had thought it would be for men only, with women serving in auxiliary roles. Two blocks away from the synagogue where the Germantown minyan met, he bought a big, shabby three-story house with a wraparound veranda that was to be not only his home but the headquarters of the community. A handful of followers held services there with Zalman once a month. They called themselves B'nai Or ("Sons of Light"). Their main activity was retreats, held several times a year during the Jewish holidays at Fellowship Farm, an old farm turned retreat center outside Philadelphia.

On Simkhat Torah ("Rejoicing in the Law"), when the annual cycle of Torah readings begins again with Genesis, there was a ritual that became a B'nai Or tradition. We stood in a large circle on the grass, with the scroll of the Torah unrolled, and each of us supporting a section—a wonderful symbol that we, as a community, owned the Torah and were responsible for keeping it aloft. Then Zalman walked around the circle, reading a line from the section under each pair of hands to give each of us a personal Torah message for the year ahead.

I began to incorporate a few snippets from the B'nai Or approach into my life. At retreats, some of us would pray outdoors at sunrise, combining the morning prayers with dancelike motions. I began getting up early to do the morning prayers, relishing this quiet moment of connection and communion before the day's responsibilities. Later an article appeared in *New Menorah,* the B'nai Or journal, about doing the morning prayers with yoga exercises. I started combining the prayers with either yoga exercises or the West Point calisthenics program: for example, doing a buttocks–strengthening exercise while reciting the prayer thanking God for the healthy functioning of all the tubes and ducts of the body. It was wonderful! I could experience the prayers more fully, could *mean* them better when I was combining the words with body motions. (And exercising became emotionally refreshing rather than boring.)

Zalman's personal relationship to many of the people who

gathered around him was as important as his unique retreats. We havurahniks were fond of retelling the story of the Hasid who hid under his rebbe's bed so he could see how the rebbe tied his shoelaces. In our time we had not found a leader so holy and righteous that we would want to model ourselves on every detail of his life. But Zalman had something precious: an unquenchable zest for life. We tacitly hoped that by hanging around with him, we might "catch" it. Like him, we might learn to find in all experiences—even the most wretched, like the concentration camps—the possibility of liberation.

Zalman took very seriously the role of the Hasidic rebbe as spiritual counselor, having written a Ph.D. thesis on that relationship.[8] Lubavitchers, like some other parts of the Jewish mystical tradition, believed in reincarnation. When counseling a disciple the rebbe tried to look into the Hasid's soul, seeing him in the context of all his incarnations, in order to discern his life's task. He would then counsel not just about the immediate difficulty but about the trajectory of the Hasid's life.

Zalman did something similar for me. He knew I had decided, after breaking off my engagement and returning from Canada, to try to lift my depression by taking a trip to Israel. He called me to the side at a retreat one day and urged me to make the trip a mission of personal spiritual healing. These are the things he suggested I do:

- Take a trip to Rachel's tomb, wrap a red thread around the tomb (a tradition among religious Jews), and pray for a good marriage and children. ·
- Write a petition to God on a small piece of paper and tuck it into a crack in the Wailing Wall.
- Take a trip outside Safed to the grave of a rabbi who had died unmarried (where traditional Jews go to pray that they may be granted a marriage and children).
- Visit a Jerusalem healer named Colette.
- Give charity to each beggar I saw in Israel.

• Buy a prayer shawl for my future husband.
• Buy a wedding dress.

At first I was angry with Zalman for butting into my psychic space with unsolicited prescriptions. I had thought of my Israel trip as a carefree getaway, and he had transformed it into a heavy pilgrimage. But I trusted his perceptiveness, and I was at such a low that I decided to give the whole batch of suggestions a try. Thus it was that late in the afternoon of my second or third day in Israel, I found myself standing outside Colette's basement apartment in an outer suburb of Jerusalem. A tall, statuesque woman with silver hair piled high on her head, she looked rather like a witch because of her dress, a long black gown with some sort of gilded design. I hadn't been able to call ahead—she had no phone—so I explained that Zalman had sent me. "Oh, another depressed unmarried woman in her thirties," she said. "Zalman is always sending these to me. I can't see you today. Come back Thursday."

I was angry and humiliated. It had taken me three buses and most of the day to get there, and I was sure wild horses couldn't drag me back there again. But Israel can be a tough place. I had come with a whole notebook full of names of people to look up, not just from Zalman but from other friends. By Thursday I had been stood up at two meetings, treated like an unwelcome fifth wheel at the third, and had been unable to contact most of the rest. The one old friend I had reached was deeply depressed herself; she sent me out on a series of thankless errands and told me not to come back until next week. I had been in Israel half a week, had met no one, and felt utterly alone. So, muttering to myself that I had nothing else to do and it couldn't really hurt me to be made a fool of, I made my way back to Colette's door.

Another woman was standing outside in the morning sunshine. She was waiting for Colette's self-healing class. It turned out that her two-year-old child had been injured in a kibbutz accident. The medical treatment had been mishandled; the child had been through a series of tense and traumatic major surgeries and would be terribly handicapped for the rest of his life. She had been coming for several weeks to Colette's classes, learning to accept this reversal and get on with her life. Listening to her gentle voice detailing this story, I felt my own woes diminish. If this woman felt there was something valuable in Colette's class, I would stay and try it out.

In the dim apartment, a circle of women with their eyes closed described their visions. There were angels climbing stairs, flowers, and heavens opening. Their descriptions seemed too vivid to be real. They're making this up, I thought, and I can't do it; I see nothing. As I listened, I saw before my closed eyes nothing but a shapeless gray-green expanse. Just before it was my turn to speak, though, a shape began to emerge. When I spoke, I found myself describing an old, crumbling moss-covered wall, and clinging to it some old, dried roses as green and colorless as the wall. That was how I felt: moldy, useless, and withered of soul. But as I described my picture, I felt my spirits lift. I was sad, but the sadness had its symbol. I could see something in my shapeless mist, and what I saw had its own tentative beauty.

When I walked back down the hill to the bus stop, I was startled at how different the street looked. All the walls and apartments were golden, lit by the noon sunshine. Every house had a garden of bright, fragrant flowers and hovering butterflies. Children were shouting. Gardeners were listening to music on radios, or singing to themselves. How could all this have escaped my notice when I walked up the hill that morning?

Without my understanding how it had happened, the trip seemed to have become a spiritual voyage. More than ever before in my life, I was forced to confront my aloneness—and then to heal it.

By the end of my trip, I had traveled from one end of Israel to the other alone. I had visited Rachel's tomb, tucked a petition into the Wailing Wall, prayed at the tomb of the bachelor rabbi (on a luminous, flower-spangled meadow outside the ancient town of Safed), and given out handfuls of jingling charity in the winding stone streets of old Jerusalem.

I still had to buy a prayer shawl for the husband I would meet someday. I looked first in a row of shops just outside Mea She'arim, an ultra-Orthodox section of old Jerusalem. They asked me the size of the man I was buying for, and when I couldn't say and attempted to try it on myself, they ordered me out of the store. I was trudging up the hill to the YMCA to pack my bags when, just before closing time, I saw a beautiful, gently striped soft wool *tallis* in a window. When I finally did meet my husband a year later, it turned out to be just right for him. I had taken the first step, an act of faith in God and my own recovery.

Going to the airport the next morning, I realized I had never dealt with the hardest item on my list: Zalman had told me to buy my wedding dress. I checked in at the airport and learned I could postpone my return to a later flight. There wasn't time to go back to Jerusalem, so I wandered through the outdoor market near the Tel Aviv bus station. There were lots of expensive American-style satin dresses I couldn't imagine myself wearing. I was feeling more and more foolish, when, again just before closing time, I saw a lovely, unpretentious cotton and lace dress which felt like me. In my wallet was exactly the amount of cash I needed to pay for it.

At the airport I remembered that my friend Sheyna had asked me to bring her a menorah (a branched candlestick) from Israel. I saw one I liked, but it had human figures, Hasidim dancing. Sheyna was more religiously observant than I was, and I wasn't sure whether this menorah violated the prohibition against making graven images. I went into the little airport chapel. A group of cleaning men, their brooms propped against their chairs, were studying between shifts. In my halting Hebrew, I asked for their opinion. "A *sh'elah* [question]!" they exclaimed delightedly. They directed me to a row of plastic seats outside the chapel where I sat, reading my prayerbook, waiting for their answer. One of the cleaning men came out and sat beside me. "You should never miss an opportunity for study," he said, proffering a stack of prayerbooks that he had found left behind on airplanes. "What language do you speak? French? German? English? We will study together."

While we studied, a woman from the airline ticket counter came up and said my luggage tag had been written improperly, so I would have to transfer my suitcase myself in Zurich. I got angry. If they had noticed the tag was improperly written, I demanded, why couldn't they just rewrite it? After she left, my cleaning-man teacher gently chided me. "You should thank her, not berate her; without her, your suitcase would have been lost. She is a messenger, a *shaliach*. And I am a *shaliach*. Everyone you will meet in your life is a *shaliach*."

I felt as if I had been speaking with Elijah the prophet, who (according to Jewish tradition) comes in humble guise to test people's kindness and see if they are ready to receive the Messiah. From that moment on I began to see the messengers, in other people and in my experiences. Instead of judging and criticizing, I tried to ask: What is this person, or this moment, intended to teach me? In my new openness, I could see many times in my life where I was being taught, warned, or taken care of. The prayers that praise God for protecting and guiding us began to make sense to me. I no longer felt so alone.

When I got back to the States, I continued to use Colette's visualization technique. I went back to that crumbling wall I had seen in my mind's eye and found a paved-over garden, with just a few brave lines of grass struggling up through the cracks. As I jogged, I pictured myself chopping out the concrete with a jack-hammer one day, breaking up the hardened soil the next, then fertilizing it, planting it, and watering the vines until they clambered over the wall, covering it with brilliant flowers. I planted borders with rows of flavorful vegetables and young, flowering fruit trees. And I experienced the miracle of my own healing: I felt God close to me, pouring the healing through my own hands and eyes and heart, through my inner vision so that I would have the gift of believing in myself.

I recognized that healing my anger and despair was a sacred process. If I were ever to become the loving and giving person I wanted to be, the person Judaism taught me to be, I would have to heal myself. I realized that the roots of my anger were much deeper than one failed relationship. Like many people, I had stormy relationships with my parents, my bosses, my boyfriends. I felt as if these clashes were rooted in generations of anger. I remembered the line Art Green had asked me to think about for my bat mitzvah: Those who love God shall be fulfilled to the thousandth generation; those who hate God shall be fulfilled (or, as I had read it, made whole) in the third or the fourth generation. How many generations would it take before I and my descendants could heal this anger and become whole, at peace? Surely it was up to me to make a serious effort.

I read books about healing one's relationships. I wrote. As I jogged, I carried on imaginary conversations with the people I was angry at, and with God. I shouted about the hurts I was holding; I imagined loving responses, forgiving responses. As I worked on healing my relationships and the angry places inside me, I discovered that I was also healing my images of God. Even God the Ruler, God the Father, and God the Judge were no longer totally excluded from the pantheon of metaphors I used to draw an emotional connection between myself and God. Jogging and praising God, jogging and healing my anger—my two journeys were intimately bound up with one another.

The journey of healing is far from over. When I had children, I found myself fighting the same battles against anger and self-judgment I fought during that transforming year. But I don't think it's any accident that a year after my trip to Israel I met the man who became my husband.

While I was changing, B'nai Or was changing. Art Waskow moved to Philadelphia, merging his newsletter, *Menorah,* with the

B'nai Or journal to create *New Menorah*. His longtime friendship with Zalman deepened and became transforming for both of them. Waskow's politics became infused with a mystical vision; he spoke not only of justice but of wholeness. Zalman began to integrate Waskow's political perspective—the concern with ecology, peace, and justice—into his spiritual vision, conceiving of a planet alive with divinity but in need of healing. At a workshop for *Tikkun,* Michael Lerner's political magazine and would-be movement, Zalman said the era of peace and justice we are seeking will not come as long as we think "we" are right and "they" are wrong. It will not come until our politics is infused with the realization that all people, and the planet itself, are parts of a single organism; that we can only heal as one.

The feminist movement increasingly influenced the thinking of Zalman and his followers. One outward sign was a change of name from the male noun B'nai Or ("Brotherhood of Light") to the neutral P'nai Or ("Faces of Light").

P'nai Or was also changing as an organization. Gradually, Zalman collected around him a talented group of rabbinical students, psychotherapists, and others who applied their skills to developing creative Jewish rituals and took over more and more of the retreats. A series of executive directors was hired. This partial transfer of leadership crystallized when Zalman and his family went to Israel for a year, and the retreats went on without him. There were pluses and minuses to this transfer of power. There were some wonderful creative moments, and Zalman's energy was saved for some new directions. New projects were undertaken that Zalman didn't have the time or administrative ability to shepherd through alone.

But none of his disciples and assistants had Zalman's deep grounding in traditional Judaism. When Zalman played with the texture and format of the service, a knowledgeable person could always see the threads and parallels that connected the activities to the tradition. Some of the new retreats seemed to me like a disconnected series of pseudo-psychological exercises. Some-times I felt like a member of a drill team, being ordered to face left, face right, stretch, and march. In addition, Zalman himself blew hot and cold. There were times when his talks touched me to the marrow. At other times he seemed to wander, and I ques-tioned whether he still remembered what point he had intended to make.

My own situation had changed. My husband, from a more tra-ditional background, wasn't comfortable with the P'nai Or style. For a number of years I didn't go back to the retreats.

But P'nai Or was there when I needed it. Once, after the birth and death of a premature baby, when I had learned that I would not be able to bear any more children, I came to a retreat hoping to find in its free-form blend of prayer and gestalt psychology a healing that was eluding me in the traditional synagogue prayers. In one exercise, a woman who specialized in psychotherapy through visualization had us draw pictures of a part of our body we felt badly about. I drew a picture of my womb: gray, lumpy, and withered. Then she had us dance about the room with our picture, holding it up in the air and asking the Shekhina, the nur-turing feminine aspect of God, to send Her healing energy to our bodies and our souls. With our eyes closed, we were to picture those beams of energy transforming us—and I felt it, that healing golden warmth. Then we sat down and drew a new picture of the damaged body part; I took a pink crayon and drew a plump pink womb. When I went home I felt that a burden had lifted, and I was able to start the process of adoption that brought my husband and me our deeply loved daughter.

With my daughter's arrival, my spiritual life entered a new stage that took me even further away from P'nai Or. I was very busy with both my writing career and a new baby, and I was dis-tracted during services with child-chasing. Most of all, though, my heart seemed to be in a new place. I was happy being part of a community and anxious to contribute to it, but the yearning and loneliness that had fueled my earlier spiritual searches were gone. I neither believed nor disbelieved. I no longer had much sense of God's presence in my life, nor did it seem to matter.

Often during my life, the need for spiritual search had seemed to well up from within as my life turned in new directions. This time the impetus came from outside. My first book, on intermarriage, had introduced me to many Jews who were out of touch with their own spirituality. I could see (but they didn't seem to) that even if they didn't believe in God, they were deeply spiritual and very Jewish persons. They were committed to the sacredness of their task as parents, nourished by experiences in nature, fulfilling their deepest convictions through activist politics, or simply keeping alive their connection to the Jewish people through the books they read or their annual Passover seders.

I decided to write a book about the way that many Jews of uncertain faith were finding themselves spiritually nourished by Judaism. As part of my research I would have to go back to P'nai Or, where I had received so much spiritual nourishment. I discovered that since I had last been involved with P'nai Or, it had grown a great deal. Zalman's followers had started twelve new havurot following his eclectic model in places ranging from Ft. Lauderdale, Florida; Boulder, Colorado; and New York City to Amsterdam, Holland. Zalman himself was trying something new: a "mystery school" or "wisdom school," a yearlong series of monthly retreats at Fellowship Farm for serious New Age seekers. In March 1989, shortly after I began work on my new book, he agreed to let me attend a weekend.

Beside the old white barn that would double as a synagogue this weekend, a goat bleated, peering curiously through the fence when I arrived. A warm breeze tickled the white-garbed arrivals embracing in the parking lot. I stepped into a meeting hall and glimpsed in the corner shadows a man lying on his back, wrapped in a multicolored prayer shawl and meditating. As sunset turned to dusk, one end of the dining hall bloomed with forty or more flickering candles.

This was the fifth weekend of the school. Each month the group had focused on one or two books of the Hebrew Bible, seeing the text not only through the lens of traditional Jewish teaching but through the parallel prisms of many other faiths. Tentatively, the participants had explored the bridge back to their Jewish roots via Zen Buddhism, yoga, Sufism, and other mystical paths where they had been traveling, often for years. A show of hands indicated that in this group, more people had read the works of the yoga masters than had read the Hebrew Bible.

Zalman had traveled virtually every path represented in the group. He spoke their language. During this retreat he explained one idea through a Hasidic parable, the next by belting out a line of a gospel song ("Hey, Sinner Man"). He quoted from the Roman Catholic mass and told a story from the Babylonian Gilgamesh epic.

When we gathered for the Friday evening service, sitting cross-legged on the floor of the barn, Zalman told us our task for this weekend. Each of us was to build a sanctuary, a place in which to meet God. Zalman's co-teacher, Eve Ilsen, explained that as we studied the biblical book of Leviticus we would try to recapture the mindset, the awe and mystery of a culture and time when people really believed in holiness and impurity; when objects, actions, animals, and plants were either sacred or taboo; when the world throbbed with a sense of the power and presence of God.

Zalman said that the Hebrew word *mishkan* ("sanctuary"), though taken from the word for dwelling, contains the Hebrew word *ken* ("yes"). We are trying to build a place, he told us, not only where God can dwell but where we feel so safe, so loved, so embraced that we can say, "Yes, God. Now. Your way." For most humans it is too overwhelming to try to meet God in the open, he added. In reaching toward the cosmic, we would feel our boundaries dissolve; we would be annihilated. The sanctuary, with its walls and its intimate space, can help us feel the

Shekhina, the Presence, the One Who Dwells With Us or Within Us, the "yes-maker."

Throughout the weekend we were given various tasks, various experiments in achieving a sense of the holy, which were interspersed with sections of the traditional Jewish prayer service. In one of the most powerful experiments, we created a "sanctuary" from a large white silk parachute. The women gathered under its folds, veiled from the men, to recall the moments of life when they had most strongly felt a sense of holiness: rocking a child to sleep, or gently bathing the body of a mother who had died and was being prepared for burial. The conversation was both intimate and public; each woman spoke into a microphone so that everything could be heard by the men standing at a distance outside in a circle around us. Then the men, touched by the intimacy of the women's conversation, gathered under the parachute and talked in gentled voices about their own holiest moments, many of which were also quiet times with children. Afterward, many men said they had never before talked so personally in a group of men.

At Shabbat dinner, I talked with Shoshana. Raised in a very Orthodox Lubavitch family, she had always played the role of dutiful daughter. Her father died when she was a teenager and her mother had become increasingly stringent, even grim, afterward in her observance of the religious rules and prohibitions. Shoshana felt stifled. When she finally left home (despite the disapproval of her family, because she was not married), her repugnance toward the traditional wing of Judaism was so great that whenever she saw the black coat of an ultra-Orthodox Jew coming down the street toward her she felt compelled to cross to the other side of the street. Yet the stamp of her upbringing was strong. Though she never entered a synagogue, in her own apartment she continued to keep kosher, to observe the Sabbath, and to live an Orthodox Jewish life.

Shoshana had struggled for years, through dance therapy, to open herself emotionally and cast off some of the numbness she had felt ever since her father's death. The last year had been one of exhilarating breakthroughs. She had come to the "wisdom school" hoping that this warmth that was thawing out her spirit could be extended to her frozen relationship to Judaism. P'nai Or, however, was not an easy environment for her. To hear the Sabbath service pasted together like a patchwork quilt with bits from other traditions was jarring to her, as was seeing tape recorders, microphones, and electronic music used in casual violation of the traditional Sabbath laws. "I said to myself, is this paganism, or is it something real? I didn't know if I should stay," she said. But she did stay, because "I knew that they had something here I wanted and needed. I wanted the joy juice. I wanted to inject this joy juice into my dead Jewish life."

Like Shoshana, I found myself thinking a number of times during the weekend, "Is this paganism, or is it a more-alive, fresher brand of Judaism?"

The regular Wisdom School participants had been told to bring "sacred objects" from home with which to construct an altar. Many of them had some sort of altar at home: a Buddhist shrine, a yoga meditation corner, a Wiccan (witchcraft) ceremonial table—legacies from spiritual journeys that they were now seeking to integrate with their Jewish roots. The idea made me uneasy. It seemed perilously close to idolatry. Besides, I hadn't known about this altar-building assignment. I made a quick survey of my car and brought to the barn the only objects in it that I could remotely classify as holy to me: my two-year-old daughter's hairbrush and one of her scribbled drawings. I walked around the barn, looking at the collections of objects lovingly arrayed on low tables or colored cloths: photos of mountain retreats and spouses, sparkling faceted nuggets of colored quartz, holy texts and icons. I found myself touched by the struggles of these people to find inner peace, an experience of the divine.

When I came to my own little "altar," it suddenly hit me that these little tokens of my daughter really *were* holy to me because of my intense love for her. And in this midlife period, when I had felt very busy and not particularly spiritual, it occurred to me that my love for my daughter and my trust in my husband were the most intense experiences of God I had ever had. So in the midst of my skepticism and discomfort at this possible "idolatry," suddenly I learned something helpful and sustaining about my own spirit and faith.

After that weekend I no longer felt that my faith was in hibernation. Instead I saw it where it was: no longer in communal prayer but in the sanctuary I was building in my own home. Whenever I felt frustrated trying to hold down my little girl long enough to tame her curls, I would do what Zalman prescribed and take a "sanctuary break," remembering (as I pinned her down with my elbow) that all this wriggling energy comes from God.

The decade and a half that brought me from age thirty-five to fifty brought Zalman from fifty-five to seventy. He began to think about his spiritual legacy. He left the day-to-day running of P'nai Or to others and concentrated on being mentor to a new generation of rabbis. In addition to being a teacher of many rabbis ordained through the Reconstructionist Rabbinical College, he privately ordained many others. Among them were Michael Paley, the Havurat Shalom student who became chaplain of Columbia University; Lynn Gottlieb, the feminist dancer and storyteller; and Leah Novick, ordained at age fifty-five after a career in Democratic and feminist politics.

In Philadelphia, Reconstructionist rabbi Julie Greenberg started the Jewish Renewal Life Center, a New Age learning program, offering a year of study with Reb Zalman, Waskow, and other teachers. Students lived with actively Jewish families, participated in various experimental Jewish groups, and developed skills as Jewish community activists.

P'nai Or began holding national Kallot (weeklong intensive summer retreats) and reaching out to young people who hadn't yet been born during the mystical and political ferment of the 1960s. ALEPH was created as an umbrella organization for a variety of New Age groups spawned by Reb Zalman, Waskow, and their comrades. Elat Chayyim, the Jewish retreat center in Woodstock, New York, ran eclectic summer programs bringing together Zalman and his associates with feminists, healers, and teachers from Eastern spiritual disciplines.

Zalman began a program of "spiritual eldering" in which he taught people of retirement age how to reevaluate their lives, appreciate their spiritual strengths, and become mentors to a new generation. In doing his own life review, Zalman affirmed the experimenting he had done in the 1960s, even with what he now sees as some of its excesses. It was a time of real spiritual democracy, he said. He realized that "in order to feel free to move toward the future, there were ways I cut myself off from keeping alive connections from the past, because it was cumbersome. If you stay with people on the *frum* [Orthodox] side, they make claims on you, on your life, what you may or may not do. It was easier to cut oneself off from that community. I feel now that it would have been worth while to have kept something up of that connection."

In August 1991, three years before the Lubavitcher Rebbe's death, Zalman took his youngest son, Yotam, to meet the man who had once been his teacher. "I realized that we didn't have much time left. I wanted to see him and to be seen by him." They stood in a long line with Hasidim waiting to see the Rebbe. Zalman was dressed as usual in sandals "and a funky cap," wrote Seth Fishman, who drove him in.[9] "I wanted to say, 'This is who I am,'" said Zalman.

To each person in the line, the Rebbe gave a dollar bill to be used for charity. When he saw Zalman standing in front of him, he stopped in surprise and smiled. Zalman handed the Rebbe a copy of his book, *Spiritual Intimacy*, about the relationship between rebbe and Hasid, and asked for the Rebbe's blessing. The Rebbe handed Zalman not one but three dollar bills. He said, "The High Holidays are coming. You are a *Kohen* [a descendant of the priests of the ancient Temple]. You will be blessing the people. Keep me in mind also."

To Zalman, it seemed he was saying that "you had to go where you had to go, and that was okay. You were needed where you went, and I couldn't say go there. I threw you out of the nest, but I recognize you as my offspring."

The new generation of rabbis mentored by Zalman includes many who had a spiritual awakening outside of Judaism and then felt a need to connect it with their roots. Sheila Peltz Weinberg, influenced by Camp Ramah and the Conservative synagogue of her childhood, had staked her Jewish identity on emigrating to Israel and helping to build the land. But her husband hated being in Israel, and so they came back to Scranton, Pennsylvania. The failure of their plans was a devastating blow to Sheila. She took a job with the Jewish Community Relations Council, ran a conference about the Holocaust, and loved teaching about and working with Judaism. The rest of her life, though, felt disconnected and out of place; she had two small children, and her marriage was falling apart. While trying to figure out what to do with her life, she took a philosophy course from a teacher of the Gurdjieff path, and felt her heart open. In Israel, she and her husband had considered themselves secularists. Through her involvement in the Gurdjieff path, she began to feel that she was a spiritual person, destined to be a spiritual teacher.

But Sheila's Jewish identity was so strong she couldn't imagine being a teacher in any other spiritual tradition but Judaism. That meant she should become a rabbi, a career she had just learned was open to women. A friend told her about the Reconstructionist Rabbinical School in Philadelphia, which accepted unconventional students like herself. Leaving her husband, Sheila took her two small children and went to Philadelphia, where she encountered Reb Zalman, the Germantown minyan, and a world where her own special mix of Jewish identity and questing spirituality seemed perfectly at home. As a single mother she could not afford to stop working to go to school, so she got a job as director of Temple University Hillel Foundation and scraped by for seven years until she had accumulated enough savings to fulfill her dream. She completed rabbinical school and is now rabbi of a congregation in Amherst, Massachusetts.

All the time she inched toward her dream of becoming a rabbi, Sheila continued to explore other spiritual traditions. Zen Buddhism and the twelve-step path used by Alcoholics Anonymous, Overeaters Anonymous, and other self-help groups became the two most important supplements to Judaism in the recipe she created for her own spiritual sustenance. "What drove me to these paths?" she wrote in an article for the *Reconstructionist* magazine. "I always had a desire to change myself and the world, and to probe the nature of reality. . . . I was drawn because I sought a way of being that entailed less suffering, less angst, less fear."[10]

In Buddhist retreats Sheila met many Jews who had deserted Judaism. Buddhism offered them a powerful transforming meditative discipline, a sense of being connected to divinity without all the theological questions of good and evil, sexism, science versus religion, and authority versus autonomy posed by the traditional personal God of Judaism. Buddhism didn't have hanging over it the scars of authority struggles, boredom, and hypocrisy that many Jews associated with the religion of their childhoods. Nevertheless, Jews would always remain cultural outsiders in Buddhism. Their meditations helped many Jewish Buddhists realize that they would have to go home and make peace with their roots; their Buddhist teachers encouraged them to do so.

Weinberg began to ask herself if there was any way to bring the positive experiences she and others found in Buddhism into Judaism without threatening the continuity of Judaism. She personally felt so deeply Jewish that everything she learned through Buddhist meditation she immediately translated into Jewish terms. She thought her Buddhist meditation helped her to understand Jewish texts and practices more deeply. But Jews have had to struggle for so many centuries to maintain their way of life. Given today's rampant assimilation, any conscious borrowing or synthesizing from other religions is seen as a threat by the Jewish mainstream.

Weinberg asked herself: Is the integration of Buddhist and Jewish ideas a form of idolatry? She thought not. Jews have always borrowed, consciously or unconsciously, from the spiritual traditions of the cultures surrounding them. The second commandment, "You shall have no other gods before me," she says, "bids us to see how we make things into our gods and worship them. . . . In this culture—which worships money and glamor, the trendy, the passing and fleeting, the quick fix—which worships power and force, the false, the glossy, the clever—which venerates running away from the moment, deadening the pain, covering up—in this culture, we are called to repudiate all this as idolatry."[11]

Any spiritual path that could help people find a living connection with other people and the earth was the opposite of idolatry, she thought. "If a renewed, reconstructed Judaism can help us advance our capacity to root out idolatry from the midst of our hearts, I welcome it. . . . I hope to heed the voices warning me to respect the integrity of the tradition I have received. I know, too, that I am nurtured, healed, enlivened when I step beyond the gates of home and invite into my heart the beauty of spiritual openness, flowing from other doorways."[12]

Reconstructionist rabbi Shefa Gold says that the way she was taught about Judaism as a child "made me feel that Judaism was a great noble burden. That it put me in touch with the suffering of the world." Though it taught her compassion, "at some point in my life, I couldn't bear it any more, and I made a very conscious dedication to joy." Having participated in the rituals of other religions helped her to see more clearly the beauty and potential of her own Jewish tradition, she says. From her experiences with the sweat lodge ceremony, she had learned "the preciousness of all life and the fact of its inter-relatedness."[13] From Buddhist meditation, she learned "mindfulness . . . to experience the unique gift of this moment." The Jewish blessings that accompany so many actions of the day became occasions to use this practice of mindfulness. Shabbat became a day of mindfulness. From Buddhist meditation, she learned the skill of "letting go," which allows her to let go of weekday concerns on Shabbat, to stop doing and simply be.[14] Most recently, modeling on a Sufi practice, she has developed a chanting service in which participants focus deeply on just a few lines or words from a Jewish text.

While I was working on this chapter, Eve Penner Ilsen, who had been Zalman's partner in teaching the Wisdom School, became his fourth wife. Zalman was gracious enough to give me another interview just one week before the wedding, and I was invited to the celebration immediately after the ceremony. For many of us who attended, it was like that old TV show, "This Is Your Life," with a parade of characters from all the stages of our Jewish evolution. There were people I had known from the first B'nai Or retreats, people who had been my companions at the Germantown minyan and in New Jewish Agenda. There was Andi Cohn-Kiener, who had introduced me to Rosh Hodesh celebration, and Malka Goodman, who had taught me about mikveh. People I'd met at the Wisdom School were there as well. Barry Barkin from the Aquarian Minyan, in a silver vest that reminded me of Shlomo Carlebach, was master of ceremonies. There were people I'd been angry with and reconciled to, people I treasured and was treasured by.

Zalman, dressed in the white tunic worn at weddings and for burial, gathered us into a circle around him and Eve. Embracing us with his smile, he said he'd like to give us a small teaching. "Why does our text say, 'And you shall know the Lord *your* God?'" he asked. "In our prayers we say God of Abraham, God of Isaac, and God of Jacob. Why don't we just say, 'God of Abraham, Isaac, and Jacob'? Our sages say that's because Abraham's God is not the same as Isaac's God nor as Jacob's God. Each person must find God for him or her self. . . . I have tried to help you come to know *your* God."

CHAPTER 13

MEDITATION

Nothingness and Self

I f young American-born Jewish mystics like rabbis Larry Kushner and Mitchell Chefitz tried to act like rebbes, they would
be clones instead of originals. Kushner, Chefitz, and others draw
on the same legacy of Kabbalistic and Hasidic ideas as Zalman
and Shlomo, but they convey them in a very different idiom.
Kushner speaks with a dry, droll humor and writes in a cryptic,
poetic style, with metaphors from dream analysis and gestalt and
Jungian psychology.

If we want to encounter God in our experience, we have to be
aware, says Kushner. The burning bush was a test of Moses's attention span. If God had really wanted to grab Moses's attention,
He would have used a volcano instead of a burning bush. One
day, sitting in front of his fireplace, it struck Kushner: "Do you
know how long you have to watch kindling burning to notice
that it's not being consumed? Five to seven minutes. There could

252

be a miracle in your fireplace, and you probably wouldn't notice. God was trying to see if He was dealing with someone who could pay attention for five to ten minutes. With that kind of person, He could do business."

Kushner is reticent about the experiences that drew him toward a mystical path. But others of the new generation of mystical rabbis can point to a clear moment of spiritual awakening.

Mitch Chefitz was a rabbinical student at Reform Judaism's Hebrew Union College, struggling to write a thesis about the *Merkava* mystics, who wrote many of the prayers in the traditional Jewish prayerbook. He found their works impenetrable. Suddenly it became clear to him that the prayers were the coded record of a meditative journey. These mystics had found the chariot of God, the *Merkava,* at the deepest point of a descent into the depths of the psyche. If he were to understand them, he would have to follow. Reconstructing their mystical techniques from their writings and from close examination of the prayer texts, he began to try them out. It felt dangerous and exhilarating; it was the kind of spirit-opening journey for which one needed a guide. When he became a rabbi, he guided others who wished to journey.

Rami Shapiro was a teenager in the late 1960s, taking a course in Zen meditation. One day in meditation, he suddenly knew: it was all One. There was no it and me, no Rami and "out there." Individuality was illusion; the Oneness was Reality. He felt a great peace and sureness that has never left him. But he was Jewish, not Buddhist, he thought to himself. No problem. If this Oneness was reality, surely this is what Judaism, with its proclamation that God is One, was really all about. When he was a rabbi, he would be able to let people in on the secret. "Hasidism is Jewish Zen," Shapiro said. "To be totally awake to the ultimate Reality."

Shohama Weiner's daughters were preparing for bat mitzvah. Shohama felt guilty. She herself had abandoned the idea of God when she was a teenager. She hated going to synagogue. How could she hand the Torah to her daughter on the day of the bat mitzvah without being an utter hypocrite? Recently, while going through a midlife crisis, she had taken a course in meditation to learn how to relax. In doing so, she had encountered something unexpected: what felt to her like a living Divine Presence.

She made a bargain with this Presence. "It's possible You are there," she said. "I am willing to go to synagogue and pray with a prayerbook as if I'm talking to You. If You answer me, I'll keep doing it."

On the first day of Sukkot (the fall harvest holiday) in 1978 Weiner went to services, read the prayers, and suddenly felt that she had been heard. She decided to study for her own bat mitzvah so that she would be ready to hand the Torah to her daughter. During that Shabbat service she had made a true leap of faith, from being unsure whether there was a God to planning her life around what she thought was God's will for her. Four years later she entered the Academy for Jewish Religion, a rabbinical school. She is now its president.

Each of these rabbis felt the mystical encounter in a different way: Mitch Chefitz talks of a partnership with God, Shohama Weiner of receiving guidance, Rami Shapiro of a boundariless Oneness of all existence. Kushner says the theology that appeals to a given person is probably a matter of personality. Humans have two different needs, he says: a need to be individual and separate, and a need to merge. People who have a greater need for connection (and there may be more women than men in this category) may imagine an oceanic God in which all is contained, while people with a greater need to individuate (more men may fall into this category) may think of a mountaintop God who urges us to scale obstacles to move toward Him. People who imagine a mountain God may think God demands obedience and efforts of will. People who imagine an oceanic God may think it requires submerging of ego, a quieting of self, to become aware of the connection that is already there. Rami is a classic

proponent of the oceanic God, Mitch of the God we journey toward, the I–Thou God with whom we are in partnership.

In January 1990 I flew to Miami to spend time with Rami in
Congregation Beth Or and Mitch in the Havurah of Southwest
Florida. I jumped off the plane, snatched the keys to my rental
car, and roared down the highway trying to be on time for
Rami's Friday evening service. Suddenly I noticed the bumper
sticker on the car in front of me: "Are you looking for God in the
wrong places?" On my radio, a rabbi was intoning sonorously,
"Help us to see the bush that is burning in front of us."

Both Rami and Mitch are interested in meditation as a way to
see what is in front of us, or inside us. Near the end of the Shabbat service, the congregation bows "before the King of Kings."
Rami tells his congregation that these are our spiritual exercises,
our Jewish yoga: we are making ourselves flexible, ready to receive God's presence.

Mitch taught his havurah class in "practical mysticism" with a
light, wry touch. The night I attended he was teaching the technique of meditating on an object. It could be any object, he told
the class, plunking a white styrofoam cup onto the table to serve
as the focus of meditation. I found this informality reassuring.

The previous summer I had taken a class on Kabbalah with
Mitch at the Havurah Institute. I had found the guided meditation scary. At a certain point in the meditation I stopped, fearing
that if I went one step further I would come to nothingness—a
nothingness from which I might not emerge. Yet that is the point
of both the guided meditations Mitch leads and the sitting meditations Rami leads: to reach that nothingness. In an article titled
"The Boundariless Universe," Rami writes of molecules, atoms,
electrons, "the vast emptiness within" all things, balancing the
endless reaches of space, "the vast emptiness without."[1]

"You and I and all things exist at the tension point between
these two infinities," wrote Rami. "Better still: you and I are the
tension point between these two infinities. . . . We insist that the

emptiness within and the emptiness without are not real. We are real, and we create boundaries to prove it. . . . Yet Reality is otherwise: the relative and the absolute are themselves part of each other and a greater whole we call God."

One of the Kabbalists' names for God is Eyn Sof ("Without End"). A more radical name for God, says Hershe Matt's son Daniel Matt, a professor of Jewish mysticism, is Ayin ("Nothingness").[2] God tells Moses, you cannot see My face and live; you can only see My back, My attributes, what I do in the world. "The deep mystical stuff can't happen unless you are willing to die in that moment," says Zalman. "My sense was often that if I take another step in the direction of God, I will be wiped out. My counter-ploy to that was, so what. If I die in the moment of *dvekut* [of cleaving to God], that's not so bad."

I did not have the courage—or the foolhardiness—to step into that abyss, but I watched Mitch guide a traveler deeper and deeper. In that depth the traveler learned what she needed to know to make the next step in her spiritual journey, and then she came back. The descent, said Mitch in his thesis, is a trip first into the deepest self and then into the collective unconscious, or perhaps something more. It takes self-discipline and humility to make a safe descent and return. It is a process of confrontation so intense that some mystics spoke of fire issuing from one's flesh: confrontation, reconciliation, and eventually transformation.

Nothingness can be comforting rather than terrifying, says Rami. "Find the still point," Rami told people at the start of the fifteen-minute meditation that began one class. "You're not meditating to get somewhere; you're already there. But you're also there when you're brushing your teeth or scrambling eggs. . . . If you can really say nothing is happening, you'll be surprised what's happening."

New Age rabbis like Mitch, Zalman, and Rami were not the only ones teaching meditation as a Jewish path to God. Judaism abounds with meditation techniques, said the late Orthodox rabbi Aryeh Kaplan, who has collected them in several books.

But they have been lost in the modern era; he had to dig into obscure untranslated Hebrew texts to find them. Meditation is looked at askance by most of mainstream Judaism today. This is a serious loss to Judaism, said Kaplan: Up to 75 percent of the devotees in some ashrams are Jewish, and large numbers of Jews follow disciplines such as Transcendental Meditation. "Jews are by nature a spiritual people, and many Jews actively seek spiritual meaning in life, often on a mystical level."[3]

Meditation, said Mitch, is a way of turning your antenna toward God. "When you go to the no-place, you come back with your antenna changed. You come back with an understanding of God you never had before. You don't know how it got there. You get your head on more or less right, and God takes care of the rest. It's called grace."

Rami rewrites the traditional prayers to create evocative liturgies that speak to people's hearts. But for him personally, meditation rather than prayer provides the connection to God. Prayer is more a connection with history and culture, an evocation of feelings, than a central way of connecting to God. "I feel a different kind of intimacy [with God]; I feel absolutely connected to whatever God is, but I don't talk to it as I would something separate from me."

Rabbi Everett Gendler found his God-connection in nature. He liked to meditate on a tree, or on his own breathing, as a gift of the life force, *Chei Ha-Olamim* ("Life of the Worlds"). "I was not into other reality realms," he said. "Listen, here I am, there must be some reason, so let's live here." As a rabbi-farmer, he meditates "while working the soil, helping food grow, participating in the mystery of the seed."

He tries to help his congregation make the connection between their indoor world of prayer and the agricultural calendar from which Judaism sprang. By installing a skylight and solar power panels on the roof of the synagogue, they have allowed nature's light to light their congregation. Every year they plant grain, watching it grow taller during the period of the omer between Passover and Shavuot, then harvesting it. They celebrated the 28-year cycle of the sun with prayers on the beach, holding high a circular mandala. Like Alfred North Whitehead and Charles Hartshorne (with whom he had studied at the University of Chicago), Gendler thinks of divinity as a process, "becoming" rather than being.

In each community I visited I did my research as a participant-observer, trying to experience fully the world of each group I encountered. Letting myself be receptive to a variety of spiritual teachers was renewing. But when I began experiencing my own gift of the spirit, my own spontaneous inner imagery, I didn't know what to make of it at first.

In May 1989, shortly after I started research on this book, I attended a Memorial Day retreat of Achiyot Or ("Sisters of Light"), a feminist community. I had come to this retreat center in the Poconos to do research about feminist spirituality, not about mysticism. The first day we had focused on the experience of God within us. On the second day, however, we were sharing our experiences of God as transcendent, beyond us. I didn't really know if I had any experiences that would qualify. My workshop leader, Carol Rose, a big, ruddy woman from Winnipeg, led us on a guided meditation. I was frustrated because I couldn't see any of the things she was telling us to visualize. Then she told us to go outdoors for about twenty minutes, find a congenial spot, have a transcendent experience, pick up three objects that would symbolize the experience, and come back to share it.

Sure. Just go out, have a transcendent experience, and be back in twenty minutes. Well, I would try. I lay down on the grass in the warm sun in front of a low dome of branches like the skeleton for a Native American hogan. I closed my eyes and focused on the splashes of red painted on the insides of my eyelids by the spring sun. What happened next left me breathless. The red began to undulate like scarves waved by an exotic dancer, giving way to green and then brilliant purple, color after color. From within the colors I sensed a presence—one that was brilliant, female, and laughing at me. This divine presence, whom I sensed as powerful, creative, fecund, and amoral, invited me into a dance. I felt scared, but the presence answered my fear almost as if she was in conversation with me: "You're scared? I'll be as close or as distant as you like. This is for you."

I entered the dance, but without coming too close. My guide took me journeying. She displayed civilizations, carven images, tapestried patterns in wood and gold, intricate mosaics, and pagan images, flipping them in front of my eyes like so many cards in a deck or samples in a sheaf of wallpaper. Under her guidance I visited, in a series of dazzling images, long-ago times, distant lands, other planets. She said, not in so many words but with the arch smile of her presence, "This is my glory. And this is only the barest sample of the worlds upon worlds I could show you."

Somehow I knew that my half-hour was up; my divine guide brought me back. I descended into myself and opened my eyes. Looking around, I quickly found my symbols: a charred bit of rock from the campfire, a bit of metal melted and twisted from the heat, a flower.

When I went back to my group and told my story, I wondered aloud: Is this just my projection? Eyelid images gone wild? And if not, what do I do with the profound sense of a presence, a powerful divine presence, who isn't anything like what I have been taught of the Jewish God?

The group urged me not to repudiate my vision but to embrace it as a holy gift. For the next few weeks, I felt a residue of that presence almost as if she was floating in the air beside me. Almost as a way of keeping trust, I felt I had to say the blessings in the feminine, even though my Hebrew grammar was so bad that I didn't know what to say after *Brucha At Shekhina* ("Blessed are You, Divine Presence"). I felt as shy to talk about my experience as someone newly in love. When I couldn't sleep at night, I would invite the Presence and spend time with Her, letting the glorious and flaming images roil across the space between my closed eyelids and the Milky Way.

At the P'nai Or Kallah (weeklong retreat) later that summer, I went to a Friday night gathering of reverent atheists. It turned out that several people in the group, even though they did not believe in God, had gone through mystical experiences. They, too, urged me not to rationalize or repudiate my vision. Even if it were only my own imagination, it was still a holy gift, they said; it still had something to teach me. But what?

Later that summer I wrote in my journal, "I was feeling comfortable with a certain theological stance: I don't know if God exists, but I am spiritually nourished by acting as if He/She does. . . . My experience at Achiyot Or has called that whole status into question. On the one hand, I feel newly pressed to affirm a decision: Does God exist? Does a personal God exist? Or do I ascribe that experience to my being blessed with the ability to visualize—to 'trip' (without drugs)?" If I said this is just my imagination, I wouldn't have to do anything about the experience. But then I would be calling into question all of my previous religious feelings.

This vision also challenged my commitment to Jewish law and observance. "If God presents Herself to me as delighting, as fertile, as joyous, and loving those qualities in me," I wrote, "then when I'm faced with the choice of following strict niddah [abstaining from sex during the week following the menstrual period] or having one more love-making with my husband before going away on a trip, I summon my experience of Shekhina and it becomes obvious that I am to make love. Further, it seems that niddah and other aspects of the law are a man-made structure that shackles, rather than liberates. So I find myself increasingly impatient—with the endlessness of Shabbat morning services (though at other times I've found them rich), with the minutiae of keeping kosher, with the we've-found-the-true-answer attitude of some of the observant. The very structure of communal prayer doesn't allow opportunity for the kind of God-experience I've had, and posits a very different kind of God. Teshuvah [repentance] seems onerous and heavy and life-denying."

At the same time I felt that praying to Shekhina—to a feminine, immanent presence of God—was as narrow and partial as the patriarchal image. Was staying with this vision a kind of idolatry, like the *Asherot* (the Canaanite fertility goddesses), taking one aspect of God for the whole?

When I visited Mitch in Florida, I asked if he could help me interpret the vision. He suggested I read the biblical chapters on Ezekiel's vision. I noticed that the language was all "as ifs," seeming to imply that the mystical experience itself was a symbol, a messenger pointing not to itself but to something beyond itself. Even though I usually shied away from Kabbalistic terminology, not feeling that I understood it or was comfortable with it, I began to think of the words *tiferet* (beauty), and *hod* (praise) from the Kabbalistic list of the attributes of God. Perhaps God was letting me know that my images of God as source of morality, of caring Parent, even as Creator, were only a small part of it all— that God was not only the Creator of beauty, but *was* beauty, *was* glory. And I, too, embodied these attributes. After all, my name was Yehudit ("God's praise").

Once I had crossed the threshold of visionary experience, I could open myself to such experiences whenever I had sufficient solitude to meditate, especially when I could go outdoors. I found it increasingly easy to integrate these experiences into my Jewish life and my Jewish concept of God. At Carlebach's Ruach retreat, I meditated outdoors at sunrise before Shabbat services. I felt infused with and carried on a rippling banner of golden light out across the forest—a wonderful preparation to feeling I was praying in the presence of a luminous and benevolent love.

From my own struggles I realized that mystical experience, which uses the pathways of the deep unconscious mind, doesn't necessarily follow the images prescribed by religious dogma. It can be hard to integrate mystical experience into an established religious framework, hard to tell the difference between revealed truth and the private symbolism of one's own mind.

From reading Kushner's books, I got a new perspective on

why traditional Judaism reserved learning about mysticism for people (men, actually) over forty. When I first read Kushner's *Honey from the Rock* nearly fifteen years ago, it didn't speak to me; it seemed like a series of disconnected musings. When I reread it as part of the research for my book, however, it made sense. His observations reflected and confirmed my experience: that we have to go into the wilderness in order to become open, to become ready to receive; that openness itself is a wilderness (of course); that there are entrances to holiness everywhere, and messengers; and that "the hands of heaven" are always guiding us. Having learned these things on my trip to Israel, I could read what Kushner wrote and nod my head in understanding. Perhaps you can only learn what you already know.[4]

But you can learn it in a new way. One of the most troubling things in my spiritual search was the sense of paradox. When I thanked God for my blessings, I always found myself adding a postscript: I am blessed, but so many people suffer. I feel You existing in my life, permeating my life, but that's only my projection because I feel so blessed. You can't really exist, because if You did, there wouldn't be so much suffering; or, if You exist, You have no power. You either can't listen, can't act, or don't care. The duality that I had tried to resolve as a mental construct when I first began to pray came back forcefully now that I was really feeling God as a presence in my life.

This was even more true after Steve and I lost two babies in the second trimester of pregnancy. I'd held those doomed babies—looking like tiny mirror images of my husband—while they gasped vainly for breath. I argued with God: That's the way it is, I said, with all your creation. You let us have it, glimpse it, and then snatch it away. You tell each of us we must make some kind of bargain with you, what we will win and what we will lose. Was God then less of a real presence? No, but I felt less loving concern, more brilliance and beauty and paradox. I thought the pagans or Hindus had something, in envisioning fertility and destructiveness as intimately connected. Caring, erotic fecundity, and destruction were all aspects of the same power, but we humans, encountering them a facet at a time, might find it awfully hard to understand how and why one God might do all this. My husband gave me *When Bad Things Happen to Good People,* the book that Rabbi Harold Kushner wrote after his son died of a disfiguring genetic disease. Sometimes I embraced Kushner's notion of a loving but limited God who weeps with us but cannot change the natural order. Sometimes I was just mad.

I talked with Zalman about how this "Yes, but" attitude interfered with my prayers. He said, "If you only criticize God when you pray, then it's probably something you do to keep yourself from praying." I thought about it, and what he said was true. Yet books by the other Kushner, Rabbi Larry, affirmed that what I was feeling was true, too. Paradox, duality, intertwined good and evil—these are the essence of reality. That is the mystery we confront when we affirm, in spite of it all, that God is one. As I write this, I realize my personal visions have also taught me, to put it quite simply, that there is more. Beyond my preconceptions, beyond my imaginings, beyond what I have been taught or could possibly have been taught, there is more.

As I wrote this chapter I asked myself, "What was I supposed to learn from Rami and Mitch and Zalman?" If in my life they were messengers, what was the message? Perhaps it was playfulness, a certain lightness or sense of humor in relating both to the tradition and to the search for God. "As long as you think you're on a serious spiritual quest, there's no hope," says Rami. "Humor is the only way to wake up."

An obvious question remained: Were these visions gifts, evidence (however difficult to interpret) of some greater spiritual dimension in the cosmos, or just a mind game I was getting good at? To trust them seemed like self-indulgence or solipsism. But to dismiss them seemed like a tacit decision that, beyond being grateful for the comforts of our lives, human connection to and experience of God was impossible. And yet if I accepted my nonmaterial experience as real, what were the boundaries?

Who could know the difference between heavenly guidance and craziness?

I posed this last question to Shohama, because she seemed to have come to a point of being reasonably sane and grounded after experiences that in large parts of our culture would be dismissed as insanity. In deep moments of prayer or meditation Shohama began to experience guides, which she interpreted as manifestations of God, or angels. Though some great rabbis of former eras described experiences with guides, it took faith in oneself and in God to cultivate such visions in late twentieth-century America.[5] Studying Kabbalah with Zalman helped validate her mystical experience. She trusted her visions. In her day-to-day work as dean of a rabbinical school, she kept quiet about them.

How does she explain her varied visions of God? "I'm enough of a Kabbalist to know God is 'Eyn Sof'—without end, beyond knowing. But God is revealed to us in ways we can apprehend. Since I treasure intimacy in all my relationships, God comes to me in an intimate way.

"When I get a spiritual message, I ask, does this make sense? If [the message had] told me to go to China, I wouldn't have gone. When I go with the guidance, I get tremendous strength, courage, joy, and success. Things work out well. When I came to the Academy, there were five faculty and eight students; now we have thirty faculty and fifty students. How do you judge [whether] someone [is] spiritual [or] loony? See how it manifests in their life work."

I had started my research for this chapter in 1989 with a little book of Zalman's, "A First Step," which is part of the first *Jewish Catalog*. It is a small group of spiritual disciplines, Hasidic meditations to do just before bed at night and on rising in the morning. In January 1995, as I was completing my research, I picked up the book and tried out Zalman's suggestions again. Sitting in my office with a typewritten copy of the instructions on my lap, I began. (I was trying to be a participant-observer, but could I really meditate and take notes about it?)

In "A First Step" Zalman suggests you start by "placing yourself in God's presence."[6] Elsewhere I had read that one must begin prayer by knowing before Whom you stand. How could I truly feel myself in God's presence? Truly know before Whom I stand? My mind moved from speculation to prayer: "If You are the Source of All and My Source, what does that mean?" I imagine the burst of light from the Big Bang, bright beyond brightness, coalescing into stars and planets—shells (as the Kabbalists put it) for that great light and heat, still coursing outward—and gradually the condensing of seas, the swirling beginnings of life, sea creatures, grasses, all flowing outward from You. I see one-celled animals dividing, corals and sponges multiplying, fish spawning, and then something radically different: In a grove somewhere, a deer licks its fawn. Now there is tenderness, nurture, the possibility of loss and grief. So of course when humans begin to care for their babies and teach them, the still-flowing Source is present and delighting. History unrolls. There are Jews, holding their children on their laps, feeding and teaching them. There are my parents loving and teaching me. When I see it this way, how could I doubt that You, my Source, love me? Loving is the fulfillment of all this flow. This is before Whom I stand.

As I do this meditation, in my lap I have two pages on which I have typed Zalman's outline of the service according to the mystical four worlds or four levels of being (derived from the four letters of God's name). The first part of the service, rooted in the physical world and the body, I have already felt in this meditation—God's creation flowing through me, in my muscles (I stretch), in my breathing. Now, as Zalman suggests, I try to breathe while visualizing the Hebrew letters of God's name. I chuckle at this crazy balancing act, of trying to visualize the letters of God's name superimposed on my body, the breath flowing into and out of my head (*yud*, י), my shoulders and arms (*hey*, ה),

my trunk (*vav*, ו), hips and legs (*hey*, ה). As I do this, I can feel the divine energy flowing through me, creating and recreating me, illumining me. My body tingles with light. Now I am to go on to the emotional part of the prayer, and I realize that I have already been there, too. I have despaired and asked how a person so full of anger could be lovable, and then realized: You are my Source; of course you love me!

The second page on my lap is Zalman's interpretation of the Amidah, the standing prayer that is the heart of the Jewish service. It's almost with regret that I touch back down to earth to follow the structure of the Amidah. When I do, however, there are new riches to be found. The prayer begins, "God of Abraham, God of Isaac, God of Jacob"; Zalman suggests I "recognize the chain that connects you to your ancestors." I have been seeing that chain. Now, though, I suddenly get a new insight on the Torah portion I wrestled with during my bat mitzvah. Art Green asked me to figure out why it says that those who love God are fulfilled to the thousandth generation, and those that hate God to the third and fourth generation. In the unfolding love of generations of families, parent to child and parent to child, I see that fulfillment to the thousandth generation. The anger that I struggle with—the anger that I would like to put to rest in my lifetime and not pass on to my children—is only a puny matter of three or four generations; it will pass. It pales beside this history of love.

I glance down at Zalman's outline again. Now I am to ask for what I need, beginning with the wisdom to know what I need. God, you know what I need: to overcome this anger, to live in your image of restraint and kindness and unconditional love. The prayer anticipates my feeling of "Who the hell am I to ask for this?" and I pray to feel worthy of prayer—to be forgiven, to be forgiving, to feel worthy of forgiveness, to forgive myself. I see that it is a sin to destroy even one cell, by my anger, of the self-esteem that will allow my children to know that they are in the image of God. Zalman's prayer-outline puts into words my thoughts and feelings: "It is such a struggle to live. I have so many things that are sick inside me."

Sitting in front of my computer in my paper-littered office, I have bared my heart. I have done a *teshuvah,* a turning, as deep as any in my thirty-five years of Yom Kippur fasts. I feel a great healing.

I realize that, as Rabbi Shefa Gold has said, my true spiritual growth comes when I refuse to be bound by either-or choices and instead seek my own path. Whether God truly exists or doesn't exist, whether the mystical experiences are windows into a greater reality or absurd, these are not the essential questions. But what is my path? I realize my path is to find and affirm unity, in God and in myself. It is to use whatever tools I find, in the mystical tradition and outside it, to bring wholeness in the world and in my heart.

The Kabbalists said the Messiah would come when the *Kadosh Baruch Hu* ("Holy Blessed transcendent God") was reunited with the *Shekhina* (God's presence in the world). I find myself taking the Sh'ma, the declaration of God's unity, as a challenge. I see dualities, trinities, separations everywhere and try to imagine how they all fit together. When I say the blessing "*Barukh Atah Adonai, Elohaynu, Melekh Ha-Olam,*" I imagine *Adonai* as the God of Earth, of Foundations, of all that is dependable in my life. I imagine Adonai my Master-Teacher,[7] the source of my morality and my private struggle to be a good person. I imagine *Elohaynu,* Our God, the God we encounter and seek together in community. I imagine *Melekh Ha-Olam,* King of the Universe, who spun out the vast reaches of the cosmos and created the intricate framework of natural law, the music of the spheres by which stars spin. And I know all these images, these names of God are inseparably one. In the Sh'ma itself, with its threefold repetition of names, I hear the same trinity, and as I acknowledge its unity I chuckle, noticing that my attempt to enter more deeply into my own people's language has helped me to be more understanding of the Christian language of trinity. Perhaps, despite the centuries of animosity, the fragments in which they seek unity are not so different from ours.

That night at bedtime, I try the second step in the prayer process Zalman has prescribed: an accounting of the soul, *Heshbon HaNefesh*. I am supposed to forgive completely anyone who has wronged me and pray for that person's welfare. I must affirm God's oneness, affirm my longing to love God, and read the Sh'ma. I must review the actions of my day and ask God to heal me. Again, therefore I must confront my anger. This time I encounter a trinity of angers, a trinity of forgiveness. I have to forgive my son for throwing tantrums, both mirroring my anger and provoking it; to forgive myself for becoming angry; and to forgive everyone who has been angry at me. (Which means understanding that they are angry in part because people have been angry at them. How far back does this go? To Cain and Abel in the Bible?)

Lying in my bed, I cast about for a way to make this forgiveness real. I remember Shohama telling me that when she worked to help people overcome their anger, she would focus a beam of the light of Shekhina all around them. At this point in our interview, I thought to myself, "What nerve! To imagine that any person could focus a beam of Shekhina on another. I don't believe this!" Now I realize that whether I believe this or not, I can do it. So on some level it is real. I imagine beams of loving Shekhina-light flowing down upon my son, my parents, and myself. I wish us all a good sleep, a peaceful night.

The next morning, when my son starts working up to his tantrum, I try to imagine the same Shekhina-light, the arms of Shekhina surrounding him. I suddenly realize that instead of trying to argue or scold him out of his anger, I should embrace him. My arms are the arms of Shekhina.

It's just one moment of insight; it doesn't solve the problem forever. But for that moment, I too am standing in the light.

CHAPTER 14

PUTTING IT ALL TOGETHER
—FOR NOW

When I went back to college for my twentieth reunion in 1986, there were T-shirts on sale that said, "Don't trust anyone over 30 [crossed out], 40 [crossed out], 50." Just after I finished writing this book, I crossed off the last number on the shirt and replaced it with a question mark. Even at the half-century, I feel as if a lot of my life, particularly my spiritual life, is an experiment. And that feels quite lovely.

Reb Zalman says that because twentieth-century life is so full of changes, people in our time need a bar or bat mitzvah every thirteen years. I didn't plan it that way, but that's how it turned out for me.

During my childhood years in a Reform Sunday school, I got an infusion of the Bible stories that can serve as metaphors and frameworks for understanding one's adult life. Then there was a hiatus in my learning. Having not had a bat mitzvah at age twelve or thirteen, I had one at age thirty-six. Thirteen years later, after several years of preliminary interviewing and writing, I began work on this book. So it happened that in the fiftieth year of my life, I had the opportunity to stop and reflect on what it means to be a postmodern Jew and how I (and we) got here.

I did my research as a participant-observer. I kept a journal, and in it I reflected on my twenty years of experiments with Judaism, as well as the experiments of this spiritually tumultuous year. Looking back, I could see that I have grown not only in knowledge of prayers, texts, and traditions, but in how I experience my life as a Jew. When I started with the havurah in Dayton, I loved Shabbat as a day of community in what had been a lonely life, as a day of poetry after a week of prose. Gradually it became a day of being imbedded in the cycle of Jewish time and Jewish history. After I had children, it became a day when Mommy got to take a nap. Shabbat gave me a chance to start over, refreshed and whole, able to be the kind of Mom I wanted to be.

Even after twenty years of observing it, I keep discovering new meanings of Shabbat. Only during the writing of this book did the discipline, the restrictions of Shabbat observance, begin to take on spiritual meaning for me.

The Shabbat before the manuscript of this book was due, I found it extremely difficult mentally to hang up on my work for a day. I was so close to my deadline, so close to the end of the project, and had worked such long and intensive hours in the last few weeks that I felt like a juggernaut. It was hard for me to slow down, but I willed myself to let go and stop thinking about all this. And then the Shabbat magic occurred: As soon as I stopped trying to think and worry, I saw the whole structure of the book (in fact, the whole structure of modern American Jewish history and how my book fit into it!) in one glorious panorama. Of course, I couldn't write it down, because it was Shabbat.

It was so hard for me to slow down that particular weekend that I had to stop and ask: What is Shabbat all about for me anyway? I realized that for me the essential quality of Shabbat is taking time out for a meeting with God. An agnostic might call it a meeting with the deepest level of oneself, a reconnection with the deeper meanings of life. And how had I come to understand the way Shabbat heightens my awareness of God's presence? In part through trivial experiments with Shabbat restrictions: using liquid soap and not tearing toilet paper—and suddenly realizing that there was not a single activity, not a second of the day, when I was not in the presence of God.

I check in with God a dozen times every day—when I get up in the morning, when I eat, when I laugh with delight at my children's bouncing walks, or when I cast out a quick prayer not to lose patience with their whining or insolence. But I need a meeting of a different order. It's like my husband Steve and me: We see each other every day, we sleep together, we hug and talk each night, and these elements are really the essence of the relationship, the times when things flow and we pass easily into humor and companionship. But when we make love, there's another kind of meeting. In the sharing of that heightened sensibility, we symbolize the deep commitment, trust, tenderness, and wonder that underlies those everyday conversations. In a sense, we are affirming the foundation under our love. Shabbat plays the same role in my relationship to God.

Prayer was another aspect of Jewish life that had grown from the barest wisp of a plant into a luxuriant vine with tendrils in every corner of my consciousness. I began my journey by trying to construct an image of God I could pray to. Years of saying blessings transformed my vision. I began to see the image of God everywhere, not only in the physical blessings of blue sky and trees, the order and vastness of the universe, but flowing through all my experience: the love of friends and family, the "Aha!" of a new insight just as I'm typing the old insight into the computer. And beyond that, I began to sense that I am being guided, taken care of, and loved in everything that I do. Prayer is a reminder. Like walking down a tree-lined street on a sunny day, it helps lift that awareness, that gratitude, that trust above the weedy garden of

my consciousness. The feminist experiments with God-language
have given me metaphors, words with which to say thank you.

Living the seasonal and emotional cycle of the holidays feeds
that trust and gratitude. As I became gradually attuned to the
cycle of the natural world, I felt a broader attunement in all my
life, an acceptance of world and myself.

I have emerged from this process with an identity. I am an
American Jewish woman. And because I have been part of a
movement in Judaism that accepts me both as a woman and as a
product of American culture, all these strands of me are knit together, in harmony and not at war. From a place of fragmentation
and isolation, I have come to a place of wholeness and connection. I have been empowered to see Judaism as a living and growing culture to which I can contribute. I am excited to be a part of
the feminist thinking that is helping Judaism emerge into its next
great age.

In moments of crisis and change as well as in daily life, Jewish
tradition has given me tools for coping. From Jewish tradition I
have learned the importance of ritual and ceremony, not only as
decorations on the weave of life, but as stitching to hold the fabric of identity together at the seams. The T-shirt ceremony was
one example. When I was forty-nine, I interviewed Phyllis
Berman and learned about her seder for turning fifty. I thought,
"I should do something like that." When I turned fifty, though, I
just wasn't ready to come to terms with it. It took me the whole
year to wrestle with this turning point, to figure out a healthy, af-
firmative way to acknowledge that I was growing older. Finally, I
had a party two weeks before my fifty-first birthday, using Phyllis's seder of the seasons of life. It was a funny, moving, joyous, and
liberating event.

Like Phyllis and others in this movement, I have learned to use
the tools of Jewish tradition—the story and symbols of the seder,
for example—to create new traditions. The new ceremonies that
people in this movement have created are now part of the tradi-

tion I can draw on. As Judith Plaskow says, we are continuing the centuries-old process of making Torah, adding the voices of women, of elders, of those who have not been heard. Certain aspects of Phyllis's ceremony were drawn from a different ceremony devised by Mitch Chefitz; in turn, I felt free to add my own touches.

During my research for this book I had interviewed Savina J. Teubal, a Bible scholar who has developed feminist interpretations of the stories of Sarah and Hagar (the wife and concubine of the patriarch Abraham, respectively). Teubal had celebrated her sixtieth birthday with what she called a "croning ceremony" or *simchat hochmah* ("celebration of wisdom").[1] Singer Debbie Friedman and Teubal collaborated to create a theme song for the occasion, a feminist version of the words God said to Abraham (and to his wife, Sarah, whether she liked it or not) when they were commanded to leave their home and go to a new land: "L'chi Lach [Go, in the feminine form] to a land that I will show you. Leich L'cha [Go, in the masculine form] to a place you do not know. L'chi Lach, on your journey I will bless you. And you shall be a blessing. L'chi Lach" (Genesis 12:1–2).[2]

I used that song in my ceremony. It expressed perfectly the mixture of fear-at-not-knowing and hopefulness and adventure that I felt at launching this next phase of my journey.

In striking symbolism, Savina Teubal, when she read from the Torah at her ceremony of maturity, had donned a *kittel* (the white tunic which a man wears at his wedding, on Yom Kippur, and in which he is buried). I, too, understood the power of symbolic clothing in a ritual of transition. Instead of putting a *kittel* over my long, lovely party dress, I chose to slip on my twentieth-reunion T-shirt. My husband, Steve, solemnly crossed out the "50" with a red felt pen and inscribed a large question mark on my chest. I took my place on the raised porch in the company of the elders, looking down at the mere thirty- and forty-year-olds and the kids chasing fireflies on the lawn below. Then I slipped on a different T-shirt: one with a World War II–era picture of Rosie the Riveter showing her muscle, with the logo "We Can Do It." We all had a hearty laugh. I felt liberated from the barely suppressed anxiety that had dogged me ever since that day when I held a medicine bottle at the end of my outstretched arm, realized that I couldn't read it even by squinting, and picked up the phone to make an appointment for bifocals. I've always been an earnest, serious person. For me to take my own aging lightly—to acknowledge it, celebrate it, and poke fun at myself—was wonderfully healing.

Since I had done most of my Jewish journeying in the comforting lap of an accepting and tolerant Jewish movement, a movement of people similar to me, this final year of research was also a chance to compare my Jewish life with those who had chosen differently: those with a more rigorous commitment to Jewish law, as well as those who were more skeptical and less drawn to the spiritual than I. I was able to see that regardless of the path we choose, each of us is on a journey. As we travel, each of us must decide, as a twentieth-century American, what to draw from the deep well of Jewish tradition.

It was also a year in which to look backward. Having been more and more fulfilled by the Jewish way of life, I found it exciting to place what I was doing in historical context. As I read about the complex ways in which we Jews have constructed our community over the last four thousand years, I understood that we weren't just victims. In spite of the pressure of hostile surrounding societies (or the lure of accepting ones), we were busy creating our own history and culture. An ingenious culture. A thoughtful, sensitive, clever culture. A passionate and compassionate culture. Reading of the many ways Jews conceptualized God through the centuries, I realized that in my struggle with the hard spiritual questions of good, evil, death, and purpose, I could turn to the works of many Jewish comrades-in-search.

This year also brought helpful insights into my recurring question about the relationship between Jewish practice and morality, between immersing myself in Jewish culture and trying to become a good person. I learned more than I ever had before about how one can use the raw materials of Jewish culture and religion to become that good person. (Not that I've gotten there, but I have some good tools.)

Looking closely at my own inner life helped me to see more vividly the main idea that Judaism has been teaching me all these years: Taking what I am given in this life—the blessings and the curses—and trying to respond to them honestly, constructively, thoughtfully, and joyfully is a holy process. In short, living life is a holy process.

At my fiftieth birthday celebration, I wanted to share with my friends some of the insights that had come to me during the six years of researching this book and the more intensive seventh year of writing it. Judaism, it now seems to me, is at every level a religion about the possibility of radical transformation in our everyday lives. Our stories, from the patriarchs through Moses, are about people making journeys—outward journeys that parallel inward journeys. Our prophets called for the transformation of society, the creation of a just and humane world. The Passover seder and Shabbat help us feel the possibility of change in our *kishkes* (guts). We are taught that everyday life can be radically different, and that we are capable of making it that way. Laws like the Jubilee give us a vision of how to get from here to there. I had experienced this transformation in my own life. Looking at the smiling, loving faces of friends who had been with me on the journey, at the raised arms holding up their plastic goblets full of kosher champagne, I could acknowledge my own transformation and rejoice.

As I interviewed people who had also been journeying, I realized that even though I'd arrived at a new place of wholeness, this would not be the end of the journey. There were spiritual questions I had not begun to tackle. I have arrived at a place where I can see the blessings of my life, but not at the place Rachel Adler talks about—where somehow I can acknowledge that all, even the cruelty, disease, distortions, and curses, comes from God. I'm fearful of the challenges that will force me to confront that question, but I suspect they will come.

In the ten years and two books' worth of time I have spent talking with Jews about their spiritual lives, I have become convinced of three things: First, spirituality is a basic need of human beings, as basic as the needs for companionship and love; second, Judaism as a culture has an amazing range of ways to nurture and express that spiritual urge; and third, Jews, as products of that culture, have a passionate need to do something meaningful with their lives. Many of the Jews I talked to did not believe in God, yet all were people of faith, living life as if it made a difference. Through Judaism or their connection to the Jewish people they gained the spiritual sustenance to find, and make, meaning in their lives.

When Shohama Weiner started her spiritual journey, she felt a need to take a new name, a Hebrew name. She meditated and found it. I was blessed to be born with my name: Yehudit, the praise of God, which is also Yehudit, a Jewish woman. I don't need a new name: I need to become more fully the person I already am, to find and affirm God's unity and my own wholeness, and to affirm that they are one.

Unlike some of the people I interviewed for this book, I am not perfectly clear about God or anything else in the spiritual life. But my teachers have widened my spiritual horizons. Each one has nudged me gently, as if to say, "Hey, if you move forward just a bit, you'll be able to see something you can't see from where you're standing now."

It occurs to me that all these elements of my Jewish life—the mystical exercises, the blessings, Shabbat itself—are simply tools to help lengthen my attention span, to expand my ability to take note of the miracles. The burning bush is always in front of me. I myself am the bush, continually burning yet not consumed.

I have not conquered my anger, my division, my despair, or my doubt. After the days that went so beautifully there have been lots of days that didn't go so well, when I was almost cut off from my inner light. But I have been given so many tools, so many hints, so many possibilities. Once again, I am beginning.

PART III

BEGINNING

NOW IT'S YOUR TURN

Steps Toward Defining Your Jewish Self and Shaping Your Jewish Community

"Provide yourself with a teacher; get yourself a companion. . . . And do not keep aloof from the community," say two great sages of the Talmud.[1] They might well have been giving a prescription to the modern person who wonders how to connect, or reconnect, with Jewish tradition.

Finding a teacher and a community should not be hard. Thanks to the intrepid Jewish peddlers of eighty and one hundred years ago, there are clusters of Jews in every city and state and in nearly every town in the United States. And wherever there are two Jews, one will know enough (or think she knows enough) to teach the other something.

There are lots of places in the established Jewish world to seek teachers. Check out the lunch-and-learn opportunities and adult education classes offered through the local synagogues (you don't have to be a member to study), Jewish Community

Center, or Board of Jewish Education. Your local or regional Federation of Jewish Philanthropies/United Jewish Appeal can bring in a teacher from CLAL, the National Jewish Center for Learning and Leadership. CLAL's teachers cross denominational barriers and help people discover and explore the real spiritual issues of their lives. Orthodox groups such as Ohr Samayach and Aish HaTorah sponsor study programs in various parts of the country. The Orthodox Lubavitch movement also sends teachers to all kinds of groups and places. They are glad to teach non-Orthodox Jews.

You can bring teachers from other communities to your town through the adult education programs of your synagogue or Jewish Community Center. The National Havurah Committee and ALEPH (the Alliance for Jewish Renewal) both have speakers' bureaus. If you can get people to help you organize it, bringing in an artist or musician like Debbie Friedman or Shefa Gold to lead a weekend retreat can galvanize a community. Ask your scholar-in-residence to spend at least part of the time meeting with community leaders to help you organize an ongoing study program.

To get a quick introduction to basic Judaism or enough knowledge of Hebrew to follow a service, you can import a teacher from Rabbi Noah Golinkin's Hebrew Literacy Network, or Rabbi Ephraim Buchwald's National Jewish Outreach Program. You can also go to where the learning is: at a CLAL regional workshop, a National Havurah Institute, or a Kallah held by the Reform movement or ALEPH. Spend a week at Elat Chayyim retreat center, or a Discovery weekend with the Orthodox Aish HaTorah. If your life is flexible enough, you could spend a year at the Jewish Renewal Life Center in Philadelphia, a summer or a year at Pardes or another more Orthodox yeshiva in Israel, go on a study tour of Israel, or take a course at Hebrew University.

Just seeking out a teacher puts you on a trajectory where you will meet other teachers, including the one you eventually click with. Even if you don't immediately meet a teacher who speaks to you on a deep level, learning itself can provide a spiritual opening.

What if you can't find a compatible community? In Lexington, Kentucky, Judith Baumann, who was on the board of her Conservative synagogue, was frustrated. Even though the Rabbinical Assembly had voted to permit women to be called to the Torah and counted in a minyan, the local rabbi refused to allow it. Baumann and other dissatisfied members didn't want to leave the synagogue, because they wanted a Jewish education for their children, and they didn't want to divide the community. But they felt "we needed a more interesting religious life." Someone joked, "Couldn't we hold our own services on Thursday nights?"

They invited *Jewish Catalog* coauthor Sharon Strassfeld to speak at their synagogue. They started meeting in people's homes, with five families, each of whom had a member on the synagogue board. Jewishly, they were a pretty well-educated group: Judith had gone through Hebrew High School in Cleveland; two members had graduated from Hebrew College; and one member was the child of a Conservative rabbi. They started by holding their own creative service for the second day of Rosh Hashana. Then they formed a havurah that held services once a month and on holidays. Some members of the havurah belonged to the Reform temple, some to the Conservative synagogue, and some didn't belong anywhere until they started participating with the havurah.

Everyone was encouraged to help lead services; people who had more Jewish experience were paired as leaders with people who had less. Participants ranged from university professors to a computer expert and a local television personality. On High Holidays everyone takes at least some role in the services. Once a year, they have a retreat; they bring in teachers from the National Havurah Committee teachers' bureau.

The Lexington havurah is not a phenomenon of the alienated fringe; among its 32 families are eight or nine former presidents of the local Hadassah chapter, chairs of the Israel bond drive, and the United Jewish Appeal fund campaign. One of its members is the morning prayer leader at the Conservative synagogue when he is not at the havurah. But there are also members who would have no Jewish connection if not for the havurah. It is a highly organized group, with committees on services, social action, and education, as well as its own newsletter. It is affiliated with the United Synagogue of Conservative Judaism and has a representative on their local Jewish Federation board.

Eventually the Conservative synagogue hired a new rabbi, and women are now permitted full participation. But by this time the havurah has been in existence for nearly twenty years and is like an extended family. Baumann's children (who were five, eight, and eleven years old when the havurah started) grew up in the havurah and had their bat and bar mitzvahs there. Every year, Baumann goes to the National Havurah Institute and brings back ideas to use in havurah services; she also studies in order to do her share. Being responsible for helping to put on havurah services has been "the most positive adult Jewish education experience I've ever had," said Baumann. "It's helped me grow as a Jew."

Though the first havurot were in East and West Coast cities, the havurah idea has helped Jews in small towns that can't afford a rabbi to maintain a vital Jewish life. Pianist Jack Winerock and his wife, Sue Elkin, a writer-editor and social service professional, spent a year coming to the Germantown minyan while Jack was on sabbatical from his job teaching music at the University of Kansas. When they got back to Lawrence, Kansas, they organized a havurah there. Their daughters have grown up in it.

Natalie Richman came back from a week at Elat Chayyim retreat center feeling that the style of Jewish celebration she encountered there was something she wanted in her life. Since there was no New Age Jewish community in Highland Park, New Jersey, she decided to organize one. As she mentioned the idea to people she knew, one response led to another. Her chiropractor, who was connected to the world of herbalists and healers, mentioned it to some people he knew. Another friend spoke to some members of her Reconstructionist synagogue. Others heard and joined: dissatisfied members of the Highland Park minyan; people who had been to Elat Chayyim; an active member of P'nai Or Philadelphia who had just moved to Highland Park; a woman who had converted to Judaism and was uncomfortable in traditional services; and some gay men and lesbians looking for a Jewish connection.

The fledgling group, which called itself the Jewish Renewal Havurah, asked P'nai Or Philadelphia to send someone to lead several Shabbat morning services. These became models as Natalie and others took turns leading services. The group held community meetings to come to consensus on what they were trying to create. A committee volunteered to paste together a prayerbook that would reflect the services they'd found most meaningful. The members have been holding services for more than a year at this writing. In the process of organizing the havurah, Natalie discovered that she had gifts as a leader of services, and she has grown confident in that role. To her surprise, while still very much a learner, she became a mentor for others in the group.

If you don't feel able to organize your own havurah, some sympathetic rabbis may be willing to help. Since Los Angeles Conservative rabbi Harold Schulweis brought the havurah idea into mainstream synagogues in the early 1970s, many synagogues have formed havurot. Usually these meet for study, Shabbat dinners, holiday celebrations, or social events rather than for services. Some synagogues have also permitted independent havurot to hold services on the premises. In fact, some synagogues (notably Ansche Chesed in New York and the Germantown Jewish Center in Philadelphia) have become pluralist enterprises, with a common board and committee structure, but different member-led and rabbi-led services meeting in various rooms all over the building in order to serve the needs of different segments of the congregation.

Organizing a study havurah is a good way to stimulate spiritual freshness in a synagogue that may have gone stale. A rabbi or professor of Jewish studies may help you work out the reading list, but it's important that laypeople take turns leading the group; you begin to learn and to make a spiritual investment when you have the responsibility to lead. The Torah portion of the week is a natural curriculum for the first few years of discussions. (If your rabbi is open to it, you might have a congregational discussion during services in place of or as part of the sermon.) Or your study group might choose to pick up where the Torah leaves off, reading your way through Judges, the prophets, and the rest of the Bible. You could study the Shabbat or weekday service, looking at the overall structure and discussing the meaning of each prayer. Shabbat afternoon is the traditional time for discussing *Pirkei Avot* (*Ethics of the Fathers*).

You can organize a discussion around topics, letting each person in the group lead from his or her area of strength. The history buff, for example, can find a book on Jewish history and lead discussions about it. The business executive can lead discussions on what Jewish texts have to say about business ethics. Parents can lead discussions on Jewish parenting. Those with elderly parents can lead discussions on Jewish attitudes toward the elderly. The leader should pose some question to the group. Some of the best discussions get started by focusing on what troubles you, what you find puzzling or downright obnoxious about a text or a law. Be prepared to brainstorm about other ways of understanding that troubling part, or ways of challenging it. Always try to talk about how the text relates to your life.

Make sure everyone gets a chance to speak and no one monopolizes the discussion. You can suggest people limit themselves to two-minute comments if necessary, and that no one speak a second time until everyone has spoken. Sometimes it's helpful in a mixed group to make a rule that men and women must alternate.

If the idea is congenial to the group, think about beginning and ending with a song, a simple ritual or a *kavannah* (intention). For example, you could light candles and say, "May what we learn illumine our lives."

Many Orthodox and Conservative synagogues hold a service, study session, and light meal (Seudah Shlishit, or "Third Meal") just before the close of Shabbat. This more intimate setting is a good place to get to know people who are most interested in having a spiritual life within Judaism. If your synagogue doesn't have Seudah Shlishit, you could start it.

Another suggestion is to organize a social action havurah. Begin each meeting by studying something about Jewish social action values, then discuss the project you're working on. If you feel comfortable doing so, begin and end with a blessing or prayer for your work. Try to communicate with national Jewish groups or groups in other communities who are doing similar work.

Or you could organize some other subgroup in the synagogue that meets your special needs: a Rosh Hodesh group, a Shabbat walking group, a group for parents of toddlers, or a meditation group (slowly reading a psalm and focusing on one verse or phrase that speaks to you makes a wonderful guided meditation and preparation for services). Whatever you do—adding a blessing, reading a paragraph or two from a Jewish text, or doing a ritual as simple as holding hands in a circle and wishing each other a good week—can deepen the meaning and help you bond together. (If you have refreshments, try putting the bread in the center and have everyone touch it with one hand as you say the blessing together.)

From organizing a Rosh Hodesh group in Highland Park, I learned that the organizers have to put in a lot of energy for at least two years. One or two people have to push to get others to put out a reminder mailing, plan the meetings or services, and call to follow up on people who stop coming. Learning to delegate is a saving grace. After awhile, as the group becomes important in people's lives, other people will take over the role of pushing things along.

You can also build a group around a teacher or leader whose worldview touches you. In central New Jersey, a unique congregation, String of Pearls, formed around a charismatic and un-conventional Reconstructionist rabbi, Susan Schnur. When Klonda Speer's husband, Alan, died young, neither of them had any connection with organized religion. Klonda had been raised Methodist, Alan in a nonobservant Jewish family; neither was re-ligious. Schnur had conducted their wedding and counseled Alan, Klonda, and their young daughters during the seven months he was dying from lymphoma; now she led the funeral. Schnur had a gift for acknowledging intolerable mysteries, like why a young man in his prime would die. To the group of friends who gathered to help Klonda mourn, she spoke deeply.

Many of this group were friends because their children went to the same creative Waldorf school. Many, like Alan and Klonda, were involved in interfaith marriages and had no connection to organized religion; Klonda says they were the type who would "hyperventilate" if they came into a standard religious service. For three nights, with Schnur guiding them, they came together to sit shiva, sometimes softly singing songs and chants she taught them, sometimes speaking quietly and sporadically about their memories of Alan. A deep bond formed. "By the third night, it was almost joyous," said Klonda. They shared food and talked quietly; no one wanted to leave.

It was also a special moment for Schnur, who joked, "I would-n't mind being rabbi to a Waldorf school." Some of the Waldorf parents asked Schnur if she would create a Waldorf-style Hebrew school for their children. She countered that a school in isolation from a community wasn't enough. If they would organize them-selves as a community, and promise to handle all the administra-tive work, she would be their part-time rabbi.

Schnur had been freelancing both as writer and as rabbi (con-ducting weddings was one of her specialties). After a short stint as a congregational rabbi, she had decided that role was not for her. If she were to lead a congregation again, it would have to be a very different kind of congregation. In her proposal for the new community, she wrote:

The word "religion" comes from the Latin and means "to bind together." . . . The most important thing is to remember that *this is a
community based on generosity of spirit* and on *good will.* . . . To want to
be in this particular Jewish community, you need three things:

—you need to be interested in introspection, in exploring the
meaning of life, in thinking about what matters to you.

—you need to be willing to put away all religious "shoulds"—
that this or that *should* be done in accordance with Jewish tradition.
(For example, people can wear jeans, if that's how they feel closest to
God.) . . .

—you need to be willing to do a lot of singing and chanting. . . .

I have had many offers to work with other communities over the
years, but, as you know, I am committed to a radically different, radically homely paradigm of Jewish practice. I am deeply hoping that
my fantasy (of a Judaism that really *works*—for us) can find its warm,
spiritual, intentional heart right here.

Members of the community went through a year of intense
bonding and rededication to Judaism. Then Schnur, who suffered
from lupus erythematosis, a potentially deadly disease of the im-
mune system, became very ill. She pulled herself out of bed to
dance them through a soaring set of High Holiday services, but
announced that afterward they would have to find someone else
to be their leader. It was a hard act to follow, and the community
has gone through three rabbis in the three years since. They have
become committed to each other as a community, however, and
they are continuing with or without their charismatic leader.

Even if you seek out a rabbi to lead you, the richness of your
experience with Judaism often depends on how much of your
Jewish life you take into your own hands. In the small town of
Hammonton, near the southern tip of New Jersey, a synagogue
that had once served a community of Jewish chicken farmers had
dwindled to the point where it couldn't attract a minyan for the
Sabbath. Members contacted Reconstructionist rabbi Goldie
Milgram to lead them in saying kaddish for the congregation be-

fore they folded. Instead, she encouraged them to reorganize it by reaching out to Jews whose needs weren't being met by more conventional congregations. They posted notices in supermarkets and health food stores, advertised in weekly suburban shopper newspapers, and eventually got the critical mass to re-create the congregation. Some members drive more than an hour to attend from places like Cherry Hill, which have lots of Jewish congregations but not ones where they feel comfortable. A number of the families are working-class and felt out of place in more posh synagogues. Some members have a rebel streak that could only be satisfied by a fairly freewheeling form of religion.

The reborn congregation is very much a do-it-yourself affair. When the synagogue needed renovations, they did it with their own hands, directed by a couple of members who had their own small-scale construction companies. One Sabbath a month, Goldie leads the services; one Sabbath a month, a member of the congregation leads. One Sabbath they meet as a social action committee, deciding how to put their religious life to work in the world. And one Sabbath a month they go out to a diner and just schmooze, keeping the social and personal connections alive. Because most members of the congregation had little or no Jewish background, they asked Goldie to establish an adult Sunday school where they could learn alongside or at the same time as their children.

If you're not the organizing type and you can't find a group to connect to, can you deepen your connection to Judaism on your own? Sure, if that's your style. Rabbi Max Ticktin, the chair of Judaic Studies at George Washington University, suggests beginning with some reading. One of Heschel's works might be a good place to start. You can even do some learning by cruising the Jewish interest groups on the Internet. But you're likely to find that eventually, to develop your Jewish identity and to grow spiritually within Judaism, you will have to find a place to connect face to face with other Jews. Just finding one other person to be your study partner and to share holidays can make a big difference.

Study is not the best entry point for everyone. Like the Hebrews who stood at Mt. Sinai, saying "We shall do and we shall hear," I had to do Judaism before I could hear it.

Rabbis Mitch Chefitz and Art Green teach that the most important thing a person interested in Judaism can do is to start observing Shabbat—not necessarily in an Orthodox way, but in a way that consecrates it and sets it apart from other days. Light candles, and then have some period of time when you do not work, do laundry, or anything else you find aggravating. Do nothing but be with family, friends, and community.

I would add that it's important to celebrate Shabbat, and holidays, with friends. If you have children, have friends there for them; Shabbat in my family feels most like Shabbat when it feels that way to the kids as well as the adults. Singing is an important part of Shabbat, and it's easier to sing with friends.

After Shabbat, my next step was to take on the cycle of the Jewish year, holiday by holiday. To do this you must definitely find a community or friends with whom you can celebrate. If there aren't any Jews around, you could go to a retreat for holidays, or be hospitable and introduce your holiday to non-Jews with whom you are friendly. It helps to pick up the *Jewish Catalog,* some recipe books, craft books, storybooks, and adult discussion books, the tools you need to make your holiday celebration an expression of your self.

Once you cross the threshold, once you begin the experiment of living a Jewish life, how do you keep growing spiritually? Or, to put it in non-theistic terms, how do you keep aliveness in your way of life?

I have to understand the meaning of what I do, to put everything in context. That is how I come to really live what I do. Study and reflection are the light that allow me to see what I would otherwise be doing in the dark.

I'm not much of a student. I have to have an occasion, like preparing to lead the Torah discussion at my minyan, to push me to read. After twenty years of adult Jewish practice, I have a pretty solid Jewish identity. My reading helps me to understand the foundations of this way of life I have been given.

And it *is* a gift. To have an identity, to know where you came from, to make choices about where you're going, to feel yourself woven into the fabric of history—these are some of the gifts that can come from bringing one's Jewish heritage to life.

As Rabbi Max Ticktin told me some years ago, the essential spiritual question for Jews is not "Do you believe?" but "You have been given an appointment with destiny. What do you choose to do about it?"

GO AND LEARN

What is hateful to you, do not do to your neighbor: this is the whole Torah. The rest is commentary; now go and study.
—Hillel, Babylonian Talmud, *Shabbat* 31a.

FINDING A TEACHER: A SAMPLING OF RESOURCES

BASIC JUDAISM AND BASIC HEBREW SKILLS

National Programs

One-day and six-week crash courses in Hebrew and basic Judaism: Hebrew Literacy Network, Rabbi Noah Golinkin, 56-39 Thunder Hill Rd., Columbia, MD 21045; 410-964-ALEF (964-2533). Texts available include introductions to the prayerbook and Haggadah.

National Jewish Outreach Program, Rabbi Ephraim Buchwald, 485 Fifth Ave., Suite 212, New York, NY 10017; 1-800-44-TORAH or 1-800-44-HEBRE(W). Tapes available.

293

Regional Programs

New York Area

Derekh Torah (see the 92nd Street Y, below).

Washington, DC

Jewish Study Center, 1747 Connecticut Ave., NW, Washington, DC 20009 202-265-1312.

ONGOING CLASSES, LUNCH AND LEARN, EVENING PROGRAMS

National Programs

CLAL, National Jewish Center for Learning and Leadership, 99 Park Ave., Suite C-300, New York, NY 10016-1599; 212-867-8888.

Lubavitch movement (Orthodox). Chabad houses in most university towns and medium-to-large cities. Lubavitch will assign mentors to people wishing to learn to live by Jewish law.

Ohr Somayach (Orthodox), 21550 W. Twelve Mile Rd., Southfield, MI 48076 (810) 352-4870. Programs in Baltimore, Chicago, Cleveland, Detroit, Miami, Milwaukee, New York, Toronto.

Regional Programs

New York Area

The 92nd Street YM-YWHA, 1395 Lexington Ave., New York, NY 10128; 212-996-1100 or 415-5630 (senior program).

The Jewish Community Center of the Upper West Side, 15 W. 65th St., New York, NY 10023; 212-580-0099.

The Jewish Theological Seminary (Conservative Judaism) Franz Rosenzweig Lehrhaus (community learning program), 3080 Broadway, New York, NY 10027; 212-678-8996.

New York Kollel of the Hebrew Union College-Jewish Institute of Religion (Reform), Brookdale Center, One West Fourth St., New York, NY 10012-1186; 212-674-5300, ext. 272.

West Coast

The Brandeis-Bardin Institute, 1101 N. Peppertree Lane, Simi Valley, CA 93064; 805-582-4450.

Women's Institute for Continuing Jewish Education, 4126 Executive Drive, La Jolla, CA 92037; 619-442-2666.

Washington, DC Area

Jewish Study Center, Washington, DC (see above)

Am Kolel Judaic Resource Center (classes on Jewish culture and Jewish spirituality) and Ma'alot (training in Jewish music and arts); 15 W. Montgomery Ave., Suite 204, Rockville, MD 20850; 301-309-2310, fax 301-309-2328; David Shneyer, director.

All regions: Check local synagogues, Jewish Community Center, YM-YWHA, Jewish Family Service, Board or Agency of Jewish Education.

SPEAKERS' BUREAUS AND SPECIAL-INTEREST PROGRAMS

National

CLAL (see above)

Havurah-Style Learning

National Havurah Committee, 7318 Germantown Ave., Philadelphia, PA 19119; 215-248-9760; e-mail: 73073.601@compuserve.com

Mystical or New Age

ALEPH, The Alliance for Jewish Renewal, 7318 Germantown Ave., Philadelphia, PA 19119-1720; 215-247-9700; e-mail: ALEPHajr@aol.com

Practical Spirituality, Marthajoy Aft and Ann Asnes, P.O. Box 545, Brookline, MA 02146; 617-277-9838.

Feminist and Women's Issues

New York Area

Jewish Women's Resource Center, New York section, National Council of Jewish Women, 9 E. 69th St., New York, NY 10021, 212-535-5900.

Lilith Magazine Talent Bank, Naomi Danis, 250 W. 57th St., Suite 2432, New York, NY 10107, 212-757-0818.

Ma'yan (the Jewish Women's Project) and Jewish Feminist Research Group, Jewish Community Center of the Upper West Side (see above).

West Coast

Los Angeles Jewish Feminist Center, American Jewish Congress, 6505 Wilshire Blvd., Suite 417, Los Angeles, CA 90048.

San Diego Women's Institute for Continuing Education (see above).

Boston Area

Nishmat Anashim, Matia Angelou, 508-358-7237; Hebrew College, 43 Hawes St., Brookline, MA 02146, 617-232-8710.

Environment and Social Action

Religious Action Center of Reform Judaism (see below).

The Shalom Center, now a project of ALEPH (see above).

The Shefa Fund, 7318 Germantown Ave., Philadelphia, PA 19119-1720, helps foundations develop giving strategies based on Jewish values.

Shomrei Adamah (Guardians of the Earth), 527 W. Carpenter Lane, Philadelphia, PA 19119; 215-844-8150.

Tikkun Magazine, 251 W. 100th St., New York, NY 10025; 212-864-4110. National conference for social activists, local groups.

RETREATS AND WEEKEND AND WEEKLONG LEARNING

National Havurah Committee Summer Institute (see above).

Brandeis-Bardin Institute (see above).

Discovery Seminars, Aish HaTorah (Orthodox), 1220 Broadway, Suite 610, New York, NY 10001; 212-643-8800; Rabbi Noah Weinberg.

Elat Chayyim Retreat Center, The Woodstock Center for Healing and Renewal, P.O. Box 127, Woodstock, NY 12498; 800-398-2630.

Heart of Stillness Retreat Center (meditation retreats), Rabbi David Cooper, P.O. Box 106, Jamestown, CO 80455; 303-459-3431.

Machne Israel, Lubavitch Youth Organization, 770 Eastern Parkway, Brooklyn, NY 11213.

Metivta (meditation retreats in New Mexico and Los Angeles with Rabbis Jonathan Omer-Man and Judith Halevy, 1047 South Point View, Los Angeles, CA 90035; 213-934-7066.

P'nai Or Kallah, ALEPH (see above).

Reform Kallah, Union of American Hebrew Congregations. Contact Rabbi Sanford Seltzer at the Boston regional office, 617-499-0404. Regional kallot: contact the nearest UAHC regional office.

Rose Mountain Center, Andrew and Shefa Gold, P.O. Box 355, Las Vegas, NM 87701; 505-425-5728.

Ruach, c/o Rabbi Meir Fund, 1049 E. 13th St., Brooklyn, NY 11231; 718-338-8442.

RESIDENTIAL LEARNING

Bais Chana (Lubavitch movement, for women), 15 Montcalm Court, St. Paul, MN 55116; 612-698-3858; Rabbi Manis Friedman.

Jewish Renewal Life Center (progressive study program), Rabbi Julie Greenberg, B202, 6445 Greene St., Philadelphia, PA 19119; 215-843-4345.

The Open University of Israel, American Friends of the Open University of Israel, 330 N. 58th St., 401, New York, NY 10019; 212-713-1515.

Pardes (traditional but liberal yeshiva in Israel, where men and women study together), American Pardes Foundation, P.O. Box 926, Avon, CT 06001; 860-675-1431.

Orthodox Kollel programs for men in many large U.S. cities and Jerusalem. Some provide free tuition, room and board.

IN-DEPTH LEARNING

Drisha Institute for Jewish Education (Liberal Orthodox learning program for women), 131 W. 86th St., New York, NY 10024; 212-595-0307.

Jewish Spiritual Leadership Program (egalitarian) Chomat HaLev, 2140 Shattuck Ave., 403, Berkeley, CA 94704; Nan Fink, 510-704-9687.

Jewish Institutions of Higher Learning (many also offer lower-level adult and high school education):

Baltimore—Baltimore Hebrew University
Boston—Hebrew College, Brookline, MA; Brandeis University, Hornstein Program, Waltham, MA
Chicago—Spertus College
Cincinnati—Hebrew Union College
Cleveland—Cleveland College of Jewish Studies
Los Angeles—University of Judaism (Conservative); Hebrew Union College (Reform)
Montreal—McGill University Jewish Teacher Training Program
New York—Academy for Jewish Religion (nondenominational); Hebrew Union College (Reform); Jewish Theological Seminary (Conservative); Yeshiva University (Orthodox)
Philadelphia—Gratz College, Melrose Park, PA; Reconstructionist Rabbinical College, Wyncote, PA
Judaica, Jewish Studies or Religion departments at many universities.

TO ORGANIZE YOUR OWN STUDY GROUP

Choose a text. Read it together aloud, in small chunks, so you don't have to depend on people reading it at home. Have people raise questions about it, or about particular phrases, words, ideas. Discuss how it applies to your life, how it seems to complement or contradict other ideas. Discuss it on a literal level, a symbolic or metaphoric level, and as a source for insights about moral questions.

1. Study the weekly Torah portion. Jewish calendars in the Saturday column list the name of the portion for each week. They are available in synagogue gift shops or Jewish bookstores, or from United Synagogue in New York and other denominations.

Helpful commentaries: Nehama Leibowitz, *Studies in the Weekly Parasha* (six volumes covering the five books of the Torah), Jerusalem, World Zionist Organization, 1962–80 (can be ordered through Jewish bookstores).

You will need a *Chumash,* the first five books of the Bible arranged according to the weekly Torah portion, with the Haftarah (weekly reading from the prophets). Helpful translations and commentaries: *The Jewish Publication Society Torah Commentary;* Rabbi W. Gunther Plaut, ed., *The Torah: A Modern Commentary,* Union of American Hebrew Congregations, 1981; *The Soncino Chumash* (the Rev. Dr. A. Cohen, ed.); Everett Fox, trans., *The Five Books of Moses,* Schocken Books, New York, 1995.

For fun, act out, and discuss with: *Sedra Scenes: Skits for Every Torah Portion,* Stan J. Beiner, Alternatives in Religious Education, Inc. (ARE), 1992; 3945 S. Oneida St., Denver, CO, 80237.

The Reform movement's Commission on Jewish Education has a guide called "Welcome to the World of Torah." UAHC, 838 Fifth Ave., New York, NY 10021.

2. Go through the prayerbook, discussing each prayer or group of prayers. Helpful commentaries: Evelyn Garfiel, *Service of the Heart: A Guide to the Jewish Prayer Book;* B. S. Jacobson, Meditations on the Siddur. *Kol Haneshamah,* the series of prayerbooks for Shabbat and holidays by the Reconstructionist Press, also has extensive commentaries. The Metsudah *siddur* has line-by-line translations that are helpful in connecting the Hebrew and English words.

3. Study and celebrate each holiday in the Jewish year. Helpful commentaries: Rabbi Irving Greenberg, *The Jewish Way: Living the Holidays*; Michael Strassfeld et al., *The Jewish Catalog;* Michael Strassfeld, *The Jewish Holidays;* Arthur Waskow, *Seasons of Our Joy* (citations in bibliography below).

4. Read and discuss *The Ethics of the Fathers (Pirkei Avot).*

5. Read and discuss Jewish ideas by topic. Resources: Rabbi Joseph Telushkin, *Jewish Wisdom: Ethical, Spiritual and Historical Lessons from the*

Great Works and Thinkers, William Morrow, New York, 1994; Francine Klagsbrun, *Voices of Wisdom: Jewish Ideals and Ethics for Everyday Living,* Pantheon Books (Random House), New York, 1980; Hayim Nahman Bialik and Yehoshua Hana Ravnitzky, eds., *The Book of Legends (Sefer HaAggadah); Legends from the Talmud and Midrash,* Schocken Books, New York, 1992.

6. Barry W. Holtz has written or edited three helpful study guides, all of which have extensive bibliographies: *The Schocken Guide to Jewish Books,* Schocken Books, New York, 1992; *Finding Our Way: Jewish Texts and the Lives We Lead Today,* Schocken, New York, 1990; *Back to the Sources: Reading the Classic Jewish Texts,* Summit Books, New York, 1984.

USING THE INTERNET

Shamash, The Jewish Networking Project; http://shamash.nysernet.org

Dr. Chaim Dworkin, The New York-Israel Project, Chai Computer Associates, 115 East Mt. Airy Ave., Philadelphia, PA 19119-1715; 215-242-6843; Internet: chaim@israel.nysernet.org or chaim@linc.cis.upenn.edu

The Aleph Network, P.O. Box 1232, Mendocino, CA 95460, 707-937-4022, on-line bulletin board linking teenagers from small isolated Jewish communities. From "Reb Responsa" (a Jewish "Dear Abby") to Swap Meet to on-line discussion and learning.

Jewish Social Justice Network: http://shamash.org/hc/jsjn or just browse the lists at shamash.org.

The Electronic Havurah, National Havurah Committee: havurah@shamash. nysernet.org. Send in comments and thoughts; a digest of comments received will be sent out.

Rabbi Rami Shapiro of Congregation Beth Or in Miami, the Rasheit Institute for Jewish Spirituality: "Havurah on the Net." Teaching material, discussions, real-time conversations with scholars. The e-mail address is not yet available, but Shapiro's address is 76252.517@compuserve.com.

Rabbi Judith Abrams, through her school Maqom, has organized *hevruta* (study in pairs) on the Internet. One can lurk (read what others have written) or participate. To participate, send a brief description of yourself to Abrams by e-mail. She will send you a list of people looking for study partners. Your name is kept on this list until you and someone else on the list agree to study together. Abrams posts a text at the website. You and your partner discuss it. You e-mail your discussions to Abrams, and she prepares a digest and summary of all the discussions and posts it at the website. Topics are flexible: when Israeli Prime Minister Yitzhak Rabin was assassinated, the group discussed a Talmud text about saying blessings when bad things happen. "If Talmud isn't relevant to your life, what's the point?" said Abrams.

Rabbi Abrams's e-mail address is maqom@compassnet.com; the World Wide Web site is http://www.compassnet.com/~maqom/.

Maqom, P.O. Box 31900-323, Houston, TX 77231; 713-728-8200.

MUSEUMS AND ARCHIVES

Balch Institute, 18 S. Seventh St., Philadelphia, PA 19106; 215-925-8090.

B'nai B'rith Museum, 1640 Rhode Island Ave., NW, Washington, DC 20036; 202-857-6583.

The Holocaust Museum, 100 Raoul Wallenberg Place, SW, Washington, DC 20024; 202-488-0400.

The Jewish Museum, 1109 Fifth Ave., NY 10128; 212-423-3200.

National Museum of American Jewish History, 55 N. Fifth St., Philadelphia, PA 19106; 215-923-3811.

Jewish Women's Resource Center (see above).

MAKING CONNECTIONS, FINDING COMMUNITY

SOCIAL ACTION GROUPS AND CONGREGATIONS

The Ark, 6450 N. California Ave., Chicago, IL 60645; 312-973-4362.

American Jewish World Service, 15 W. 26th St., New York, NY 10010; 212-683-1161 (economic development and disaster relief for anyone in need).

Americans for Peace Now (American support for Israeli peace group Shalom Achshav), 27 W. 20th St., 9th Floor, New York, NY 10011; 212-645-6262.

Dorot (homelessness prevention and serving Jewish elderly), 316 W. 95th St., New York, NY 10025; 212-666-2000.

Jewish Fund for Justice, 260 Fifth Ave., New York, NY 10001; 212-213-2113 (community development for urban and rural poor).

Kehilla Community Synagogue, 941 The Alameda, Berkeley, CA 94707; 510-527-5452, 528-4636.

Mazon: A Jewish Response to Hunger, 12401 Wilshire Blvd., Los Angeles, CA 90025; 310-442-0020. New York office: 197 East Broadway, 6th Floor, New York, NY 10002-5507; 212-475-5427.

Mishkan Shalom Congregation, c/o Stratford Friends School, 5 Llandillo Rd., Havertown, PA 19083; 610-446-4068.

New Israel Fund, 1625 K St. NW, Washington, DC, or P.O. Box 91588, Washington, DC 20090-1588; 202-223-3333. In New York: 165 E 56th St., Second Floor, New York, NY 10022; 212-750-2333.

Project Ezra (serving Jewish elderly), 197 East Broadway, New York, NY 10002; 212-982-3700.

Religious Action Center of the Union of American Hebrew Congregations (Reform), 2027 Massachusetts Ave. NW, Washington, DC; 202-387-2800.

Student Struggle for Soviet Jewry, 240 Cabrini Blvd., NY 10033; 212-923-3313.

Tikkun Magazine (see above).

FEMINIST GROUPS

Ma'yan and Jewish Feminist Research Group (see above). Los Angeles Jewish Feminist Center (see above).

FINDING A HAVURAH

National Havurah Committee (see above).

Network of Jewish Renewal Communities; 510-841-3747; Ahuva Steinhaus. Network of Independent Jewish Communities and Havarot (DC area); 301-309-2310.

RURAL JEWS

Conference on Judaism in Rural New England, c/o Sarah Lisniansky, R.D.1 Box 56, East Montpelier, VT 05651, 302-223-2962.

FINDING A CONGREGATION

Conservative: United Synagogue of America, 155 Fifth Ave., New York, NY 10010; 212-533-7800. Regional offices: New York, Los Angeles, Chicago, Houston, Philadelphia, Toronto, Montreal, Oakland, CA, Rockville, MD, Hillside, NJ, Milton, MA, Plantation, FL, Farmington Hills, MI, Amsterdam, NY, West Hartford, CT, Sioux City, IA. Yellow Pages listing: Synagogues—Conservative.

Reconstructionist: The Jewish Reconstructionist Federation, Church Rd. and Greenwood Ave., Wyncote, PA 19095; 215-887-1988; e-mail:jrfnatl @aol.com.

Reform: Union of American Hebrew Congregations, 838 Fifth Ave., New York, NY 10021; 212-249-0100. Regional offices: New York, Chicago, Los Angeles, Philadelphia, Washington, St. Louis, San Francisco, Miami, Dallas,

Toronto, Brookline, MA, Beachwood, OH, Paramus, NJ. Yellow Pages listing: Synagogues—Reform.

FOR COLLEGE STUDENTS

B'nai B'rith Hillel Fdtn, most colleges.

Brandeis-Bardin Institute, Los Angeles area.

HUMANIST AND SECULARIST

Congress of Jewish Secular Organizations, Executive Director, Roberta Feinstein, 19657 Villa Drive North, Southfield, MI 48076; 810-569-8127.

Society for Humanistic Judaism, 28611 W. Twelve Mile Rd., Farmington Hills, MI 48334; 810-478-7610.

GAY AND LESBIAN

World Congress of Gay and Lesbian Jewish Organizations, P.O. Box 3345, New York, NY 10008. In addition to the U.S. organizations listed below, there are organizations in Israel, Australia, France, England, Sweden, Hungary, Germany, Austria, Belgium, the Netherlands, and South Africa.

New York

Congregation Beth Simchat Torah, 57 Bethune St., New York, NY 10014; 212-929-9498.

Mid-Atlantic

Beth Ahavah, P.O. Box 7566, Philadelphia, PA 19101; 215-923-2003.

Bet Mishpachah, P.O. Box 1410, Washington, DC 20013; 202-833-1638.

New Jersey Lesbian and Gay Havurah, P.O. Box 2576, Edison, NJ 08818; 908-549-6032.

West Coast

Beth Chayim Chadashim, 6000 W. Pico Blvd., Los Angeles, CA 90035; 213-931-7023.

Kol Ami, 8400 Sunset Blvd., Suite 2A, West Hollywood, CA 90069; 213-656-6093.

Response for Gays, Lesbians and Their Families, 15739 Ventura Blvd., Encino, CA 91436; 818-788-6000.

Kol Simcha, P.O. Box 1444, Laguna Beach, CA 92662; 714-499-3500.

Long Beach Lesbian and Gay Havurah, Jewish Community Center, 3801 E. Willow St., Long Beach, CA 90615.

Shalom Chavurah (parents of gays and lesbians), 1617 Chevy Chase Dr., Brea, CA 92621; 714-529-4201.

Sha'ar Zahav, 220 Danvers St., San Francisco, CA 94114; 415-861-6932.

Yachad, P.O. Box 3457, San Diego, CA 92163; 619-492-8616.

Tikvah Chadashah, P.O. Box 2731, Seattle, WA 98111; 206-329-2590.

New England

Am Tikva, P.O. Box 11, Cambridge, MA 02238; 617-926-2536.

Am Segulah, P.O. Box 271522, West Hartford, CT 06127.

Am Chofshi, c/o Horowitz, RR1 Box 688, S. Harpswell, ME 04079.

Southeast

Bet Haverim, P.O. Box 54947, Atlanta, GA 30308; 770-642-3467.

Beth Rachameem, c/o Fackelman, 3617 Creek Way Court, Plant City, FL 33567; 813-754-9465.

Etz Chaim, 19094 W. Dixie Highway, North Miami Beach, FL 33180; 305-931-9318.

Yeladim Shel Yisrael, 4938 S. Davis Road, Lake Worth, FL 33461; 407-987-4267.

Midwest

Or Chadash, 666 W. Barry Ave., Chicago, IL 60657; 312-248-9450.

Simcha, P.O. Box 652, Southfield, MI 48037; 810-353-8025.

Chevrai Tikva, P.O. Box 18120, Cleveland, OH 44118; 216-932-5661.

St. Louis Gay and Lesbian Havurah, c/o Central Reform Congregation, 77 Maryland Plaza, St. Louis, MO 63106; 314-361-3919

Spinoza, P.O. Box 6112, Bloomington, IN 47407.

304 APPENDIX

South and Southwest

B'nai Shalom, P.O. Box 6861, Louisville, KY 40206; 502-696-0475.

Beth El Binah, P.O. Box 191165, Dallas, TX 75219; 214-497-1591.

Mishpachat Am, P.O. Box 7731, Phoenix, AZ 86011; 602-966-5001.

Mishpachat Alizim, P.O. Box 960136, Houston, TX 77298; 713-748-7079.

Tikvat Shalom, P.O. Box 6694, Denver, CO 80206; 303-331-2706.

Canada

Keshet Shalom, Box 6103, Station A, Toronto, Ontario; 416-925-1408.

TEACHERS/MENTORS APPEARING IN THIS BOOK

Abrams, Rabbi Judith, Maqom, 5444 Rutherglen, Houston, TX 77096-4032; 713-721-8906.

Ackelsberg, Martha, Dept. of Government, Smith College, Northampton, MA 01063, 413-585-3533; e-mail: mackelsberg@smith.smith.edu.

Adelman, Penina V., 243 Upland Rd., Newtonville, MA 02160.

Adler, Rachel, adjunct faculty, Hebrew Union College-Jewish Institute of Religion, 3077 University Ave., Los Angeles, CA 90007-3796; 213-749-3424.

Agus, Arlene, 808 West End Ave., New York, NY 10025; 212-222-5203; e-mail: aa162@columbia.edu.

Alpert, Rabbi Rebecca, co-director, Women's Studies Program, Temple University, 617 Gladfelter Hall, Philadelphia, PA 19122; 215-204-6953; e-mail: rebecca@vm.temple.edu.

Azen, Margot Stein, New Legends (feminist musical/drama) and MIRAJ (feminist folk liturgical music), 608 West Upsal St., Philadelphia, PA, 19119; 215-848-8036.

Bell, Roselyn, 134 Highland Ave., Edison, NJ 08817; 908-819-0593.

Berman, Phyllis, 6711 Lincoln Drive, Philadelphia, PA 19119; 215-844-5008; e-mail: bermanp@aol.com.

Buchwald, Rabbi Ephraim, National Jewish Outreach Program, (above).

Cardin, Rabbi Nina Beth, c/o CLAL (see above).

Chefitz, Rabbi Mitchell, Havurah of South Florida, 9315 SW 61st Court, Miami, FL 33156; 305-666-7349; e-mail: 73067.233@compuserve.com.

Cohen-Kiener, Andrea, 134 Saint Charles St., West Hartford, CT 06119; 860-233-6838; e-mail: ahuva@trincoll.edu.

Elwell, Rabbi Sue Levi, Ma'yan (see above).

Falk, Marcia, 2905 Benvenue Ave., Berkeley, CA 94705; fax 510-548-1736.

Fein, Leonard, 134 Beach St., Boston, MA 02111; fax 617-426-7513; e-mail: lfein@interramp.com.

Feld, Merle, 565 West End Ave., Apt. 12-C, New York, NY 10024; 212-874-9026.

Frankel, Ellen, 6670 Lincoln Drive, Philadelphia, PA 19119; 215-843-0228.

Friedman, Rabbi Manis, Bais Chana (Orthodox, Lubavitch movement, for women), 15 Montcalm Court, St. Paul, MN 55116; 612-698-3858.

Fuchs, Rabbi Nancy, Reconstructionist Rabbinical College, Greenwood Ave. and Church Road, Wyncote, PA 19095; 215-576-0800.

Fund, Rabbi Meir, 1049 E. 13th St., Brooklyn, NY 11231; 718-338-8442.

Geller, Rabbi Laura, Temple Emanuel, 8844 Burton Way, Beverly Hills, CA, 90211; 310-274-6388.

Gendler, Rabbi Everett, Temple Emanuel, 101 West Forest St., Lowell, MA, 01851; 508-454-1372.

Gold, Rabbi Shefa, P.O. Box 355, Las Vegas, NM 87701; 505-425-5728.

Goldfarb, Yehudit and Reuven, Aquarian Minyan, 2020 Essex St., Berkeley, CA 94703, 510-848-0965.

Goodman, Malka, 45 Carpenter Lane, Philadelphia, PA 19119, 215-844-1679; e-mail: MalkaBGood@aol.com.

Gottlieb, Rabbi Lynn, 3309 Mountain Road, NE, Albuquerque, NM 87106; 505-343-8227.

Green, Rabbi Arthur, NEJS Dept., Brandeis University, Waltham, MA 02254; 617-736-2971.

Greenberg, Rabbi Irving and Blu, CLAL, National Jewish Center for Learning and Leadership, 99 Park Ave., Suite C-300, New York, NY 10016-1599; 212-867-8888.

Greenberg, Rabbi Julie, Jewish Renewal Life Center, 6445 Greene St., B-202, Philadelphia, PA 19119; 215-843-4345; e-mail: julieGberg@aol.com.

Holtz, Barry, Jewish Theological Seminary, 3080 Broadway, New York, NY 10027; 212-678-8034.

Jacobson, Rabbi Burt, Kehilla Community Synagogue, 941 The Alameda, Berkeley, CA 94707; 510-527-5452.

Kleinbaum, Rabbi Sharon, Congregation Beth Simchat Torah, 57 Bethune St., New York, NY 10014; 212-929-9498.

Koller-Fox, Rabbi Cherie, Congregation Etz Haim, 134–136 Magazine St., Cambridge, MA 02139; 617-497-7626; e-mail:efox@vax.clark.edu.

Kroner, Rabbi Eric, Ohr Somayach (Orthodox), 21550 W. Twelve Mile Road, Southfield, MI 48076; 810-352-4870.

Kushner, Rabbi Larry, Congregation Beth El of the Sudbury River Valley, Hudson Road, Sudbury, MA 01776; 508-443-9622.

Lerner, Michael, *Tikkun* Magazine, 251 W. 100th St., New York, NY 10025; 212-864-4110.

Leviton, Susan, Levworks (art, calligraphy, and klezmer music), 3417 N. Fourth, Harrisburg, PA 17110; 717-236-0146.

Litman, Rabbi Jane, Department of Continuing Education, University of Judaism, 15600 Mulholland Drive, Bel Air, CA 90077; 310-476-9777.

Matt, Daniel, 27 Parnassus St., Berkeley, CA 94708; 510-848-9779.

Milgram, Rabbi Goldie, Academy for Jewish Religion, 15 W. 86th St., New York, NY 10024; 212-875-0540.

Novick, Rabbi Leah, 5315 Carmel Valley Road, B-310, Carmel, CA 93923; 408-648-3832.

Omer-Man, Rabbi Jonathan, Director of Religious Outreach, Los Angeles Hillel Council; 213-934-7066; or c/o Metivta (see above).

Paley, Rabbi Michael, Wexner Heritage Foundation, 551 Madison Ave., New York, NY 10022, 212-355-6115, or Bard College, 914-758-6822.

Plaskow, Judith, Dept. of Religious Studies, Manhattan College, Bronx, NY 10471; 718-920-0123; e-mail: jplaskow@manvax.cc.mancol.edu.

Prager, Rabbi Marcia, 228 W. Hortter St., Philadelphia, PA 19119; 215-849-9227; e-mail: marciaprag@aol.com.

Richter, Glenn, Student Struggle for Soviet Jewry, 50 W. 97th St., 3-S, New York, NY 10025; 212-663-5784.

Riemer, Rabbi Jack, 18212 Clearbrook Circle, Boca Raton, FL 33498; 407-883-0736.

Rovner, Dr. Jay, Jewish Theological Seminary, or 115 Highland Ave., Highland Park, NJ 08904; 908-572-3879.

Saperstein, Rabbi David, Religious Action Center of the Union of American Hebrew Congregations (Reform), 2027 Massachusetts Ave., NW, Washington, DC 20036; 202-387-2800.

Schachter-Shalomi, Rabbi Zalman, ALEPH, The Alliance for Jewish Renewal, 7318 Germantown Ave., Philadelphia, PA 19119-1720; 215-247-9700.

Schneider, Susan Weidman, *Lilith* Magazine, 250 W. 57th St., Suite 2432, New York, NY 10107; 212-757-0818.

Schulweis, Rabbi Harold, Congregation Valley Beth Shalom, 15739 Ventura Blvd., Encino, CA 91436; 818-788-6000.

Serotta, Rabbi Gerry, George Washington University Hillel Foundation, 2300 H St. NW, Washington, DC 20037; 202-296-8873.

Shapiro, Rabbi Rami, Temple Beth Or and the Rasheit Institute for Jewish Spirituality. P.O. Box 161238, Miami, FL 33116; 305-235-1419; e-mail: 76252.517@compuserve.com.

Shneyer, David, Am Kolel Judaic Resource Center; Network of Independent Jewish Communities and Havurot; Kehilla Chadasha Havurah; Ma'alot school of Jewish music; 15 W. Montgomery Ave., Suite 204, Rockville, MD 20850; 301-309-2310, fax 301-309-2328.

Siegel, Danny, Ziv Tsedakah Fund, 301-468-0060, 263 Congressional Lane, Apt. 708, Rockville, MD 20852; fax 301-468-6923.

Steinsaltz, Rabbi Adin. Steinsaltz lives in Israel; to find out about his frequent U.S. visits, contact Aleph Society, 25 W. 45th St., Suite 1405, New York, NY 10036; 212-840-1166.

Strassfeld, Rabbi Michael, Congregation Ansche Chesed, 251 W. 100th St., New York, NY 10025; 212-865-0600.

Teubal, Savina J., Santa Monica, CA; 310-459-5503; e-mail: savina555 @aol.com.

Ticktin, Rabbi Max and Esther, 2311 Connecticut Ave. NW, Washington, DC 20008; 202-462-3392.

Umansky, Dr. Ellen M., Fairfield University, North Benson Road, Fairfield, CT 06430; 203-254-4000, ext. 2065.

Walt, Rabbi Brian, Mishkan Shalom Congregation, c/o Stratford Friends School, 5 Llandillo Road, Havertown, PA 19083; 610-446-4068.

Waskow, Rabbi Arthur, ALEPH, The Alliance for Jewish Renewal, 7318 Germantown Ave., Philadelphia, PA 19119-1720; 215-247-9700.

Weinberg, Rabbi Sheila Peltz, Jewish Community of Amherst, 742 Main St., Amherst, MA 01002; 413-256-0160.

Weiner, Rabbi Shohama, The Academy for Jewish Religion, 15 W. 86th St., New York, NY 10024; 212-875-0540.

Weissler, Professor Chava, Dept. of Religion Studies, Lehigh University, 9 W. Packer Ave., Bethlehem, PA 18015; 610-758-3372; e-mail: lew1@lehigh.edu.

Wenig, Rabbi Margaret, Beth Am, The People's Temple, 178 Bennett Ave., New York, NY 10040; 212-927-2230.

COMMUNITIES DESCRIBED IN THIS BOOK

Ansche Chesed, 251 W. 100th St., New York, NY 10025; 212-865-0600.

Aquarian Minyan, Berkeley, CA; 510-848-2003.

Congregation Beth Simchat Torah, 57 Bethune St., New York, NY 10014; 212-929-9492.

Fabrangen, 1747 Connecticut Ave. NW, Washington, DC 20009; 202-667-7829.

Germantown Minyanim, c/o Germantown Jewish Center, Lincoln Drive and Ellet St., Philadelphia, PA 19119; 215-844-1507.

Havurah of Southwest Florida, c/o Rabbi Mitchell Chefitz, 9315 SW 61st Court, Miami, FL 33173; 305-666-7349.

Havurat Shalom, 113 College Ave., Somerville, MA 02144; 617-623-3376.

Mishkan Shalom Congregation, c/o Stratford Friends School, 5 Llandillo Road, Havertown, PA 19083; 610-446-4068.

P'nai Or, c/o ALEPH, 7318 Germantown Ave., Philadelphia, PA 19119; 215-247-9700.

Upstairs Minyan, Newberger Hillel Center, University of Chicago, 5715 Woodlawn, Chicago, IL, 60637; 312-752-1127.

LOCATING JEWISH BOOKS AND TAPES

Try Jewish bookstores, synagogue gift shops, or the mail-order catalogs below. ALEPH (see above) has Jewish renewal tapes not available elsewhere.

MAIL-ORDER CATALOGS

1-800-JUDAISM.

Behrman House, 235 Watchung Ave., West Orange, NJ 07052-5520; 201-669-0447.

J. Levine Co. (bookstore and Judaica), 5 W. 30th St., New York, NY 10001; 212-695-6888.

Jonathan David Books, 68-22 Eliot, Middle Village, NY 11379; 718-456-8611.

JEWISH PUBLISHERS

Jason Aronson, 230 Livingston St., Northvale, NJ 07647.

Biblio Press (women's and feminist), 1140 Broadway, New York, NY 10001; 212-684-1257.

Jewish Lights, P.O. Box 276, S. Woodstock, VT 05071.

Jewish Publication Society, 1930 Chestnut St., Philadelphia, PA 19301-4599.

Schocken Books, 201 E. 50th, New York, NY 10022; 212-751-2600.

SELECTED READING

This bibliography is intended to open a variety of gates to a deepened Jewish identity. It cannot pretend to completeness or even representativeness. Among other things, I haven't tried to cover mediaeval or modern Jewish literature. Holtz's guides, listed on page 299, are one place to get started on the great spectrum of Jewish books.

MAGAZINES

Sh'ma: A Journal of Jewish Responsibility, c/o CLAL, National Jewish Center for Learning and Leadership, 99 Park Ave., Suite C-300, New York, NY 10016-1599; 212-867-8888.

Moment Magazine, 4710 41st St. NW, Washington, DC 20016; 202-364-3300.

The Reconstructionist, c/o The Reconstructionist Rabbinical College, Church Road and Greenwood Ave., Wyncote, PA 19095.

Reform Judaism, 838 Fifth Ave., New York, NY, 10021; 212-249-0100.

International Jewish Monthly, B'nai B'rith, 1640 Rhode Island Ave., NW, Washington, DC 20036; 202-857-6646.

Conservative Judaism, c/o Jewish Theological Seminary, 3080 Broadway, New York, NY 10027.

Jewish Renewal

Response: A Contemporary Jewish Review, 27 West 20th St., New York, NY 10011.

New Menorah, ALEPH (see above).

Politics / Social Action

Tikkun Magazine (see above).

Feminist

Bridges, P.O. Box 24839, Eugene, OR 97402; 503-935-5720.

Lilith Magazine (see above).

Neshama: Encouraging the Exploration of Women's Spirituality in Judaism, P.O. Box 545, Brookline, MA 02146; 617-965-7350.

Women's Zionist

Hadassah Magazine, 50 W. 58th St., New York, NY 10019; 212-355-7900.

BASIC JUDAISM

Diamant, Anita, and Howard Cooper, *Living a Jewish Life: Jewish Traditions, Customs and Values for Today's Families,* HarperCollins, New York, 1991. (From a Reform or liberal perspective)

Donin, Rabbi Hayim Halevy, *To Be a Jew: A Guide to Jewish Observance in Contemporary Life,* Basic Books, New York, 1972. (Orthodox)

Einstein, Stephen, and Lydia Kukoff, *Every Person's Guide to Judaism,* UAHC Press, New York, 1989. (Reform)

Greenberg, Blu, *How to Run a Traditional Jewish Household,* Simon and Schuster, New York, 1983.

Neusner, Jacob *The Way of Torah: An Introduction to Judaism,* Wadsworth Publishing, Belmont, CA, 1988.

Olitsky, Kerry M. and Ronald H. Isaacs, *The How-To Handbook for Jewish Living,* KTAV Publishing House, Hoboken, NJ, 1993.

Rosenberg, Rabbi Roy A., *The Concise Guide to Judaism: History, Practice, Faith,* Meridian Books (Penguin), New York, 1994. (From the perspective of a Reform rabbi)

Steinberg, Milton, *Basic Judaism,* Jason Aronson, Northvale, NJ, 1987.

Telushkin, Rabbi Joseph, *Jewish Literacy: The Most Important Things to Know About the Jewish Religion, Its People, and Its History,* William Morrow, New York, 1991.

HISTORY
General

Dimont, Max I., *The Amazing Adventures of the Jewish People,* Behrman House, New York, 1984.

Eban, Abba, *Heritage: Civilization and the Jews,* Summit Books, New York, 1984.

Eban, Abba, *My People: Abba Eban's History of the Jews, Vols. I and II,* adapted for educational use by David Bamberger, Behrman House, New York (1978, 1981) from *My People: The Story of the Jews,* Random House, New York, 1968.

Potok, Chaim, *Wanderings: Chaim Potok's History of the Jews,* Fawcett Crest (Ballantine), New York, 1983.

Seltzer, Robert, *Jewish People, Jewish Thought: The Jewish Experience in History,* Macmillan, New York, 1980.

Eastern Europe

Dawidowicz, Lucy S., *The Golden Tradition: Jewish Life and Thought in Eastern Europe,* Beacon Press, Boston, 1968.

Heschel, Abraham Joshua, *The Earth Is the Lord's,* Farrar, Straus and Giroux, New York, 1978.

Zborowski, Mark, and Elizabeth Herzog, *Life is With People: The Culture of the Shtetl,* Schocken, New York, 1962.

American Jews

Howe, Irving, *World of Our Fathers: The Journey of the East European Jews to America and the Life They Found and Made,* Harcourt Brace Jovanovich, New York, 1976.

Roth, Henry, *Call it Sleep,* Avon Books, New York, 1976. Powerful fiction about immigrant family.

Holocaust

Dawidowicz, Lucy, *The War Against the Jews,* Holt Rinehart & Winston, New York, 1973.

More, Arthur D., *While Six Million Died: A Chronicle of American Apathy,* Random House, New York, 1968.

Holocaust Novels and Memoirs

Anne Frank: The Diary of A Young Girl, Pocket Books, New York, 1985.

Flinker, Moshe, *Young Moshe's Diary,* Board of Jewish Education, New York, 1965.

Gutman, Israel, *Resistance: The Warsaw Ghetto Uprising,* Houghton Mifflin, Boston, 1994.

Hillesum, Etty, *An Interrupted Life: The Diaries of Etty Hillesum,* Pocket Books, New York, 1985.

Levi, Primo, *Survival in Auschwitz,* Collier (Macmillan), New York, 1958.

Schwarz-Bart, Andre, *The Last of the Just,* Athaneum, New York, 1973.

Suhl, Yuri, *They Fought Back,* Schocken, New York, 1975.

Wiesel, Elie, *Night,* Avon, New York, 1958.

Soviet Jews

Wiesel, Elie, *The Jews of Silence: A Personal Report on Soviet Jewry,* Holt Rinehart & Winston, New York, 1966.

CLASSIC TEXTS AND MODERN COMMENTARIES

(See Barry Holtz, *Back to the Sources* and *Finding Our Way*, and recommended Torah extracts in "To organize your own study group," above.)

Abrams, Rabbi Judith, *Talmud for Beginners, Vols. I* (Tractate Brachot: highlights and structure) *and II* (Megillah: How do you approach a text); *The Women of the Talmud; Learn Talmud: How to Use the Steinsaltz Talmud, English Edition;* w/Steven Abrams, *Jewish Parenting: Rabbinic Insights,* all published by Jason Aronson, Northvale, NJ.

Alter, Robert, *The Art of Biblical Narrative,* Basic Books, New York, 1981.

Ginzberg, Louis, *Legends of the Bible,* Jewish Publication Society of America, Philadelphia, 1975.

Leibowitz, Nehama, *Studies in Genesis* (separate volumes for Exodus, Leviticus, Numbers, and Deuteronomy), World Zionist Organization, Jerusalem, 1981.

Neusner, Jacob, *Invitation to the Talmud,* Harper & Row, San Francisco, 1989.

Neusner, Jacob, *Learn Mishnah,* Behrman House, West Orange, NJ, 1978.

Neusner, Jacob, *The Mishna: An Introduction,* Jason Aronson, Northvale, NJ, 1989.

Sedra Scenes (see above).

Soncino Bible, individual volumes with commentary.

The Talmud, Steinsaltz translation.

Waskow, Arthur, *God-Wrestling, Round 2: Ancient Wisdom, Future Paths,* Jewish Lights, Woodstock, NY, 1995.

JEWISH WAY OF LIFE AND OBSERVANCE

Donin, Rabbi Hayim Halevy, *To Be a Jew: A Guide to Jewish Observance in Contemporary Life,* Basic Books, New York, 1972.

Klein, Isaac, *A Guide to Jewish Religious Practice,* Jewish Theological Seminary, New York, 1979.

Siegel, Richard, Michael Strassfeld and Sharon Strassfeld, eds., *The Jewish Catalog: A Do-It-Yourself-Kit,* Jewish Publication Society of America, Philadelphia, 1973. See also the Second and Third Jewish Catalogs and Michael Strassfeld's *New Jewish Catalog,* forthcoming from Schocken.

Waskow, Arthur, *Down-to-Earth Judaism: Food, Money, Sex and the Rest of Life,* William Morrow, New York, 1995.

HOLIDAYS

Greenberg, Irving, *The Jewish Way: Living the Holidays,* Summit Books, New York, 1988.

Kitov, Eliahu, *The Book of Our Heritage,* Feldheim, New York, 1978.

Strassfeld, Michael, *The Jewish Holidays: A Guide and Commentary,* Harper & Row, New York, 1985.

Waskow, Arthur I., *Seasons of Our Joy: A Handbook of Jewish Festivals,* Bantam, New York, 1981.

SPIRITUAL LIFE

Buber, Martin, *Hasidism and Modern Man,* Humanities Press International, Atlantic Highlands, NJ, 1988, or Harper & Row, New York, 1966.

Buber, Martin, *Israel and the World: Essays in a Time of Crisis,* Schocken, New York, 1963.

Buber, Martin, *On Judaism* (Nahum Glatzer, ed.), Schocken, New York, 1972.

Cohen, A., and P. Mendes-Flohr, *Contemporary Jewish Religious Thought,* The Free Press, New York, 1988.

Gillman, Neil, *Sacred Fragments: Recovering Theology for the Modern Jew,* Jewish Publication Society, Philadelphia, 1990.

Green, Arthur, *Seek My Face, Speak My Name: A Contemporary Jewish Theology,* Jason Aronson, Northvale, NJ, 1992.

Hartman, David, *A Living Covenant,* The Free Press, New York, 1985.

Heschel, Abraham Joshua, *God in Search of Man: A Philosophy of Judaism,* Farrar, Straus and Giroux, New York, 1955.

Heschel, Abraham Joshua, *Man is Not Alone: A Philosophy of Religion,* Farrar, Straus and Giroux, New York, 1951.

Heschel, Abraham Joshua, *Man's Quest for God: Studies in Prayer and Symbolism,* Charles Scribner's Sons, New York, 1954.

Heschel, Abraham Joshua, *The Sabbath: Its Meaning for Modern Man,* Farrar, Straus and Giroux, New York, 1975.

Holtz, Barry, *Finding Our Way: Jewish Texts and the Lives We Lead Today,* Schocken, New York, 1990.

Kushner, Harold S., *When Bad Things Happen to Good People,* Schocken, New York, 1981.

Lerner, Michael, *Jewish Renewal: A Path to Healing and Transformation,* Grosset/ Putman, New York, 1994.

Neusner, Jacob, *Between Time and Eternity: The Essentials of Judaism,* Dickenson Publishing Co., Emmaus, PA, 1975.

Rosenzweig, Franz, *On Jewish Learning* (N. N. Glatzer, ed.), Schocken, New York, 1965.

Shapiro, Rami, *Dvekut: Theory and Practice of God-Consciousness in Judaism,* forthcoming from Belltower Press (Random House), New York, 1996.

Shapiro, Rami, *Shirt Pocket Wisdom* and *Light House Books,* two series of tiny, pungent books about spiritual ideas, Temple Beth Or, Miami.

Soncino, Rifat, and Daniel B. Syme, *Finding God: Ten Jewish Responses,* Union of American Hebrew Congregations, New York, 1986.

Steinsaltz, Adin, *Teshuvah: A Guide for the Newly Observant Jew,* Free Press, New York, 1987.

Waskow, Arthur, *These Holy Sparks: The Rebirth of the Jewish People,* Harper & Row, San Francisco, 1983.

Wolf, Arnold Jacob, ed., *Rediscovering Judaism: Reflections on a New Theology,* Quadrangle Books, Chicago, 1965.

The B'nai B'rith History of the Jewish People contains three helpful anthologies, all edited by Simon Noveck: *Creators of the Jewish Experience in the Modern World; Great Jewish Thinkers of the Twentieth Century;* and *Contemporary Jewish Thought,* B'nai B'rith Books, Washington, DC, 1985.

ETHICS AND POLITICAL ACTION

Bush, Lawrence, and Jeffrey Dekro, *Jews, Money & Social Responsibility: Developing a "Torah of Money" for Contemporary Life,* The Shefa Fund, 1993.

Fromm, Erich, *The Art of Loving,* Bantam, New York, 1963.

Gopin, Mark, Mark H. Levine and Sid Schwarz, *Jewish Civics: A Tikkun Olam/World Repair Manual,* Coalition for the Advancement of Jewish Education and the Washington Institute for Jewish Leadership and Values, 1994.

Heschel, Abraham Joshua, *The Insecurity of Freedom: Essays on Human Existence,* Farrar, Straus, New York, 1967.

Heschel, *The Prophets,* Harper & Row, New York, 1969 and 1971.

Lerner, Michael, ed., *Tikkun Anthology,* Tikkun Books, Oakland, CA, 1992.

Roots of Jewish Nonviolence, Jewish Peace Fellowship, New York, 1985.

Schwartz, Richard H., *Judaism and Global Survival,* Atara Publishing Co., New York, 1987. A broad and impassioned survey of the relevance of Jewish texts to social and political action.

Siegel, Danny, *Gym Shoes and Irises,* 1987, *Munbaz II and Other Mitzvah Heroes,* 1988, *Mitzvahs,* 1990, *Good People,* 1995, and for young readers, *Tell Me a Mitzvah* and *After the Rain,* all from Town House Press, Spring Valley, NY.

Vorspan, Albert, and David Saperstein, *Tough Choices: Jewish Perspectives on Social Justice,* UAHC Press, New York, 1992.

Waskow, Arthur I., *The Bush is Burning!: Radical Judaism Faces the Pharaohs of the Modern Superstate,* Macmillan, New York, 1971.

JEWISH MYSTICISM

Green, Arthur, and Barry W. Holtz, *Your Word is Fire: The Hasidic Masters on Contemplative Prayer,* Schocken, New York, 1987.

Kaplan, Aryeh, *Jewish Meditation: A Practical Guide,* Schocken, New York, 1985.

Kerdeman, Deborah, and Lawrence Kushner, *The Invisible Chariot: An Introduction to Kabbalah and Jewish Spirituality,* Alternatives in Religious Education, Denver, CO, 1986.

Kushner, Lawrence, *The Book of Miracles: Jewish Spirituality for Children to Read to Their Parents and Parents to Read to Their Children,* UAHC Press, New York.

Kushner, Lawrence, *Honey from the Rock: Visions of Jewish Mystical Renewal; Sefer Otiyot: The Book of Letters: A Mystical Alef-Bait; The River of Light: Spirituality, Judaism, Consciousness;* and *God Was in this Place, and I, i did not know: Finding Self, Spirituality and Ultimate Meaning,* all available from Jewish Lights Publishing, Woodstock, VT, 1995 editions.

Paradigm Shift: From the Jewish Renewal Teachings of Reb Zalman Schachter-Shalomi (Ellen Singer, ed.), Jason Aronson, Northvale, NJ.

Schachter, Reb Zalman, *The First Step* (in *The First Jewish Catalog*), above; *Fragments of a Future Scroll: Hasidism for the Here and Now,* available through ALEPH.

Schacter-Shalomi, Rabbi Zalman M., *Gate to the Heart: An Evolving Process,* available through ALEPH.

Steinsaltz, Adin, *The Thirteen-Petalled Rose: A Discourse on the Essence of Jewish Existence and Belief,* Basic Books (Harper Collins), New York, 1980.

FEMINIST

Adelman, Penina V., *Miriam's Well: Rituals for Jewish Women Around the Year,* Biblio Press, Fresh Meadows, NY, 1987.

Antonelli, Judith, *In the Image of God; A Feminist Commentary on the Torah,* Jason Aronson, Northvale, NJ, 1995.

Baum, Charlotte, Paula Hyman, and Sonya Michel, *The Jewish Woman in America,* New American Library, New York, 1976.

Brod, Harry, *A Mensch Among Men,* Crossing Press, Freedom, CA, 1988.

Cardin, Nina, *Out of the Depths I Call to You: A Book of Prayers for the Married Jewish Woman,* Jason Aronson, Northvale, NJ, 1992.

Elwell, Sue Levi, ed., *The Jewish Women's Studies Guide,* second edition, University Press of America, Boston, and Biblio Press, Fresh Meadows, NY, 1987.

Fine, Irene, *Midlife: A Rite of Passage* and *The Wise Woman: A Celebration,* Women's Institute for Continuing Jewish Education, La Jolla, CA, 1988.

Gottlieb, Lynn, *She Who Dwells Within: A Feminist Vision of a Renewed Judaism,* Harper San Francisco, 1995.

Greenberg, Blu, *On Women and Judaism: A View from Tradition,* Jewish Publication Society, Philadelphia, 1981.

Grossman, Susan and Rivka Haut, eds., *Daughters of the King: Women and the Synagogue,* Jewish Publication Society, Philadelphia, 1992.

Henry, Sondra and Emily Taitz, *Written Out of History: Our Jewish Foremothers,* Biblio Press, New York, 1990.

Heschel, Susannah ed., *On Being a Jewish Feminist: A Reader,* Schocken, New York, 1983.

Koltun, Elizabeth, ed., *The Jewish Woman: New Perspectives,* Schocken Books, New York, 1976.

Levine, Elizabeth Resnick, ed., *A Ceremonies Sampler: New Rites, Celebrations, and Observances of Jewish Women,* Women's Institute for Continuing Jewish Education, La Jolla, CA, 1991.

Orenstein, Debra, ed., *Life Cycles: Jewish Women on Life Passages and Personal Milestones,* Jewish Lights Publishing, Woodstock, VT, 1994.

Plaskow, Judith, *Standing Again at Sinai: Judaism from a Feminist Perspective,* Harper & Row, San Francisco, 1990.

Pogrebin, Letty Cottin, *Deborah, Golda and Me: Being Female and Jewish in America,* Crown Publishers, New York, 1991.

Schneider, Susan Weidman, *Jewish and Female: A Guide and Sourcebook for Today's Jewish Woman,* Simon and Schuster, New York, 1985.

Spiegel, Marcia Cohn, and Deborah Lipton Kremsdorf, eds., *Women Speak to God; The Prayers and Poems of Jewish Women,* San Diego Women's Institute for Continuing Education, San Diego, CA, 1987.

Umansky, Ellen M., and Diane Ashton, *Four Centuries of Jewish Women's Spirituality,* Beacon Press, Boston, 1992.

Weissler, Chava, "The Traditional Piety of Ashkenazic Women," in Arthur Green, ed., *Jewish Spirituality: From the Sixteenth Century Revival to the Present,* Crossroad Publishing, New York, 1989, pp. 245–275.

GAY AND LESBIAN

Balka, Christie, and Andy Rose, eds., *Twice Blessed: On Being Lesbian, Gay, and Jewish,* Beacon Press, Boston, 1989.

Beck, Evelyn Torton, ed., *Nice Jewish Girls: A Lesbian Anthology,* Beacon Press, Boston, 1989.

MODERN ISRAEL

Nonfiction

Hertzberg, Arthur, *The Zionist Idea,* Athaneum, New York, 1969.
Oz, Amos, *In the Land of Israel,* Vintage Books, New York, 1984.

Fiction

Michener, James, *The Source,* Fawcett, New York, 1988.
Uris, Leon, *Exodus,* Bantam, New York, 1983.

STORIES

Band, Arnold J., ed. and trans., *Nahman of Bratslav: The Tales,* Paulist Press, New York, 1978.

Buber, Martin, *Tales of the Hasidim,* Schocken, NewYork, 1975.

Frankel, Ellen, *The Classic Tales: 4,000 Years of Jewish Lore,* Jason Aronson, Northvale, NJ, 1989.

Halkin, Hillel (trans.), *Tevye the Dairyman and The Railroad Stories,* Schocken, NewYork, 1988.

Howe, Irving, and Ruth Wisse, *The Best of Sholom Aleichem,* Jason Aronson, Northvale, NJ, 1989.

Schram, Peninah, *Jewish Stories One Generation Tells Another,* Jason Aronson, Northvale, NJ, 1987.

Schwartz, Howard, *Elijah's Violin and Other Jewish Fairy Tales,* Harper & Row, New York, 1985. *Miriam's Tambourine: Jewish Folk Tales From Around the World,* distributed by The Free Press, New York, 1986. *The Diamond Tree: Jewish Tales From Around the World* (with Barbara Rush), Harper-Collins, NewYork, 1991.

CONTEMPORARY ISSUES

Contemporary Jews and Judaism

Cowan, Paul, *An Orphan in History: Retrieving a Jewish Legacy,* Bantam, New York, 1982.

Roiphe, Anne, *Generation Without Memory: A Jewish Journey in Christian America,* Summit Books (Simon and Schuster), NewYork, 1981.

Waskow, Arthur, *God-Wrestling, Round 2,* Jewish Lights, Woodstock, NY, 1996.

Weissler, Chava, *Making Judaism Meaningful: Ambivalence and Tradition in a Havurah Community,* AMS Press, NewYork, 1989.

Intermarriage

Petsonk, Judy, and Jim Remsen, *The Intermarriage Handbook: A Guide for Jews and Christians,* William Morrow, NewYork, 1988. (Quill paperback, 1990.)

Conversion

Kukoff, Lydia, *Choosing Judaism,* UAHC, NewYork, 1981.

Romanoff, Lena, *Your People, My People: Finding Fulfillment as a Jew by Choice,* Jewish Publication Society, Philadelphia, 1990.

Genealogy

Kurzweil, Arthur, *How to Trace Your Jewish Genealogy and Personal History,* William Morrow, NewYork, 1980.

NEW PRAYERBOOKS

Falk, Marcia, *Book of Blessings: New Jewish Prayers and Rituals for Daily Life, the Sabbath, and the New Moon Festival,* Harper San Francisco, 1996.

Kol Haneshamah (series of prayerbooks for Shabbat and holidays), The Reconstructionist Press, Wyncote, PA.

Or Chadash (A New Light): New Paths for Shabbat Morning, P'nai Or Religious Fellowship, ALEPH, Alliance for Jewish Renewal, 7318 Germantown Avenue, Philadelphia, PA 19119-1793. (with audiotape)

Siddur Birkat Shalom (Blessings of Peace Prayerbook) Havurat Shalom Siddur Project, 113 College Avenue, Somerville, MA 02144. Groups may buy one copy and reproduce it for their own use.

Vetaher Libenu, Congregation Beth El of the Sudbury River Valley, Sudbury, MA 01776.

MUSIC, FILMS, SOFTWARE, AND JOKES

Davka software, 7074 North Western Ave., Chicago, IL 60645; 312-465-4070.

Half the Kingdom, feminist documentary film by Francine Zuckerman and Roushell Goldstein, distributed by Direct Cinema; 1-800-525-0000.

Hester Street, film about Eastern European immigrant family by Carol Micklin Silver.

Novak, William and Waldoks, Moshe, *The Big Book of Jewish Humor,* Harper & Row, New York, 1981.

Songbooks

Friedman, Debbie, *Blessings,* Sounds Write Productions (see below), 1990.

Hirschhorn, Linda, *Gather Round: New Hebrew Canons, Rounds and Musical Settings,* Tara Publications, Cedarhurst, NY, 1989.

Pasternak, Velvel, *Israel in Song,* Tara Publications, Cedarhurst, NY, 1974.

Searles, Susan Claire, ed., *Hebrew Songs for All Seasons,* Tara Publications, Cedarhurst, NY, 1987.

Shlomo Shabbos: The Shlomo Carlebach Shabbos Songbook (Ben Zion Solomon, ed.), Kehillat Jacob Productions, 1993, distributed by Tara Publications, Cedarhurst, NY.

The Shlomo Carlebach Songbook, Zimrany Records, New York, 1970.

Audiotapes

Azen, Margot Stein, *Guarding the Garden* (feminist, ecological musical) and other tapes (see above).

The Best of Shlomo Carlebach, 1960–1990, Jerusalem Star, 30 Fisherville Ave., Willowdale, Ontario, Canada; 416-633-5441.

The Boston davening tape, havurah-style melodies for Shabbat service, available from National Havurah Committee (see above).

Friedman, Debbie, *And You Shall Be a Blessing* and other tapes c/o Randee
Friedman, Sounds Write, 6685 Norman Lane, San Diego, CA 92120; 619-
697-6120.

Gold, Rabbi Shefa, *Chants Encounters,* other tapes, see above.

Hirschfeld, Rabbi Aryeh, 1304 Quincy St., Ashland, OR 97520; 503-482-
8806.

Hirschorn, Linda, *Gather Round* and other tapes, Oyster Albums, P.O. Box
3929, Berkeley, CA 94703.

Shneyer, David, Fabrangen Fiddlers (see above).

Zeller, Rabbi David, *Ruach* and other tapes, Heartsong Productions, Box 170,
Efrat, Israel.

BASIC REFERENCE

Encyclopedia Judaica, Keter Publishing House, Jerusalem, 1972.

GLOSSARY

Adonai. Lord (traditional Jews say this only in prayer)

aleph. First letter of Hebrew alphabet

aliyah. Standing beside Torah while it is read, an honor

Amidah. Core prayer of worship service, said standing

Anti-Semitism. Racist hatred of Jews

Aramaic. Language used in Middle East from approximately 700 B.C.E. to 700 C.E.

Ashkenazi. East European

aufruf. Torah ceremony the Shabbat before a wedding

avodah. Service to God, worship

baal, baalat, baalei teshuvah. Those who become more observant

Barukh Atah Adonai, Elohaynu, Melekh Ha-Olam. "Blessed are you, Lord, our God, King of the World"; standard beginning of blessings and prayers

bat mitzvah. Girl's coming-of-age ceremony

bayit (beit), batim. House, kosher communal houses

bet din. Religious court (literally, house of judgment)

Borchu. Bless Him: the call to prayer

bracha. Blessing

Brachot. Talmud tractate on blessings

breira. Alternative

brit b'not Yisrael. Covenant of the daughters of Israel

brit milah. Covenant of circumcision

Brucha At Shekhina. Blessed are You, Divine Presence (traditional beginning of prayer translated into feminine)

Chei Ha-Olamim. Life of the worlds

chutzpah. Gall, nerve (Yiddish)

covenant. Binding agreement between Jews and God

daven. Pray

dreidel. Spinning top used in Hanukkah game

dvekut. Cleaving to God

d'var Torah. Word of Torah, sermon

emet. Truth

"Enlightenment". Nineteenth-century discovery of secular culture by formerly ghettoized Jews

eruv. A fictional border within which one could carry items

Esther. Jewish wife of Persian king, in Purim story

etrog. Lemony citron used at Sukkot

exilarch or *Resh Galuta*. Secular leader of Babylonian Jews

Exodus. Story of Hebrew slaves leaving Egypt, second book of Bible

Ezrat Nashim. Literally, "help for women"; women's section in Temple

farbrangen. Hasidic study/party with the *rebbe*

frum. Orthodox, observant

galut. Exile

"Gentleman's agreement". Agreement not to sell homes to Jews

Geonim. The heads of the academies of Babylon

get. Paper of divorce

Gmilut Hasadim. Acts of loving kindness

Goldeneh Medinah. "Golden land"; *shtetl* vision of America

Hadassah. Zionist women's organization

Haggadah, Haggadot. Text of Passover seder

halachah, halakha. Jewish Law

hallah. Braided bread eaten on the Sabbath

Hanukkah. Eight-day festival commemorating rededication of the Temple

HaShem. Literally, "the Name"; traditional name for God

Hasidism. Eastern European Jewish spiritual revival movement

Haskalah. "Enlightenment"; the nineteenth-century discovery by Jews of secular culture

Havdalah. Ceremony ending Shabbat

haver, haverim. Comrade, comrades

havurah. Fellowship

havurahnik. Member of havurah movement

Hebrew. Language of ancient and modern-day Israel

hevra kadisha. "Holy fellowship"; prepares the dead for burial

hevrusa, hevruta. Studying with a partner

High Holidays. The New Year and the Day of Atonement

Holocaust. Murder of six million eastern European Jews by Nazis

intifada. Palestinian uprising against Israeli occupation

Jubilee. Every fiftieth year, when slaves are freed and land redistributed

Kabbalah. Mystical tradition (literally, "what is received")

kaddish. Prayer said by mourners, affirms God's holiness

kadosh. Holy

Kadosh Baruch Hu. Holy Blessed God

kahal. Elected community board, ran communal administration in each town

kallah. Bride

kallah. Gathering or retreat (for study)

kavannah. Intention, in prayer and ritual

kehilla. Community, elected community council

kibbutz. Communal farm in Israel

kiddush. The blessing over the wine

kippah. Skullcap

klal Yisrael. "All Israel"; the unity of all Jews

kohen. A descendant of the priests of the ancient Temple

Kol Nidre. Mournful chant that begins the evening service of Yom Kippur; literally, a release from vows one is unable to fulfill

kosher. Food permitted by Jewish law, prepared in permitted way

landsmanshaft. Association of people from the same village

latkes. Potato pancakes, a Hanukkah treat

Mashiach. Messiah

matzoh. Flat unleavened bread eaten during Passover

maven. Expert

mazon. Food, sustenance

ma'yan. Source

Mea She'arim. Ultra-Orthodox section of old Jerusalem

mehitza. A barrier separating men and women

Melekh Ha-Olam. King of the World

menorah. Branched candlestick

mensch. Decent human being

midrash. Explanatory story expanding on Bible text

mikveh. Pool filled partly from rain or flowing stream, used for purification, after menstruation, and for conversion to Judaism

minyan. Quorum of ten adults, needed for certain prayers

mishkan. Sanctuary

Mishna. Third-century C.E. compilation of Jewish laws previously transmitted only orally

Mitnagdim. Opponents (of Hasidism)

mitzvah, mitzvot. Commandment, laws (also good deeds)

M'kor Chaim. Fountain of life

Modeh or *Modah Ani.* Morning prayer, literally, "I thank you"

neshama. Soul

niddah. Refraining from sex during and for one week after menstruation

niggun. Melody

omer. Literally, a measure of grain; the forty-nine days between Passover and Shavuos

Oneg Shabbat. Refreshments after services

Orthodox. Observing the traditional laws strictly

Pardes. Paradise; also refers to four levels of interpretation of biblical text: *p'shat* (literal), *remez* (metaphorical), *midrash* (teaching moral lessons), *sod* (secret or mystical meanings)

Passover, Pesach. Spring holiday celebrating freeing of Hebrew slaves from Egypt

payes. Long sidecurls worn by ultra-Orthodox Jews

Pharisees. Movement toward greater observance of Jewish law in first century B.C.E., forerunner of today's Judaism

pogrom. Riot directed against Jews and their homes

Purim. Carnival-like holiday celebrating defeat of anti-Semitic plot to exterminate Jews of ancient Persia

pushke. Charity box

P'nai Or. Faces of Light

rebbe. Teacher/leader in the Hasidic movement

Reconstructionism. Judaism's youngest denomination, defines Judaism as an evolving civilization

refuseniks. Soviet Jews denied permission to emigrate to Israel

Rosh Hashana. Jewish New Year, a solemn holiday

Rosh Hodesh. Festival of the New Moon

Ruach. Spirit

Sabbatical year. Every seventh year, when land is to lie fallow

Sanhedrin or Men of the Great Assembly. Highest court in ancient Judea; it judged, interpreted, and at times enacted laws

schnapps. Hard liquor

Sedra. Torah portion for the week

Sephardi. Jews from Mideast or Spanish-speaking lands

Seudah Shlishit. The "third meal" of the Sabbath

Shabbat, Shabbos. Sabbath, day of rest

Shabbaton. All-day Sabbath study retreat

shalah manot. Treats sent to friends at Purim

shaliach. Messenger; sometimes refers to angels

shalom. Peace, wholeness; greeting used in place of hello or goodbye

Shavuot, Shavuos. Spring holiday celebrating giving of Torah at Mt. Sinai

Shekhina. God's Presence, the One Who Dwells With (or Within) Us

shiva. The first week of the mourning period

Sh'mita. The seventh year, when fields lie fallow

shofar. Ram's horn blown at Yom Kippur and at other times

shomer. Observe or guard

shomeret. Guardian (f)

shtetl. European ghetto village

Shulkhan Arukh. "Set Table": authoritative summary of Jewish law

shul. School, in Yiddish; often refers to synagogue

sh'elah. Question

Sh'ma. The prayer affirming God's oneness; literally, "listen"

Sh'mirat haguf. Protecting one's own body

Siman Tov, Mazel Tov. Congratulations and good luck; song sung at weddings and other special occasions

Simkhat bat. Rejoicing in a daughter

Simkhat Torah. Rejoicing in the Law; fall holiday

Sinai. Desert mountain where Ten Commandments were given

sitzfleish. flesh on your buttocks

sukkah. Open-air hut built during harvest holiday of Sukkot

Sukkot. Fall harvest holiday

s'firot. Kabbalist concept of ten aspects of God

tallis, tallit. Fringed prayer shawl

Talmud. Sixth-century C.E. compilation of commentary on the Mishna

tefillah groups. Prayer groups

tefillin. Leather boxes with Bible verses and straps wound about head and arm, worn by Orthodox men during weekday morning prayer

Temple. Center of priestly sacrificial worship in ancient Israel

teshuvah. Returning to God, often used to mean repentance

tiferet. Beauty; one of *s'firot* (attributes of God in Kabbalah)

tikkun olam. Repair, healing, transformation of the world

Tisha B'Av. Memorial of the destruction of the ancient Temple

Torah. Literally, "teaching": the first five books of the Bible and, by extension, all Jewish law and learning

Torah l'shma. Learning Torah for its own sake

trope. Notes by which the Torah portion is chanted

tsedakah. Literally, "justice"; food and money given to the poor

Tu B'Shvat. Birthday of the trees

United Jewish Appeal. Jewish communal fundraising campaign

yahrzeit. Memorial

yarmulka. Skullcap

yeshiva. Orthodox Jewish school, often at an advanced level

Yom Kippur. Day of Atonement, solemn fast day

Yovel. Jubilee: the fiftieth year, when slaves are freed and land redistributed

Zionist. Supporter of the creation of a Jewish state, Israel

NOTES

Chapter 2. Havurah

1. As noted in Riv-Ellen Prell, *Prayer and Community: The Havurah in American Judaism,* Wayne State University Press, Detroit, 1989, p. 36.
2. Cited by Giti Bendheim in Susan Weidman Schneider, ed., *Jewish and Female: A Guide and Sourcebook for Today's Jewish Woman,* Simon and Schuster, New York, 1985, p. 237.
3. The Protestantization of American synagogues is described in "Decorum in American Judaism," Chapter 1 of Prell, op. cit., pp. 30–68.
4. Rabbi Steve Shaw of the Jewish Theological Seminary's Department of Community Education and Irving Levine of the American Jewish Committee helped provide me with perspective on this evolution.
5. Quotations and personal stories, unless otherwise noted, come from interviews by the author.
6. Jakob J. Petuchowski, "Toward a Modern 'Brotherhood'", *The Reconstructionist,* Vol. 26, No. 16, Dec. 16, 1960.
7. Jacob Neusner, "Fellowship and the Crisis of Community," *The Reconstructionist,* Vol. 26, No. 19, January 27, 1961, pp. 8–15.
8. Ira Eisenstein, "And Now the Editor," *The Reconstructionist,* January 27, 1961, op. cit.

Chapter 3. Learning as Worship

1. I've told this story from Susan's point of view, since it's her motivations that count here. But from Susan's mother's point of view, despite her atheism and her discomfort with observance, she was always affirmatively Jewish. In fact, Susan's mother eventually worked for twenty years as a secretary at a Jewish educational institution.

329

2. Goldie Kopmar, who was my teacher in this as in many other things.

3. "Study," *Encyclopedia Judaica, Vol. 15,* Keter Publishing House, Jerusalem, 1972, p. 461.

4. Adin Steinsaltz, *Teshuvah: A Guide for the Newly Observant Jew,* Free Press, New York, 1982, p. 88.

5. Rabbi Joseph Telushkin, *Jewish Literacy: The Most Important Things to Know About the Jewish Religion, Its People, and Its History,* William Morrow and Company, New York, 1991, p. 153.

6. No relation to CLAL founder Irving Greenberg.

7. Steinsaltz, op. cit., pp. 87–88.

8. Samuel C. Heilman, *The People of the Book: Drama, Fellowship and Religion,* University of Chicago Press, Chicago, 1987.

Chapter 4. Community as Sanctuary, Calendar as Catechism

1. Lawrence Kushner, Arnold Jacob Wolf, Everett Gendler, "Communities Within Synagogues," in Sharon Strassfeld and Michael Strassfeld, *The Third Jewish Catalog: Creating Community,* Jewish Publication Society of America, Philadelphia, 1980, p. 104.

2. Driving or riding on the Sabbath is prohibited by Jewish law, but many young American Jews chose to live with the contradiction of sometimes violating a law of Shabbat in order to observe the spirit of Shabbat more deeply.

3. Rabbi Samson Raphael Hirsch, *Betrachtungen zum judische Kalendarjahr,* cited in *A Treasury of Jewish Quotations,* Leo Rosten, ed., Crown Publishers, New York, 1956, p. 39.

4. Kushner et al., op. cit., p. 104.

5. Ten men in traditional synagogues; see Chapter 8.

6. Unlike either in the Orthodox world or in most Reform synagogues, both men and many women in the havurah wore skullcaps. Although people walked on the Sabbath, they used strollers, which, since there was no *eruv* (enclosure) around the neighborhood, in more Orthodox communities would be considered a violation of the Sabbath prohibition against carrying objects outside one's home.

7. Chava Weissler, *Making Judaism Meaningful: Ambivalence and Tradition in a Havurah Community,* AMS Press, New York, 1989.

8. Described in Weissler, op. cit.

9. Riv-Ellen Prell, *Prayer and Community: The Havurah in American Judaism,* Wayne State University Press, Detroit, 1989.

10. Martha Ackelsberg, "Spirituality, Community and Politics: B'not Esh and the Feminist Reconstruction of Judaism," *Journal of Feminist Studies in Religion,* Vol. 2, No. 2, Fall, 1986, pp. 109–120.

11. Ibid.

12. Ibid.

13. Rabbi J. H. Hertz, ed., *The Pentateuch and Haftorahs: Hebrew Text, English Translation and Commentary,* 1941, p. 504; note to Leviticus 19:33 cited in Richard H. Schwartz, *Judaism and Global Survival,* Atara Publishing, New York, 1987, p. 13.

14. Orthodox Rabbi Hayim Halevy Donin, in *To Be a Jew: A Guide to Jewish Observance in Contemporary Life* (Basic Books, New York, 1972), says the communal consciousness of the Jewish people was molded by the divine command "You shall be to Me a kingdom of priests and a holy nation." (Exodus 19:6)

Radical feminist Judith Plaskow, who disagrees with Orthodoxy on many points, agrees on the fundamentally communal nature of Jewish spirituality. Judith Plaskow, *Standing Again At Sinai: Judaism from a Feminist Perspective,* Harper & Row, San Francisco, 1990, pp. 79–80: "The covenantal history that begins with Abraham, Isaac, and Jacob finds its fulfillment only at Sinai, when the whole congregation answers together, 'All that the Lord has spoken we will do' (Ex. 19:8). . . . only when they receive life and teachings as a community. . . . From Sinai on, the Jewish relationship to God is mediated through this community. The Jew stands before God not as an individual but as a member of a people."

Similarly, from Reform rabbi Eugene Borowitz, "Individual and Community in Jewish Prayer," in Arnold Jacob Wolf, ed., *Rediscovering Judaism: Reflections on a New Theology,* Quadrangle Books, Chicago, 1965, p. 124: "A specifically Jewish religious life . . . means, therefore, life in and with the Jewish people, the Covenant community."

15. The following discussion is based largely on Salo Baron, *The Jewish Community: Its History and Structure to the American Revolution,* Jewish Publication Society, 1942, Vol. 2, Chap. 10, and the *Encyclopedia Judaica,* op. cit., Vol. 5, articles on "Community," pp. 808–854, "Congregation," pp. 893–896, "Consistory," pp. 907–912, "Councils of the Lands," pp. 995–1003; Vol. 3, "Autonomy," and "Judicial Autonomy," pp. 921–931; Vol. 7, "Gaon," pp. 315–323; Vol. 6, "Exilarch," pp. 1023–1034; Vol. 12, "Nasi," pp. 833–836; Vol. 14, "Sanhedrin," pp. 836–839.

16. I am indebted to my husband, Steve Eisdorfer, for putting the history into perspective for me.

17. *Encyclopedia Judaica,* article on "Community," op. cit., p. 809.

18. Ibid., p. 827.

19. Baron, op. cit., p. 35.

20. *Encyclopedia Judaica,* op. cit., Vol. 5, p. 819.

21. *Encyclopedia Judaica,* article on "Community," op. cit., p. 830.

22. While President Bill Clinton said during the 1992 presidential campaign that he had tried marijuana but never inhaled it, most of our generation admitted we had.

23. Lawrence Kushner, "The Tent-Peg Business: Some Truths About Congregations," *New Traditions*, premiere issue, Spring 1984, National Havurah Committee, New York, p. 87.

Chapter 5. Action as Prayer

1. Arthur I. Waskow, *The Bush is Burning!: Radical Judaism Faces the Pharaohs of the Modern Superstate*, Macmillan, New York, 1971, pp. 11–12.
2. Arthur Waskow, *The Freedom Seder*, Holt Rinehart & Winston, New York, 1970. Since then, Waskow has written three additional radical seders. Feminists and others have followed his lead. (See, for example, *And We Were All There: A Feminist Passover Haggadah*, American Jewish Congress Feminist Center, Los Angeles, 1993.)
3. *The Bush is Burning*, op. cit., pp. 29–30.
4. Ibid., pp. 22–23.
5. Hillel Levine, "To Share a Vision," in Jack Nusan Porter and Peter Dreier, eds., *Jewish Radicalism*, Grove Press, New York, 1973, p. 185.
6. Ibid., p. 189.
7. As Cherie Koller-Fox and others explained in the September 1978 issue of *Sh'ma*.
8. Rabbi Irving Greenberg, "The Covenant," one of the readings in the CLAL course, "Becoming a Partner in Transforming the Jewish World."
9. See Leonard Fein, "Mending the World: A Jewish Approach to Social Justice," *Commonweal*, January 14, 1994, p. 21.
10. Salo Baron, *The Jewish Community: Its History and Structure to the American Revolution*, Jewish Publication Society, 1942, Vol. 2, Chap. 10.
11. Lucy S. Dawidowicz, *The Golden Tradition: Jewish Life and Thought in Eastern Europe*, Beacon Press, Boston, 1968, p. 47.
12. Ibid., p. 48.
13. "Jewish Labor, Jewish Socialism," in Irving Howe, ed., *World of Our Fathers: The Journey of the East European Jews to America and the Life They Found and Made*, Harcourt Brace Jovanovich, New York, 1976, pp. 287–324 (electoral successes on pp. 315 and 320).
14. Porter and Dreier, op. cit., pp. xxi–xxii.
15. The following is condensed and summarized from Letty Cottin Pogrebin, *Deborah, Golda and Me: Being Female and Jewish in America*, Crown Publishers, New York, 1991.
16. Pogrebin, op. cit., p. 154.
17. *Ms.*, June 1982, reprinted in Pogrebin, op. cit., pp. 205–228.
18. Pogrebin, op. cit., p. 346.
19. Some of this history is recounted by rabbis Mark Gopin, Mark H. Levine, and Sid Schwarz in *Jewish Civics: A Tikkun Olam/World Repair Manual*,

Coalition for the Advancement of Jewish Education and the Washington Institute for Jewish Leadership and Values, 1994.

20. Fein, "Mending . . . ," op. cit., p. 23.

21. "Jewish Community and Social Action," keynote address by Rabbi David Saperstein, director of the Religious Action Center of Reform Judaism, to the 62nd Biennial Assembly of the Union of American Hebrew Congregations, October 22, 1993.

22. Leonard Fein, "What Is Required of Us," *Reform Judaism,* Spring 1991, p. 38.

23. Ibid., p. 63.

Chapter 6. Justice in Judaism

1. Rachel Adler, "The Jew Who Wasn't There: *Halakhah* and the Jewish Woman," *Response,* Vol. 7, No. 22 (Summer 1973), pp. 77–82; reprinted in Susannah Heschel, ed., *On Being a Jewish Feminist: A Reader,* Schocken Books, New York, 1983, pp. 12–18.

2. Rachel Adler, "Tumah and Taharah—Mikveh," in Richard Siegel, Michael Strassfeld, and Sharon Strassfeld, eds., *The Jewish Catalog,* Jewish Publication Society of America, Philadelphia, 1973, p. 168, and "Tumah and Tahara: Ends and Beginnings," in Elizabeth Koltun, ed., *The Jewish Woman: New Perspectives,* Schocken Books, New York, 1976, pp. 63–71.

3. Rachel Adler, "In Your Blood, Live: Re-Visions of a Theology of Purity," *Tikkun,* Vol. 8, No. 1 (January–February 1993), p. 38.

4. "On Being Jewish and Female," *Hadassah,* Vol. 76, No. 1, August–September 1994, p. 27.

5. Novelist Esther Broner's persistence in saying kaddish for her father in an Orthodox synagogue is one of the most dramatic segments in the documentary film *Half the Kingdom,* directed by Francine Zuckerman and Roushell Goldstein, distributed by Direct Cinema, 1-800-525-0000.

6. Arlene Agus, "This Month Is for You: Observing Rosh Hodesh as a Women's Holiday," in Elizabeth Koltun, ed., *The Jewish Woman: New Perspectives,* Schocken Books, New York, 1976, p. 84.

7. Ibid.

8. Ibid., pp. 84–93.

9. Susan Weidman Schneider, "Lilith Looks Back," *Lilith,* Vol. 19, No. 3, Fall 1994, p. 14.

10. Ibid., p. 15.

11. Ibid.

12. Ibid.

13. Among Maimonides's thirteen articles of faith were belief in one God, perfect, eternal, and without bodily form, who is the cause of all exis-

tence, is the author of the Torah, and will eventually bring about resurrection and the coming of the Messiah.

Chapter 7. From Exile to Homecoming

1. Judith Weinstein Klein, *Jewish Identity and Self-Esteem: Healing Wounds Through Ethnotherapy*, American Jewish Committee, New York, 1980.
2. This exercise was introduced to us by Barbara Breitman, a psychotherapist and member of our group.
3. Janet R. Marder, "Getting to Know the Gay and Lesbian Shul: A Rabbi Moves from Tolerance to Acceptance," in Christie Balka and Andy Rose, eds., *Twice Blessed: On Being Lesbian, Gay, and Jewish,* Beacon Press, Boston, 1989, pp. 214–215.
4. Rebecca T. Alpert, "In God's Image: Coming to Terms With Leviticus," in *Twice Blessed,* op. cit., pp. 62–63.
5. Ibid., p. 63.
6. Ibid., pp. 65–68.
7. Ibid., p. 69.

Chapter 8. Celebrating

1. From the archives of the Jewish Women's Resource Center, New York section of the National Council of Jewish Women.
2. Arthur I. Waskow, *Seasons of Our Joy: A Handbook of Jewish Festivals,* Bantam, New York, 1981, p. 22.
3. "Honoring the birth of a daughter," in Susan Weidman Schneider, ed., *Jewish and Female: A Guide and Sourcebook for Today's Jewish Woman,* Simon and Schuster, New York, 1985, p. 122.
4. Schneider, op. cit., p. 123.
5. Reprinted in Schneider, op. cit., pp. 124–127.
6. Laura Levitt and Sue Ann Wasserman, "Mikvah Ceremony for Laura," in Ellen M. Umansky and Diane Ashton, eds., *Four Centuries of Jewish Women's Spirituality,* Beacon Press, Boston, 1992, pp. 321–326.
7. The other women's *mitzvot* are lighting candles and setting aside a tithe for God from the hallah.
8. "M'ugelet: Pregnancy Ritual," in Elizabeth Resnick Levine, ed., *A Ceremonies Sampler: New Rites, Celebrations, and Observances of Jewish Women,* Women's Institute for Continuing Jewish Education, La Jolla, CA, 1991, pp. 5–7.
9. Judith Bleich, "Symbolism in Innovative Rituals"; the Strassfelds' ceremony is described in Amy Stone, "An Appropriate Ceremony for Daughters," *Lilith,* Vol. 1, No. 2, Winter 1976–77, pp. 22–23. The criticism and their response appear in *Sh'ma,* Vol. 14, Issue 264, December 23, 1983.

10. Susan Schnur, "An Interview with Marcia Falk, *Lilith,* No. 21, Fall 1988, p. 12.

11. The ceremony is described in Phyllis Ocean Berman, "Recreating Menopause," *Moment,* Vol. 19, No. 1, February 1994, pp. 48ff.

Chapter 9. Path or Dwelling Place

1. I later learned he was a superb teacher.

2. Richard Siegel, Michael Strassfeld, and Sharon Strassfeld, eds., *The Jewish Catalog: A Do-It-Yourself Kit,* Jewish Publication Society of America, Philadelphia, 1973, p. 9.

3. Ahad Ha-Am, cited in Rabbi Joseph Telushkin ed., *Jewish Wisdom: Ethical, Spiritual and Historical Lessons From the Great Works and Thinkers,* William Morrow, New York, 1994, p. 382.

4. Blu Greenberg, *How to Run a Traditional Jewish Household,* Simon and Schuster, New York, 1983, p. 25.

5. Although a majority of the Law Committee of the Conservative movement's Rabbinical Assembly concluded that electricity is not a form of fire and could be used, Isaac Klein, author of the standard Conservative reference on Jewish law, disagrees. See Klein, *A Guide to Jewish Religious Practice,* Jewish Theological Seminary, New York, 1979, p. 87.

6. Published by William Morrow and Company, New York, 1995.

7. Mordecai Kaplan suggested that Orthodox rabbis concerned about the unfairness of the law which permits only men to initiate a divorce could issue a ruling, modeled on Hillel's, permitting the rabbinical court to initiate divorce on behalf of the woman. So far it hasn't happened.

8. Haym Soloveitchik, "Rupture and Reconstruction: The Transformation of Contemporary Orthodoxy," *Tradition: A Journal of Orthodox Jewish Thought,* Vol. 28, No. 4, Summer 1994, p. 103.

9. Greenberg, op. cit., pp. 23, 26–28.

10. Herb Levine, "Jewish Boundaries and American Openness," *The Reconstructionist,* Vol. 59, No. 2, Fall 1994, p. 16.

11. Maimonides, Guide of the Perplexed, III: 31, quoted in Arthur Waskow, *Down-to-Earth Judaism: Food, Money, Sex, and the Rest of Life,* William Morrow, New York, 1995, pp. 150–151.

12. Mordecai Kaplan, "An Approach to Jewish Religion," in Simon Noveck, ed., *Contemporary Jewish Thought,* B'nai B'rith Books, Washington, DC, 1985, p. 337; excerpted from Mordecai Kaplan, *The Meaning of God in Modern Jewish Religion,* Behrman House, New York, 1937, pp. 2–9.

13. See Buber's letters to Rosenzweig, in Franz Rosenzweig, *On Jewish Learning* (N. Glatzer, ed.), Schocken Books, New York, 1965, pp. 111, 114–115.

14. Rosenzweig, op. cit., pp. 90, 91, 121–122.

15. Greenberg, op. cit., p. 23.

16. Greenberg, op. cit., p. 23.

17. David Hartman, *A Living Covenant,* Free Press, New York, 1985, pp. 5, 8, 14.

18. Manis Friedman, *Doesn't Anybody Blush Anymore?: Reclaiming Intimacy, Modesty, and Sexuality,* Harper San Francisco, 1990. p. 50.

19. Edward Feld, "Can Halakhah live?" *The Reconstructionist,* Vol. 59, No. 2, Fall 1994, p. 72.

20. Adin Steinsaltz, *Teshuvah: A Guide for the Newly Observant Jew,* Free Press, New York, 1987, pp. 22–42.

21. Ibid., p. 25.

22. Arthur Green, ed., *Jewish Spirituality: From the Bible Through the Middle Ages,* Crossroad Publishing, New York, 1988, p. xiii.

23. Levine, op. cit., pp. 16–17.

Chapter 10. Praying

1. Introduction to *Response* special issue on prayer, Nos. 41–42, Fall–Winter 1981–82.

2. Abraham Joshua Heschel, *Man's Quest for God: Studies in Prayer and Symbolism,* Charles Scribner's Sons, New York, 1954, p. 89.

3. As pointed out in Lenore Eve Weissler, *Making Judaism Meaningful: Ambivalence and Tradition in a Havurah Community,* University of Pennsylvania, 1982, *passim,* esp. pp. 120, 121, 125. See also Riv-Ellen Prell, *Prayer and Community: The Havurah in American Judaism,* Wayne State University Press, Detroit, 1989, pp. 13, 22–24, 107 and *passim.*

4. Heschel, op. cit., p. 51.

5. Ibid., p. 50.

6. Ibid., pp. 61–62.

7. Ibid., p. 5.

8. Symposium in *Response,* No. 9, Vol. IV, No. 4, Winter 1970–71, p. 42.

9. Ibid.

10. See discussion of *kavannot* in Weissler, op. cit., pp. 144–156.

11. Herbert Levine and Ellen Frankel Levine, "Havurah in the Ivory Tower: A Letter from Princeton," *National Jewish Monthly,* June 1977, pp. 24–27.

12. After Herb and Ellen had left, other people in Lancaster organized a havurah for study but not for services.

Chapter 11. Beyond Father and King

1. Excerpted in *Lilith,* Vol. 1, No. 4., Fall–Winter 1977–78, pp. 28–29.

2. Marcia Falk, "Notes on Composing New Blessings; Toward a Feminist-Jewish Reconstruction of Prayer," *Journal of Feminist Studies in Religion,* Vol. 3, No. 1, Spring 1987, p. 39.

3. "Eureka!" *Lilith,* Vol. 19, No. 3, Fall 1994, p. 9.

4. Falk, "Notes," op. cit., p. 41.

5. Ibid., p. 44.

6. Others suggested that referring to God as Queen evoked associations with paganism, since the prophet Jeremiah had railed at women for offering "cakes to the Queen of Heaven" (Astarte).

7. Harper San Francisco, 1996.

8. *Kol Haneshama, Shabbot Vehagim,* The Reconstructionist Press, Wyncote, PA, 1994, p. 5. The first Reconstructionist prayerbook, published in 1945, made the front page of the *New York Times* when some more traditional rabbis burned it as heresy. One of the first new congregational prayerbooks was *Vetaher Libenu,* published by Reform Congregation Beth El of the Sudbury River Valley in Sudbury, MA.

9. Gottlieb, who remembers that evening as vividly as I do, describes it in her book, *She Who Dwells Within.* But she remembers it somewhat differently.

10. Penina V. Adelman, *Miriam's Well: Rituals for Jewish Women Around the Year,* Biblio Press, Fresh Meadows, NY, 1987, p. 43.

11. Arthur Waskow, *Down-to-Earth Judaism: Food, Money, Sex, and the Rest of Life,* William Morrow, New York, 1995, pp. 67, 131.

Chapter 12. Unbinding the Boundaries

1. Ellen Singer, ed., *Paradigm Shift: From the Jewish Renewal Teachings of Reb Zalman Schachter-Shalomi,* Jason Aronson, Northvale, NJ, pp. 250–51.

2. Shefa Gold, "An Open House," *The Reconstructionist,* Vol. 59, No. 2, Fall 1994, p. 25.

3. James W. Fowler, *Stages of Faith: The Psychology of Human Development and the Quest for Faith,* Harper & Row, San Francisco, 1981.

4. Retold in Ben Zion Solomon, ed., *Shlomo Shabbos: The Shlomo Carlebach Shabbos Song Book,* Kehillat Jacob Productions, 1993, distributed by Tara publications, Cedarhurst, NY.

5. Seth Fishman, "A Trip to Brooklyn," in *New Menorah,* Second Series, No. 38, Winter 1994.

6. *Paradigm Shift,* op. cit., p. 257.

7. *Kabbalah of Tiqqun Olam,* Shiurim [Teachings] given by Reb Zalman at the Fourth P'nai Or Kallah, Bryn Mawr, Pennsylvania, July 1989, ALEPH, Philadelphia, p. 34.

8. Zalman Meshullam Schachter-Shalomi, *Spiritual Intimacy: A Study in Counseling in Hasidism,* Jason Aronson, Northvale, NJ, 1991.

9. Fishman, "A Trip to Brooklyn," op. cit.

10. Sheila Weinberg, "Many Voices in One Mind," in *The Reconstructionist,* Vol. 59, No. 2, Fall 1994, p. 53.

11. Ibid., pp. 57–58.

12. Ibid., p. 58.

13. Gold, op. cit., p. 24.
14. Ibid., pp. 26–27.

Chapter 13. Meditation

1. Rami Shapiro, "The Boundariless Universe," *The Reconstructionist,* Vol. 59, No. 2, Fall 1994, pp. 18–23.
2. Daniel Matt, "Beyond the Personal God," *The Reconstructionist,* Vol. 59, No. 1, Spring 1994, pp. 38–47.
3. Aryeh Kaplan, *Jewish Meditation: A Practical Guide,* Schocken, New York, 1985, p. vi.
4. According to one *midrash,* each soul before it is born is taught the whole Torah. At the moment of birth, an angel gently touches us on the lips (causing that little dent) and we forget. We spend the rest of our lives re-learning what we once knew.
5. Shohama Harris Weiner, "Connecting God's Names and My Name: A Spiritual Journey," *The Reconstructionist,* Vol. 59, No. 1, Spring 1994, p. 82.
6. Richard Siegel, Michael Strassfeld, and Sharon Strassfeld, eds., *The Jewish Catalog: A Do-It-Yourself Kit,* Jewish Publication Society of America, Philadelphia, 1973, p. 297.
7. I got this very helpful understanding of Adonai from Rabbi Marcia Prager's article, "Beyond Lordship: Personalizing *Adonay,*" *The Reconstructionist,* Vol. 59, No. 1, Spring 1994, pp. 32–37.

Chapter 14. Putting It All Together—For Now

1. Savina J. Teubal, "Simchat Hochmah," in Ellen M. Umansky and Dianne Ashton, eds., *Four Centuries of Jewish Women's Spirituality: A Sourcebook,* Beacon Press, Boston, pp. 257–265.
2. "L'chi Lach," in Debbie Friedman's songbook *Blessings,* Sounds Write Productions, Inc., 1990, pp. 14–15. Available on Friedman's tape, "And You Shall Be a Blessing."

Beginning

1. Joshua ben Perahya and Hillel, *Ethics of the Fathers,* I, 6, and II, 5.